Marriage and the Family

A
CHRISTIAN
PERSPECTIVE

STEPHEN A. GRUNLAN

Marriage and the Family

A CHRISTIAN PERSPECTIVE

STEPHEN A. GRUNLAN

Academie
Books Grand Rapids,
Michigan
Zondervan Publishing House

MARRIAGE AND THE FAMILY: A CHRISTIAN PERSPECTIVE
Copyright © 1984 by The Zondervan Corporation
Grand Rapids, Michigan

ACADEMIE BOOKS is an imprint of Zondervan Publishing House,
1415 Lake Drive, S.E., Grand Rapids, Michigan 49506

Library of Congress Cataloging in Publication Data

Grunlan, Stephen A.
    Marriage and the family, a Christian perspective.

    Bibliography: p.
    Includes index.
    1. Marriage—Religious aspects—Christianity. 2. Family—Religious
aspects—Christianity. I. Title.

BV835.G78   1984   261.8'358   83-19750
ISBN 0-310-36341-1

Unless otherwise indicated, all Scripture quotations are from the New International Version, copyright © 1978 by the New York International Bible Society. Used by permission.

The poem "An Ode to Marriage" on pages 291–295 is from Harold Myra, *Love Notes to Jeanette* (Wheaton, Ill., Victor Books), 1979. Used by permission.

Edited by Norma Camp and Gerard Terpstra
Designed by Louise Bauer

Printed in the United States of America

84   85   86   87   88   89 / 9   8   7   6   5   4   3   2   1

TO MY CHILDREN:

STEPHEN ARTHUR, JR.
JAIME CHRISTOPHER
REBECCA SUE

Contents

Figures

Tables

Preface

For the past six years I have taught marriage and the family classes at two Christian colleges. Each year the task of finding a suitable textbook has become more difficult. A sociological treatment of marriage and the family from a Christian perspective has not been available. The texts being produced by the secular publishers have, in my opinion, moved further from presenting data and more toward editorializing. Many positions propagated in these texts, again, in my opinion, are not consistent with a biblical world view.

I recognize that there are scholars in the evangelical community more qualified than myself to produce a text with a Christian perspective. However, since to my knowledge no such text was forthcoming, I felt the need to produce this work. As a Christian, a husband, and a father, as well as a professor, it is my conviction that our young people need to develop a Christian perspective on marriage and the family. It is my prayer that this book will help to fill this need.

Sincere Christians do not always understand biblical truth in the same way and so I recognize that there can be honest disagreement on some of the issues presented in this book. It is not my purpose to provide the "right" answers but rather to help readers think through the issues and come to their own conclusions.

PART I

THE STUDY
OF THE FAMILY

1

The Sociological Study of Marriage and the Family

So God created man in His own image,
in the image of God He created him,
male and female He created them.

God blessed them and said to them,
"Be fruitful and increase. . . ."

GEN. 1:27–28

WITH THEIR WEDDING DATE still a few months off, George broke his engagement to Carol because he felt she was too "immature" to develop a meaningful relationship. Two weeks later Carol met Carl who was thirty-two—twelve years her senior. Carl has been married twice before, his last wife divorcing him while he was in a state mental hospital for observation of aggressive tendencies (wife beating). Carol's parents are evangelical Christians and are against her marrying Carl, to whom she became engaged six weeks after they met. Carol has been raised in a Christian home, whereas Carl was baptized as an infant but has not involved himself with a church since he was a child. Carol's parents also want Carol to go to college and are concerned that Carl is a high-school dropout. Are Carol's parent's concerns warranted?

Fred and Alice have been married for three years and find that they are arguing more and more. Communication seems to have completely broken down. As Alice describes it, they seem to talk at each other rather than to each other. They both feel that they love each other and both want their marriage to work. Are there any techniques or procedures that could improve their communication with each other?

Ralph and Edith have been married for twenty-three

years and have two children, the youngest of whom will be leaving for college in a couple of months. Their other child is married. Ralph suffered a mild heart attack last year, and his doctor has restricted his activities so that Ralph had to turn down a job offer with another firm that would have meant a major advance in his career. Edith had three years of college before they were married, and now that their youngest child is leaving for college, she wants to start attending classes at a local branch of the state university to work toward a teaching degree. Ralph is upset by this because he feels he earns enough money to support the family and because his aged mother, who was just widowed, needs a place to live. Ralph would like to bring her to his home and have Edith stay home and care for her. This has led to serious tension in their relationship. Are the tensions being experienced by Ralph and Edith typical for couples in mid-life? Can these types of tensions be avoided or reduced?

As we will see, sociology is a research science rather than a helping or service discipline. However, sociological research in the area of marriage and the family investigates issues such as those raised in these three case studies. The research findings can be of great assistance to social workers, therapists, ministers, and others who work with individuals facing marriage and family problems. In this book we will examine sociological research that applies directly to these case studies as well as research related to a variety of other issues.

Each one of us is a member of a family and, according to statistics, about 96 percent of the adult population will marry. Marriage and the family is a reality that is a part of each of our lives. However, marriage and the family are not just personal realities, they are also social realities. As social realities, marriage and the family are subject matters for study by sociologists. Before discussing the sociological study of marriage and the family, the discipline of sociology should be briefly introduced.

THE DISCIPLINE OF SOCIOLOGY

While there is not a universally accepted division of the academic disciplines, many scholars divide them into two broad categories—the humanities and the sciences (see figure 1-1). The humanities, sometimes referred to as the arts, include such subjects as literature, languages, philosophy, music, and the visual arts. The sciences are usually broken down into two subcategories—the natural sciences and the social sciences. The natural sciences include such disciplines as biology, chemistry, and physics. The social sciences include disciplines such as history, economics, geography, political science, anthropology, psychology, and sociology.[1] As an academic discipline, sociology is one of the social sciences.

If we examine sociology textbooks, we will find that various writers have defined sociology as "the study of human social relationships" (Turner 1981:6); "the scientific study of human interaction" (Vander Zanden 1979:7); and "the scientific study of human social life" (Horton and Hunt 1980:482). While these definitions vary in their wording, they each contain two common ideas: first, that sociology uses the scientific method, and second, that the object of its study is human social life. We will examine the second of these ideas before discussing the use of the scientific method by sociologists.

As pointed out above, sociology is the study of human social life. Since sociology is concerned with the behavior of human beings in social contexts, a foundational question for the discipline concerns the essence of human nature. Cosgrove reminds us that "it is especially important to clarify our understanding of the nature of man because our view of human nature affects critical issues of society, such as capital punishment, abortion, and biological and psychological engineering, to name a few" (1977:12).

Secular sociologists are generally committed to the view that humans are the product of a random/chance-evolutionary process. From an evolutionary perspective human nature is not innate to a person but is acquired by a person. As Horton and Hunt state it, "The infant enters this world as a selfish little organism preoccupied with its

---

[1]Some academicians would further divide the social sciences into the social studies, including history, economics, geography, and political science, and the behavioral sciences, including anthropology, psychology, and sociology.

physical needs. It soon becomes a human being . . . through a process we call socialization" (1981:92). Broom, Selznick, and Darroch put it this way, "Socialization transforms the human animal into a human being. . ." (1981:84).

HUMANITIES		SCIENCES
	NATURAL	SOCIAL
Literature	Biology	History
Languages	Chemistry	Economics
Philosophy	Physics	Geography
Arts	etc.	Political Science
etc.		Anthropology
	·(Behavioral Sciences)	Psychology
		Sociology

Figure 1-1. THE ACADEMIC DISCIPLINES.

In contrast with many secular sociologists, evangelical sociologists generally see human nature as a God-given attribute. Responding to the contention that infants become human by the process of socialization,[2] Milton Reimer argues:

> The Christian, however, is compelled to begin with a biblical view of human nature. God created humans in His own image, and the reflection of God's image continues in all people regardless of age, sex, skin color or moral condition. The child does not *become* human when it begins to assimilate the cultural patterns of environment. Rather, the child *is* human by virtue of God's creative act (Gen. 1:26–27) (1982:21).

What is the essence of the image of God in humanity? A number of theologians suggest that the image of God refers to our ability to relate to God. This ability involves self-consciousness, reason or rationality, and responsibility. These same characteristics that enable us to relate to God allow us to relate to each other. It is our ability to

---

[2]Socialization may be defined as "the process by which persons acquire the knowledge, skills and dispositions that make them more or less able members of their society" (Brim 1966:3).

be self-conscious, to reason, and to be responsible that is foundational to human cultures and societies.

Evangelicals also recognize that the image of God was affected by the Fall. The Reformed theologian Emil Brunner says that a direct consequence of the Fall was a distortion in humanity's sense of direction. He argues that God set the direction for humankind but that people sought to become gods themselves and set their own direction (1952:125–28). It is the desire of people to be their own gods and set their own direction that is the basis for secular humanism.

Fortunately God has not left us to our own ways. While there was nothing we could do about the power of sin over our lives, God provided a way of reconciliation and renewal. As the apostle Paul writes:

> Therefore, if anyone is in Christ, he is a new creation; the old has gone, the new has come! All this is from God, who reconciled us to himself through Christ and gave us the ministry of reconciliation: that God was reconciling the world to himself in Christ, not counting men's sins against them. . . . God made him who had no sin to be sin for us, so that in him we might become the righteousness of God (2 Cor. 5:17–19, 21).

For us to understand human social life, we need to have a proper understanding of human nature:

> Any approach to sociology that ignores the biblical account of the origin of humans and its implications, as well as the effects of the Fall and the potential of redemption, will always come short of the full truth. An understanding of the scriptural view of human nature is essential for a valid sociology (Grunlan 1982:411–12).

SOCIOLOGY AS A SCIENCE

Earlier it was pointed out that most definitions of sociology have two common ideas—first, that sociology uses the scientific method and, second, that the object of its study is human social life. We have already discussed the essence of human nature and now we will turn to sociology as a science.

Some people may have a difficult time thinking of disciplines such as sociology as sciences. Many believe that only the natural sciences are true science. However, the scientific nature of a discipline is not determined by the subject matter or the setting of the study. It is determined by the methodology used to study the subject matter. The scientific method embodies the following qualities:

1. The procedures are public.
2. The definitions are precise.
3. The data collecting is objective.
4. The findings must be replicable.
5. The approach is systematic and cumulative.
6. The purposes are explanation, understanding, and prediction (Berelson and Steiner 1964:16–17).

Besides embodying the above qualities, the scientific method follows specific steps in doing research:

1. The problem is defined.
2. The literature on previous research in the area of the problem is reviewed.
3. A hypothesis is formulated.
4. A research design is planned.
5. The data is collected.
6. The data is analyzed.
7. Conclusions are drawn.

To the extent that sociology embodies the qualities of the scientific method and follows the research steps of the scientific method, to that degree it is a science. As Milton Reimer states, "As a science, sociology is committed to the use of the scientific methodology, and most scientists will do so scrupulously" (1979:7).

Some Christians are leery of sociology because what they have read or heard of sociological research appears to run contrary to a biblical view of humanity and society. However, it is important for us to distinguish between the data and the interpretations of that data. It is my conviction that there are no conflicts between the facts of science and the words of Scripture. Rather, the conflicts arise between the interpretations of the facts of science and the interpretations of the words of Scripture. We need to remember that neither the scientist nor the theologian are infallible, and either or both may misinterpret their data. We should approach both the facts of science, including sociology, and the words of Scripture with the knowledge that all truth is God's truth. As Malcolm Jeeves has put it, "As a Christian, it is my belief that what God has chosen to give to man down the ages through his special messengers will not ultimately conflict with what he has encouraged us to discover as we exercise his gifts of mind and hand in exploring the created order, including of course, man himself, his experience and his behaviors" (1976:18). We recognize that the Christian sociologist has a distinct advantage over the secular sociologist in interpreting the sociological data. The Christian sociologist has the truth of God's Word and the indwelling of the Holy Spirit to guide the analysis of the data.

SOCIOLOGICAL CONCEPTS

Sociology, like any other discipline, has basic concepts and vocabulary that it utilizes in the study of its subject matter. A brief definition of a few of the basic concepts will provide us with a foundation for the following discussions on marriage and the family.[3]

Status and Role

Status and role have been called the "basic concepts" of sociology (Vander Zanden 1979:111) and the "basic building blocks of society" (Turner 1980:111). Broom and Selznick point out that "the concepts of status and role provide indispensable starting points for the analysis of social structure" (1979:33).

A *status* may be defined as a position or place in a social system with its attendant rights and duties. A *role* is defined as the behavior that is expected from the holder of a particular status. The positions of both professor and student are statuses. We would expect a certain general behavior of the professor for a particular class, whether the professor is Dr. Jones or Dr. Smith. We would expect lectures, discussion, examinations, and so on. We would

[3]For those readers who have had an introductory sociology course this discussion will be a review. For those readers who have not previously studied sociology it will serve as an introduction to a few basic sociological concepts.

expect a certain general behavior of any given student in the class whether the student is Mary Brown or Roger Carlson. We would expect regular attendance, note taking, studying, and so on. The reason that we can expect and predict the behavior of the person holding a particular status is that roles are generally governed by a set of "rules." These "rules" are called *norms*. For example, it is a norm in North American culture to greet another person with a handshake. When a person meets another, he or she extends the right hand and expects the other to do likewise and shake hands.

Ralph Linton (1936) noted that statuses are generally acquired in one of two ways. Some statuses are assigned to an individual, often on the basis of characteristics of birth, such as sex, age, race, ethnic group, and social class. These are called *ascribed statuses*. The day I was born I was assigned the statuses of son, grandson, nephew, and American—among others. Ascribed statuses are assigned to the individual by society; other statuses are accquired by choice and effort. These are called *achieved statuses*. I am also a husband, a father, and a professor. These statuses were acquired by choice and effort. Both ascribed and achieved statuses are present in the family structure.

As you read this book, you will discover that the concepts of status and role are not only foundational to the study of sociology in general, they are also foundational to the study of marriage and the family. Every member of a family has several statuses—mother, wife, and aunt or father, husband, and uncle, for example. Each of these statuses has a role. My role as a husband differs from my role as a father, which differs from my role as an uncle. However, it is important for us to realize that these roles are not static; rather, they are constantly changing. In later chapters we will explore changing family roles.

Groups

Horton and Hunt (1980:174) see the concept of "groups" as one of the more important concepts in sociology. Sociologists use the term *group* in a more specific sense than it is generally used. In everyday speech we might speak of a group of people at a bus stop. Sociologists would refer to people waiting at a bus stop as an aggregation or a collectivity. Sociologists generally define a group as two or more persons who share some organized patterns of recurrent interaction and share a consciousness of common membership.

Sociologists distinguish between two basic types of groups—primary and secondary. A *primary group* is a small, intimate, and informal group. The members are intimately involved in each others' lives. Primary groups—such as a close set of friends, a small Bible study or prayer group, and the family—share intimate human companionship. A *secondary group* is generally impersonal and utilitarian. Secondary groups, such as a class, a club, or business associates, tend to be more formal than primary groups. Secondary groups are more concerned with the group product, whereas primary groups are more concerned with relationships.

Since families, both immediate and extended, are groups, the insights from research on groups is often applicable to the study of the family. Robert Bales and Talcott Parsons (1955) studied the family as a primary group. They had observed that groups generally work on two problems simultaneously. The first is the group's goal or product, which they call the *instrumental* problem. The second is the maintenance and smooth functioning of the group, which they call the *socioemotional* problem. In their study of families in the early 1950s they discovered that the husband generally was concerned with the instrumental aspects of the family, and the wife with the socioemotional aspects of the family. Winston Johnson points out while this was a classic study in primary groups, "the effect of the work was to reinforce stereotypical roles for the husband and wife" (1982:158). While husband-wife roles are changing, the family continues to be the classic example of the primary group.

Johnson explains for us the value of studying the family as a group when he writes:

> The family is the small group in which most of us are familiar. Understanding its dynamics and the functions and roles of its members can help build the church up as well as the family unit itself. The family is an important

interface or link between us as individuals and the society at large. In it primary values are taught and reinforced. The right use of this basic and naturally occurring group can strengthen both the individual and the groups to which a person belongs (1982:159–60).

Social Institutions

Another basic sociological concept used in the study of human social life is social institutions. As with the term *group*, the term *institution*, as used by sociologists, differs from common usage. In everyday speech, "institution" refers to the building where certain activities take place, such as a school or a hospital, or it is used to refer to a large organization, such as Bell Telephone or the United States Army. However, in sociological usage, the term refers to an organized system of social relationships that embody common values and procedures (norms) to meet certain basic needs of a society.

While sociologists argue about whether all five exist in preliterate societies, sociologists are generally agreed that all complex societies have five major social institutions. The first institution, and one that is found in all societies—preliterate and complex—is the *family*. That is the social institution on which we will focus in this book. The other four will be briefly described. The second social institution is *religion*. Religion is the way a society or members of a society organize their beliefs (doctrines) and practices (rituals) for the worship and manipulation[4] of the supernatural. Religion is another institution that is found in all societies, preliterate and complex.

The third institution is *education*. Education is the way a society organizes itself for the socialization of its members. The fourth institution is *economics*. Economics refers to the way a society organizes itself for the production, distribution, and consumption of goods and services. The fifth institution is *government*. Government is the way a society organizes itself for communal decision making and the maintenance of social control. While

---

[4]*Manipulation* is another word that differs in its sociological and common usages. Sociologically, in this context, it refers to attempting to have the supernatural act in behalf of humans.

these last three institutions are clearly present in all complex societies, in some preliterate societies their functions appear to be carried out by the family and religion. Even in complex societies, we need to recognize that there is much overlap among the institutions. As we examine the family in this book, the effects on it of religion, education, economics, and government will be explored.

THE SOCIOLOGICAL STUDY OF THE FAMILY

The U. S. Bureau of the Census defines a family as "a group of two persons or more related by blood, marriage, or adoption and residing together" (U.S. Bureau of the Census 1977:158). This definition is limited to the immediate family and does not take into account the extended family. Sociologists are concerned with both the immediate family and the extended family. On a larger scale they are concerned with the organization of the family within a society, that is, the family as a social institution. The family, as a social institution, may be defined as the way a society organizes itself for the reproduction, socialization, and care of its young, and the meeting of the sexual companionship needs of its adult members.

Social scientists have discovered several basic functions that the family institution performs in all cultures. One of these functions is *the regulation of sex*. Without the regulation of sexual activity women would either be forced into sexual unions or denied them at the pleasure of physically stronger males. Also, babies would be born without responsible parents to raise them. Another problem would be unfettered competition among males for the most desirable females. For these and other reasons, all societies regulate the sexual activities of their members. Marriage is the social mechanism used for specifying legitimate sex partners and providing responsible parents to raise children.

A second function of the family is *reproduction*. Because humans are mortal and die, societies need a system for replacing lost members. The family is the social agency for replenishing society. Reproduction includes, but goes beyond, the sex drive. It is psychological as well as physical. It is the means of survival for society.

A third function of the family is *socialization*. Society needs to transmit its culture. The goals, values, norms, and beliefs of the society need to be passed on. Children need to learn the morals and manners of their society. The family is the primary socialization agency in every society. Duvall points out that

> within the family, individual members can best learn the rules, rights, and obligations, and responsibilities essential for the survival of a society. . . . The kinds of praise and punishment experienced by a child in his earliest years instill in him the sense of right and wrong that he will carry into adulthood in his moral values and in his definitions of the good, the right, and the worthy. The family, functioning as a "choosing agency," evaluates and selects from among many ways of life, and so is the primary source of human values that spread outward into society as a whole (1977:116).

Companionship is a fourth function of the family. All humans have a need for love and affection. The family is the primary agency for meeting this need. The family provides companionship for the husband and wife and a source of love and nuturance for children. Ideally at least, "Love is a product of family living" (Duvall 1977:114).

A fifth function is *status conferring*. The family provides a newborn infant with a place in the social network. The family gives the child a name, places the child in a social class, presents the child with ethnic, national, and religious identifications. It is the family that "plugs" the child into the social system. We will examine each of these five functions in more detail in the following chapters.

Theoretical Perspectives

According to Scanzoni and Scanzoni, sociologists tend to use three basic perspectives in studying the family: "time, structure, and interaction" (1981:7). While various sociologists will emphasize one or the other of these perspectives in their research and writing, all three perspectives are needed to fully study marriage and the family. The first of these perspectives, time, utilizes the *developmental or life-cycle approach* to study the family. As Duvall explains, "Family development follows the orderly segmental changes in growth, development, and dissolution or decline throughout the entire family life-cycle" (1977:130). This approach studies the various stages the family passes through. By analyzing the statistics from thousands of families, sociologists can develop a general profile of each stage of the family life cycle. While sociologists use these profiles for descriptions and predictions, their findings are of great value to those who work with families. The fourth part of this book will utilize the life-cycle approach to study the family.

The second perspective for studying marriage and the family is the *structural approach*. Every family is a system. It is made up of parts that work together to make a unified whole. Even as we might study a transportation system, a heating system, or a system of government, we can analyze the family as a system. The concepts of status and role, as well as the concept of group, are useful in studying the family as a system. The next chapter will describe family structures in various cultures. Also as each stage of the family life cycle is discussed, the structure of the family will be examined.

The third perspective for studying marriage and the family is the *interaction approach*. This approach begins by studying the interaction that takes place between individuals. Sociologists using this approach emphasize symbolic interaction. They point out that humans interact through symbols such as words and gestures. These symbols have shared meanings. That is, the members of a society share the meaning of words and gestures. For example, in the United States the word *hammer* denotes a tool for driving nails. When I ask my son to hand me a hammer, he is able to get the correct tool because we share the same meaning for the word. Sociologists who use the symbolic interactionist approach to studying society often argue that it is shared meanings that hold society together and that these shared meanings are the beginning point for social analysis. Duvall sees this approach as particularly valuable "when applied to studying the process of communication, conflicts, decision-making, problem solving and reaction to crisis" (1977:130). This perspective will be most evident in the second and third parts of this book.

BASIC CONCEPTS IN STUDYING MARRIAGE AND THE FAMILY

In their study of marriage and the family, sociologists have developed some basic concepts. As we have already seen, scientific language needs to be precise. When I refer to "my family," am I referring to my wife and children, my parents and siblings, my grandparents and aunts and uncles—or to all of them? In order to differentiate these various family groups, specific terms are used. The unit consisting of a husband and wife and their dependent children is called *a nuclear family*. Myself, my wife, and my three children make up a nuclear family. Two or more related nuclear families are called an *extended family*. My nuclear family and my wife's parents and brother, combined, form an extended family.

Married adults are members of two families, the one they were born into and the one that was created by marriage. The family into which we are born is called our *family of orientation* or sometimes the *family of origin*. The family in which we are a spouse and parent is called the *family of procreation*. Our family of orientation and family of procreation together are part of our extended family.

Two additional terms we often encounter in the study of marriage and the family are *conjugal* and *consanguineal*. The *conjugal* relationship refers to the husband-wife relationship. The *consanguineal* relationship refers to relationships by blood, such as parent-child and sibling-sibling. In a *consanguineal* family, the emphasis is on the blood relationships.

METHODS OF STUDYING MARRIAGE AND THE FAMILY

Observation

Sociologists use various methodologies to study marriage and the family. One of these is observation. While each of us is continually observing events, scientific observation differs from casual observation. Scientific observation strives for accuracy and avoids jumping to conclusions. It is also precise. A sociologist would not report, "I saw several couples spend considerably more time than individuals spent while grocery shopping." Rather, a sociologist would state, "Fourteen couples and thirty-six individuals were observed shopping for groceries. The average time spent at this task was thirty-six minutes per couple and twenty-two minutes per individual." Scientific observation is also systematic. If we were observing people shopping for groceries, we might discover that the time of day or day of the week affected their behavior. A systematic approach would, therefore, involve observing on various days at various times.

Surveys

A more frequently used method of studying marriage and family is the survey. There are two basic survey methods—questionnaires and interviews. A questionnaire is a self-administered instrument; that is, individuals fill it out themselves. In an interview, a researcher asks the questions and records the responses. Surveys are useful for obtaining information on people's attitudes and beliefs on various issues, such as premarital sex, abortion, marriage, and childbearing. Surveys are also useful for gathering data about what has taken place or is taking place in the lives of people and families. By way of example, one of my sociology classes interviewed a sample of students at the college, asking, among other questions, their birth order and grade-point average. When the data was tabulated, it was found that the mean gradepoint average dropped with birth order. This finding was consistent with research on birth-order effect (Zajonc and Markus 1975; Steelman and Mercy 1980; Pfouts 1980). Some implications of the birth-order research will be discussed in chapter 8.

Statistical Studies

Another frequently used research method in studying marriage and the family is statistical studies. A significant amount of information of interest to researchers has already been collected by the government. All births and deaths as well as marriages and divorces are recorded. The census collects data on household composition, marital status, and other information of interest to researchers. The *Statistical Abstract of the United States* is published annually. It summarizes statistics collected by many government agencies. For example, if we wanted to know if the proportion of women who never marry has remained constant over the past century, we could derive the appropriate statistics from census data. We would find that in 1890, 24.3 percent of women never married. By 1960, the proportion of never-married women dropped to 11.9 percent. However, by 1975, it had risen again to 14.6 percent.

At this point, a word of warning about the use of statistics is important. Statistics are nothing more than organized measured facts. These "facts" may be used in misleading ways. By way of example, I recently heard a preacher speaking on the decay of the American family. To dramatize his point, he said that in the preceding year there was one divorce for each marriage in California. While those "facts" are approximately true, the statement is highly misleading. California is gaining population. Couples married in other states are moving into California. If they divorce, it shows up on California's statistics, not the state where they were married. Also, the preacher's statement compares the marriages taking place in one year with the divorces from marriages over the past fifty years or more. As Horton and Hunt warn us, "Citizens who hope to be intelligently aware of the world they live in must have some understanding of statistical interpretation, lest they be duped by every clever propagandist in sight" (1980:25).

Experiments

Another research method is the experiment. Although for both ethical and practical reasons this method has its limitations when dealing with human subjects, it is used occasionally in marriage and family research. An example is an experiment that studies sex-role socialization. A six-month-old infant was dressed as a boy and presented individually to a group of mothers. The infant was then dressed as a girl and presented to a group of mothers. The mothers smiled more at the infant when it was dressed as a girl. They also handed the infant a toy appropriate to the sex it was dressed as (Shepard 1981:240–41). As with observation, surveys, and statistical studies, experiments are utilized by sociologists in their research of marriage and the family.

TOWARD A CHRISTIAN PERSPECTIVE

Why should we study marriage and the family? Does not the Bible teach us everything we need to know about the subject? While everything in the Bible is true, not all truth is in the Bible. God has revealed much about Himself and His creation in the Scriptures, but He has also left much for us to discover. As Koteskey puts it:

> Since the world created by God was created by a rational being, it is real, it is good, and it is orderly, having patterns and regularities. These patterns are discoverable by humans since humans are made in the image of God, and they can be discovered by examining the world (1980:17).

Koteskey goes on to argue:

> Christians need to develop Christian perspectives on science and make positive contributions. Since all truth is unity . . . we need not fear truth discovered by anyone because all truth should dovetail. Too often we reject truth discovered by the non-Christian because we believe that it is not the whole truth or that there are non-Christian elements in the system (1980:14).

We need to take the truth found in God's Word and the truth found in God's world and integrate them in both doctrine and practice. Applying this idea to husband-wife roles, DeJong and Wilson point out that

> The Bible gives fundamental principles regarding the sexes and their behavior, not a full list of specific, timeless role obligations for each. And so, as with many other matters, the Christian community must take the basic principles revealed in the Bible and the attempt to apply them to life in a complex, changing society (1979:31).

We should recognize that the cultures of the biblical periods were vastly different from modern Western cultures. The study of marriage and the family from a sociological perspective can provide Christians with insights that will aid them in applying biblical principles across time and cultures. As I have previously written:

> As we study the Scriptures, we discover God's purpose and plan for marriage and the family. These purposes and plans are played out in human cultures. It is important for us to recognize that the biblical guidelines for marriage and the family may take different forms in different cultures. It is only as we become familiar with both the Scriptures and culture that we can apply the biblical teachings in a manner consistent with both Scripture and culture (Grunlan and Mayers 1979:168).

The family is the basic social unit in every society. It was the first social unit established by God (Gen. 2:18–24). The Bible gives the basis for marriage and discusses the functions and requirements of marriage and the family. As the sociological study of marriage and the family are examined in this text, the teachings of Scripture on the topic at hand will also be examined. With this approach, an attempt will be made to aid you in developing a Christian perspective on marriage and the family.

DISCUSSION QUESTIONS

1. Why is an understanding of the essence of human nature important for a valid sociology?
2. Do you believe sociology has as much right to be called a science as do such disciplines as biology and chemistry? Why?
3. What is your reaction to the author's contention that there are no conflicts between the facts of science and the words of Scripture? Why?
4. Can you find biblical support for the five functions of the family discussed in this chapter?
5. Which of the methods discussed in this chapter for studying marriage and the family do you believe are most useful? Why?
6. In what ways might a sociological study of marriage and the family contribute to your development of a Christian perspective on marriage and the family?

SUGGESTED READING

Mark P. Cosgrove, *The Essence of Human Nature* (Grand Rapids: Zondervan, 1977). A brief treatise that presents a biblical concept of the essence of human nature.

Stephen A. Grunlan and Milton K. Reimer (eds.),*Christian Perspectives on Sociology* (Grand Rapids: Zondervan, 1982). A collection of essays on sociology as a discipline, the methods of sociology, and the major subtopics of the discipline. This collection provides a variety of Christian perspectives and serves as a good introduction to sociology.

David Lyon, *Christians and Sociology* (Downers Grove, Ill.: InterVarsity, 1975). This little volume presents a Christian approach to sociology. It deals with some of the conflicts between secular sociology and a Christian world view.

Donald M. MacKay, *Human Science and Human Dignity* (Downers Grove, Ill.: InterVarsity, 1979). While this book deals more with issues related to medicine and psychology, it provides an excellent perspective on a Christian approach to the human sciences, that is, those sciences that study humans.

2

Crosscultural Perspective

The nuclear family is a universal human social grouping. Either as the sole prevailing form of the family or as a basic unit from which more complex familial forms are compounded, it exists as a distinct and strongly functional group in every known society.

GEORGE PETER MURDOCK (1949:2)

THE NAYAR ARE a Hindu warrior subcaste living in southern India. At puberty, a Nayar woman is ritually married to a young man chosen by her family. A few days later they are ritually divorced and have no further rights or obligations toward each other. Gough (1959) reports that in this matrilineal society men live with a matrilineal kinswoman. That is, the man lives with his sister or another female he is related to through his mother. Women, following their ritual marriage and divorce, engage in sexual relations with a "visiting husband," a man who arrives after supper and leaves before breakfast. A woman may have a series of these "visiting husbands." There is no legal or social bond between the woman and a "visiting husband." If a woman becomes pregnant, one of the "visiting husbands," not necessarily the genitor, publicly announces he is the father and provides a small gift for the midwife. This action is to "legitimize" the child, and the "father" has no further obligations. The child will be cared for and socialized by its mother and her brother or another matrilineal male relative.

In the Israeli kibbutz, little emphasis is placed on marriage and the family. According to Spiro (1968), there are no formal ceremonies on the kibbutz. If a couple wish to be partners, they merely apply to the community's housing committee for a common room. If children are born, they are not raised with their parents, but in a separate children's residence. The kibbutz cares for all the children's education and health needs.

In the traditional Chinese family, a man's first loyalty is to his parents, not his wife. Levy (1949, 1955) argues that in the traditional Chinese family, except for sex, the nuclear family is indistinguishable from the extended family and does not function as a distinct unit. He says that the economic and socialization functions are carried out by the extended family. Levy does not believe that the nuclear family is the basic unit in the traditional Chinese family.

The three cases just presented have all been used in attempts to challenge Murdock's assertion that the nuclear family is a universal social unit (the quotation at the beginning of the chapter). Murdock has defined the nuclear family as "a married man and woman with their offspring" (1949). Murdock argues that the universality of the family is based on its functions:

> In the nuclear family or its constituent relationships we thus see assembled four functions fundamental to human social life—the sexual, the economic, the reproductive, and the educational. Without provision for the first and third society would become extinct; for the second life itself would cease; for the fourth culture would come to an end. The immense social utility of the nuclear family and the basic reason for its universality thus begin to emerge in strong relief (1949:10).

Some social scientists have argued that the Nayar, the kibbutz, and the traditional Chinese family do not meet Murdock's definition or functions of the nuclear family. However, most social scientists today support Murdock's position on the universality of the nuclear family (i.e., Belkin and Goodman 1980; Stephens 1963; Zelditch 1964). The reason for this support of Murdock's position is that the cases cited do not make as strong an argument as might first appear. In the cases of the Nayar and the Israeli kibbutz, these are not independent cultures but rather minor subcultures within a larger society. They are tolerated deviations more than norms. Also, the practices of the Nayar have been coming more in line with the larger society for some time (Menchar 1965). As for the case of the kibbutz, even Spiro concedes that the case is not very strong. In fact, the children raised in dormitories, when asked where their home is, usually answer that it is their parents' room. This is because, in spite of living in dormitories, the children spend considerable time with their parents in their room. Also while the kibbutz provides for the children's health and education needs, ultimate responsibility still lies with the parents.

As for Levy's Chinese example, Zelditch (1964) points out that this case rests more on Levy's interpretation of the traditional Chinese family. Other researchers have not understood the traditional Chinese family in the same way. Yang (1971) points out that much familial behavior is often largely ceremonial and that closer ties exist between the husband and wife than may at first be apparent.

Murdock's assertion that the nuclear family is universal and is the basis or foundation for other familial arrangements seems to be consistent with a biblical understanding of the family. All through the Scriptures we find the husband and wife and their children as a unique social unit. In Genesis 2:24 God said, "A man will leave his father and mother and be united to his wife." God has set the nuclear family apart as a distinct unit.

TYPES OF FAMILY SYSTEMS

Monogamy

While the nuclear family is a universal social unit, it is generally not found standing alone, but rather as the basic unit in a larger familial network. There are two major types of family systems. The first is *monogamy*, which refers to a family system in which each person has only one spouse. This type of family arrangement is common to North America and most of Western Europe. The norm in these societies is a family unit consisting of a husband and a wife.

Polygamy

The second major type of family system is *polygamy*, which refers to a family system where there are multiple spouses. Polygamy takes various forms. The most common form is *polygyny*. In this type a man has more than one wife. The Old Testament Hebrews practiced polygyny. While God's law regulated polygyny (Exod. 21:1–11; Lev. 18:18; Deut. 21:15–17), it never forbade the practice. One form of polygyny involves a man marrying a woman and her sisters. This is referred to as *sororal polygyny*. Jacob, in the Old Testament, practiced sororal polygyny when he married Leah and her sister Rachel (Gen. 29:21–30). Hundreds of years later, under the Mosiac Law, the Hebrews were forbidden to practice sororal polygyny.

A polygynous family actually consists of a series of nuclear families. The husband and his first wife and their children make up one nuclear family, and so on. In other words, the husband is in a series of nuclear families, with the husband and one wife and their children being a distinct unit. In many polygynous societies each wife and her offspring have a separate hut or dwelling. This is why the nuclear family is still the basic unit even in polygynous societies.

When polygyny is discussed, many Westerners view it as a sexual arrangement. If we are honest, what we usually think of is an Arab sheik with an insatiable sexual appetite and his harem. The fact is, the basis for polygyny is not generally sexual. Among the Baganda, a tribal society in central Africa, the basis of polygyny is economic. As Queen and Haberstein point out, "Each wife becomes a source of income and constitutes an economic investment" (1967:67). The Baganda are a farming and herding society, and additional wives and children allow a man to farm more land and herd more cattle. A strong evidence of the economic basis for polygyny is the finding that in those areas of Africa that have had a subsistence economy, when wage labor is introduced, the rate of polygyny is dramatically reduced (Grunlan and Mayers 1979:37–38).

Another basis for polygyny is political. Often alliances between rulers are sealed by the marriage of one ruler or his son to the sister or daughter of another ruler. A ruler who has made several alliances could end up with several wives. Alliance marriages were practiced during the Old Testament period. We read in 1 Kings 3:1, "Solomon made an alliance with Pharaoh king of Egypt and married his daughter." Among many African tribes, political alliance by marriage is still being practiced. For example, many wives are acquired by Sudanese chiefs by the making of political alliances. In many tribal societies marriage alliances are used not only by chiefs but also by regular families for the achievement of some mutual end.

A second form of polygamy, which is quite rare, is *polyandry*. In this type a woman has more than one husband. The Todas, a pastoral tribe living in southern India, provide a classic example of polyandry. The Todas practiced female infanticide that resulted in a male population larger than the female population. Typically, the oldest son in a family would take a wife, and she would become the wife of all his brothers as well. Technically this arrangement is referred to as *fraternal polyandry*. When the wife becomes pregnant, one of the brothers, usually the oldest, is chosen to "give the bow." He makes a ceremonial bow and arrow and presents these to the wife before the relatives. He is then recognized as the "legal" father of the unborn child and any other children the wife should bear. However, if she bears more than two or three children, another brother will often "give the bow" and become the "father" of all the children born thereafter. Since early in this century, infanticide has been outlawed and the male-female ratio has been becoming more equal. This has led to more than one brother taking a wife and resulted in a form of group marriage. With the equalization of the sex ratio, the society has moved toward monogamy (Queen and Haberstein 1967). Polyandry has also been reported in parts of Tibet (Grunlan and Mayers 1979) and among the Kalapalo Indians of Brazil (Basso 1973).

Group Marriage

In a group marriage several men and women have legal sexual access to one another. There is no society where this form of marriage is a predominate model. It is sometimes a transitional arrangement as a group is changing from one type of family to another. We saw above how group marriage functioned as a transitional arrangement for the Todas. Group marriage may also be practiced by minority segments within a larger society. In American society some counterculture communes have practiced group marriage. However, on the whole, group marriage does not appear to be a viable marriage arrangement.

Polygamy and the Bible

We have already seen that the Old Testament never condemned polygyny, which was practiced by the Hebrews, but only regulated it. Some have suggested that the law of levirate marriage, which requires a man to marry a deceased brother's wife (Deut. 25:5–10), may have required polygyny in some instances (Grunlan and Mayers 1979:273). Writing in *Moody Monthly*, Graham Walker points out, "Despite King David's several wives and many concubines, he remained in fellowship with God" (1982:6).

When we turn to the New Testament, we find no references to the issue of polygyny. Some have suggested that 1 Timothy 3:2, 12 and Titus 1:6 are referring to polygyny when they say that elders and deacons should be "the husband of but one wife." However, it is most unlikely that Paul is addressing the issue of polygyny because it was not practiced by the Jews, Greeks, or Romans of Paul's day. What Paul is addressing in these passages is the nature of the marriage relationship and possibly issues such as divorce and remarriage, keeping of mistresses, and frequenting temple prostitutes. These passages are emphasizing the quality of marriage and family life (Grunlan and Mayers 1979:273).

While the Scriptures do not condemn polygyny, it is my personal conviction that God's intention in creation was for a one-man-and-one-woman relationship (Gen. 2:24). As a result of sin and the Fall, many of God's perfect intentions of creation were corrupted. With sin came death and a struggle for life. Polygyny is a functional marital arrangement for pastoral, nomadic peoples with high male mortality. While God permitted polygyny as an accommodation to societal problems, it was not His perfect plan. In polygynous societies, when people are converted to Christ, if they are in a polygynous relationship, it may be best to maintain it, but for unmarried converts the biblical ideal of one man and one woman should be taught.

RESIDENCE PATTERNS

Families are typed, not only by their marriage arrangements, but also by their living arrangements. The residence pattern we are most familiar with is called *neolocal residence*. In this type a nuclear family lives by itself rather than with either set of parents or other relatives. While some American couples live with one or the other's parents or with relatives, the ideal in our culture for a nuclear family is to have its own place.

In its strict sociological definition, an *extended family* refers to two or more related, nuclear families sharing a household (Grunlan and Mayers 1979:163; Nye and Berardo 1973:36; Zelditch 1964:468). In the *patrilocal extended family* a newly married couple takes up residence as part of the groom's parents' household. The Old Testament Hebrews practiced patrilocal residence. When Isaac married Rebekah, they lived in Abraham's household (Gen. 24). This arrangement is also illustrated by the Tiv of Nigeria, among whom the household compound

> consists of an open central area surrounded by huts and granaries arranged in a circle or oval. The compound group is headed by the senior man, the oldest male in the group, who functions as the group's leader. He usually has several wives, each of whom generally has a separate hut in the compound. Also included in the group compound are . . . his married sons along with their wives and children (Grunlan and Mayers 1979:163).

The residence pattern of a couple residing with the bride's parents is called a *matrilocal extended family*. The Navahos of the American Southwest practice matrilocal residence. Downs describes this arrangement among the Navaho for us:

> The homestead group, however, is clearly functional and easily defined. . . . Most often the group consists of an older woman, her daughters, and perhaps younger sisters.

In addition, the group will include the husbands of the married women. . . . The dominant woman may not be the eldest; an old grandmother or aunt may have a dowager position, although no longer able to contribute much labor to the group's maintenance. Essentially, then, this homestead group is a number of nuclear units related to each other by connection to the family of one of the spouses (1977:346).

Another residence pattern, called *avanculocal extended family*, involves the newly married couple's joining the household of the groom's uncle, his mother's brother. This residence pattern is practiced by the Trobriand Islanders of the South Pacific. A young man inherits land from his mother in this matrilineal society. However, because of the practice of avanculocal residence, his mother is living in the household of her husband's uncle. His mother's brother is farming the family land, so he and his wife go to live with his uncle.

KINSHIP

In its broadest sense, the family reaches beyond the nuclear family to a whole network of relationships. We refer to this larger network as a kinship system. *Kinship* is a network of biological, marital, and social ties making up a familial social system. The basis of this system is the connecting bonds between individuals. These bonds are called *kinship ties*.

Kinship Ties

There are three types of kinship ties. The first type, called *affinal ties,* refers to kinship relationships based on marital bonds. I am affinally related to my wife. I am also affinally related to her parents and brother. In North America, except for our spouses, we refer to those with whom we are affinally tied as "in-laws" or as "related by marriage."

The second type of kinship ties are those based on biological relationships or "blood." These are referred to as *consanguine ties*. My sons and daughter are consanguinely related to me. Affinal ties are made by contract, whereas consanguine ties are made by birth. Our affinal ties are achieved, but our consanguine ties are ascribed.

The third type of ties are called fictive ties. These are a socio-legal "fiction" whereby a person is legally, ceremonially, or religiously tied into a kinship network. A familiar fictive tie in our culture is adoption. When a child is legally adopted, he or she has all the rights, privileges, and responsibilities of a natural-born child.

Diagraming

In order to study kinship systems, social scientists have developed a system for diagraming them. While primarily used by anthropologists, this diagraming system is being used more and more by sociologists. Also many marriage and family counselors use the system to diagram a client's kinship network.

In the diagraming system males are represented by triangles and females are represented by circles. Affinal ties are noted by parallel lines and consanquine ties are shown by a single line. In diagraming, a reference point is needed; that is, the person from whose perspective the diagram is being viewed. A woman may be one man's wife, another's sister, and still another's mother. The reference person is referred to as *ego* and his or her symbol is darkened to indicate this. My families of orientation and procreation are diagramed in figure 2–1.

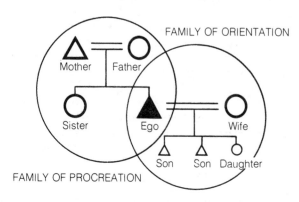

Figure 2–1. KINSHIP DIAGRAM.

Kin Terms

The terms we use to address and refer to others in our kinship system are called *kin terms*. There are two types of kin terms. The first, *terms of address*, are the terms we use to address these people. I address my wife as "Sandy" or "Honey," I address my children by their first names, and I call my mother "mom." The second, *terms of reference*, are the terms we use to refer to these people. I refer to my spouse as "my wife," I refer to my offspring as "my children," and I refer to my mother as "my mother."

Terms of address and terms of reference are not standard within a culture but often vary from region to region and with the relationship. I did a study of terms of address for parents among American college students (Grunlan 1972). In that research I divided the sample by region of the country in which students had been raised. I found that *mom* and *dad* were the most common terms of address, regardless of region. However, I also found some interesting regional secondary forms. Many females from the southeastern and south central regions of America addressed their fathers as *daddy*. Invariably, whenever a female addressed her father as *daddy*, she addressed her mother as *mother*. Several males and females from New England addressed their parents as *father* and *mother*. Again, if the person used *father*, they generally also used *mother*. In the Upper Midwest, some males used *pa* and *ma*. Another interesting finding of this research was that the term of address used for a subject's father was a better prediction of the term of address used for mother than a subject's term of address for his or her mother was of the term of address for his or her father. It might be speculated that one's relationship with his or her father may have a greater effect on one's relationship with his or her mother than vice versa. Further research in this area would be necessary before any firm conclusions could be drawn. Also, the assumption that terms of address are indicators of relationships would need to be further tested.

DESCENT RULES

My mother is getting on in years, and so the last time both my sister and I were home she asked us to pick out which particular family heirlooms, some with sentimental value and some with monetary value, we would like to have so she could list them in her will. This was a wise and somewhat normal approach to the problem of inheritance in the American culture; however, in other cultures this may have been totally unnecessary because cultural norms would have called for all property to go to me as the son or for all of it to go to my sister as the daughter. These types of norms are called *rules of descent*. Rules of descent are cultural norms that govern the determination of family line and inheritance. There are two basic types of rules of descent.

Unilinear Descent

The first type of descent is called *unilinear descent*. In this type kinship is traced through either only the maternal line or only the paternal line. When kinship is figured through the maternal line, it is called *matrilineal descent,* and the family line is traced through the female descendants. One is a member of the kin group by virtue of consanguine ties to the females of the lineage. Figure 2–2 illustrates a matrilineal kinship group. When kinship is traced through the paternal line, it is called *patrilineal descent.* Figure 2–3 illustrates a patrilineal kinship group.

Bilateral Descent

The second type of descent is *bilateral descent.* This is the system used in the American culture. With bilateral descent, one sees himself or herself as equally related to relatives on his or her mother's side of the family and his or her father's side of the family. If I were in a culture with patrilineal descent, the only "uncles" I would be related to would be my father's brothers. If I were in a matrilineal society, the only "uncles" I would be related to would be my mother's brothers. However, in a bilateral system I have four types of "uncles": (1) my father's brothers, (2) my mother's brothers, (3) my father's sister's husbands, and (4) my mother's sister's husbands. The same becomes true for aunts, cousins, and other relatives.

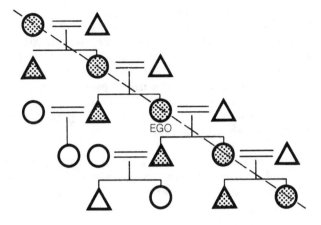

The members of the matrilineage are shaded. As with the patrilineage, matrilineage is based on consanguine ties, not affinal ties.

Figure 2-2. MATRILINEAL KINSHIP GROUP
(Grunlun and Mayers 1979: 181).

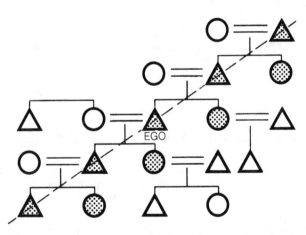

The members of the patrilineage are shaded, and these are the only persons that ego considers kind. Note that the patrilineage is based solely on consanguine ties, never on affinal ties.

Figure 2-3. PATRILINEAL KINSHIP GROUP
(Grunlan and Mayers 1979:179).

COUSIN MARRIAGE

In some states in the United States, marriage between first cousins is illegal and considered incestuous. Even in states where it is legal, it is not widely practiced. However, in many societies first-cousin marriage is the ideal relationship. First-cousin marriage takes two basic forms.

Parallel-cousin Marriage

Parallel cousins are the children of the same-sex siblings. That is, the children of two brothers would be parallel cousins as would be the children of two sisters. Parallel-cousin marriage is often practiced in unilinear societies that practice lineage endogamy; that is, persons must marry within their lineage. The Yoruk tribespeople of Turkey are a patrilineal group practicing lineage endogamy. Parallel-cousin marriage is the preferred form of marriage and very common in this society (Plog and Bates 1976:214). A parallel-cousin marriage is diagramed in figure 2–4.

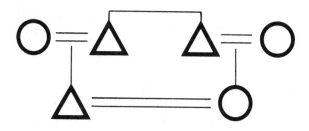

Figure 2–4. PARALLEL-COUSIN MARRIAGE.

Cross-cousin Marriage

Cross cousins are the children of opposite sex siblings. That is, the child of a woman would be the cross cousin of the woman's brother's child. Cross-cousin marriage, like parallel-cousin marriage, is practiced primarily in unilinear societies. Societies in which cross-cousin marriage is practiced are lineage exogamous. That is, persons are required to marry outside their lineage. Many African tribal groups as well as some South Pacific societies practice cross-cousin marriage. See figure 2–5 for a diagram of a cross-cousin marriage.

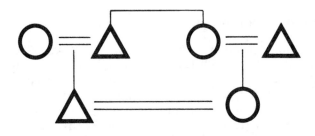

Figure 2–5. CROSS-COUSIN MARRIAGE.

KIN GROUPS

There are three major types of kin groups that serve as a basis for the social structure of many tribal societies.

Clan

The most common of the three kin groups is the *clan*, a consanguinely related group, matrilineal or patrilineal, who believe they are descended from a common, nonhuman ancestor. This is not an evolutionary concept, but rather a belief that they share the same life force or spirit as the ancestor. This nonhuman ancestor is usually referred to as a *totem*. Members of a clan may wear special insignias and generally have special rituals associated with their totem. The well-known totem pole of some North American Indian tribes are used to represent the clans of the tribe. What is less well known is that the usual practice was to place the totem of the most important clan at the bottom of the pole with the least important at the top.

Phratry

A group of two or more clans bound together by kinship or mutual interest is a *phratry*. Phratries may be endogamous or exogamous.

Moiety

When a tribe is divided into two divisions, based on birth, these groups are called *moieties*. Generally moieties have names, symbols, and rituals that aid in strengthening group solidarity. Moieties are usually exogamous in order to tie them together by kinship. When moieties are endogamous, there is usually greater rivalry between them.

OLD TESTAMENT HEBREW KINSHIP SYSTEM

The Old Testament gives us rich insights into the Hebrew kinship system. Many of the concepts we have been looking at are illustrated by the Hebrews. Let us examine the kinship system of the Hebrews during a particular period of Old Testament history.

At the time of the patriarchs (Abraham, Isaac, and Jacob) they practiced polygyny, including, in the case of Jacob, sororal polygyny. Their kinship system was patrilineal in descent, patrilocal in residence, and clan-endogamous in marriage. Parallel-cousin marriage was a preferred arrangement at this time. The ideal mate for a man was his father's brother's daughter or granddaughter (see figure 2–6). During this period they also practiced levirate marriage as illustrated by the case of Judah's sons Er and Onan (Gen. 38:6–10). It is also interesting to note that levirate marriage may still have been in existence in Jesus' day, since the Sadducees raised a question about it to Jesus (Matt. 22:24–28).

A knowledge of various kinship systems and marriage forms is a tremendous aid in understanding the Bible in general and the Old Testament in particular. The Hebrews were a product of their culture and time. Studying the kinship systems of the Egyptians and other Near Eastern societies of that period sheds rich light on the Scriptures. A knowledge of various kinship systems also is an invaluable aid to those involved in crosscultural ministry.

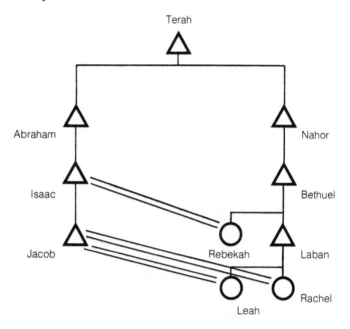

Patrilateral parallel-cousin marriage among the pastoral Hebrews of the Old Testament. The patrilineage of Terah, showing the prescribed marriage of Isaac to his patrilateral cousin Rebekah, and of their son Jacob to his parallel-cousins Leah and Rachel. (This diagram is limited to the male offspring through whom the line of descent devolved.)

Figure 2–6. PARALLEL-COUSIN MARRIAGE AMONG THE PATRI-ARCHS (Hoebel 1972:407).

DISCUSSION QUESTIONS

1. Why do you think the nuclear family is the basis for kinship systems in every culture?
2. In your opinion, why did God permit the Old Testament Hebrews to practice polygyny? What is your opinion about present-day tribal societies that practice polygyny?

3. What do you believe accounts for the differences in terms of address used by American college students as found in my research?

4. Why do you think a relationship that one culture sees as an ideal marriage another culture views as incestuous?

5. What was the advantage of practicing parallel-cousin marriage for the Old Testament Hebrews?

6. What aspects of the biblical marriage customs and practices do you see as a part of those cultures and which do you see as absolute for all cultures? Why?

SUGGESTED READING

Nelson Graburn, ed., *Readings in Kinship and Social Structure* (New York: Harper and Row, 1971). A collection of articles on kinship and social structure. This volume contains some classic articles on kinship systems and is a good introduction to the field.

George Peter Murdock, *Social Structure* (New York: Macmillan, 1949). This is a classic on kinship. It is the foundation on which all other works in the field build and is the place to begin any serious study of kinship.

Stuart A. Queen and Robert W. Haberstein, *The Family in Various Cultures* (Philadelphia: Lippincott, 1971). An overview of the variety of family systems found around the world. Covers both modern and historical cultures and contains an interesting chapter dealing with polyandry among the Toda.

Ernest L. Schusky, *Manual for Kinship Analysis* (New York: Holt, Rinehart and Winston, 1965). A basic, but thorough, introduction to kinship. An excellent source for understanding basic kinship terminology, systems, and diagraming.

PART II

DATING
AND COURTSHIP

3

Dating:
The Getting-Acquainted Process

Remember how our love began?
Years ago, I offered you my arm
  that September night we first went out.
You reached for it
  as we leaped a puddle together.
Then you walked just close enough
  to show you liked it.
I glimpsed your face under the streetlight,
  excitement splashing gently on it. . . .
No commitment—just beginnings.

FROM "AN ODE TO MARRIAGE"
HAROLD MYRA (1979:60)

WHEN I WAS in graduate school, my wife became a friend of the wife of a graduate student from India. One day they were discussing how they had met their husbands. The Indian woman explained how their marriage had been arranged by their parents. My wife described how we had met and dated. The woman from India, who was high caste and a college graduate, shared with my wife that she found the American dating system degrading. She thought it was awful to have to go out and "try out" different men to find one to marry.

In many cultures marriages are arranged as was the marriage of the couple from India. In other cultures the kinship system determines whom one will marry. For example, among some African tribes a person is expected to marry his or her father's brother's child, and among other African tribes young people are expected to marry their mother's brother's child. In North American culture, where mate selection is freer and more open, the dating process is generally used to get to know persons of the opposite sex more personally.

The terms *date* and *dating* are derived from the traditional pattern in which a man called a woman well in advance to arrange to take her to a concert, play, or other social event on a specific day or date. Dating may be defined as prearranged social activities shared by two single persons of the opposite sex. Saxton expands this definition of dating:

> It may be planned many months or just minutes in advance; it may involve only the one couple or another couple as well, or it may take place within a group. In any case, an event becomes a "date" only when one person (usually but not necessarily the male) asks the other to share in the activity. They then form a paired relation, publicly recognizable, for the duration of the event (1972:145).

How does dating differ from courtship, which will be discussed in the next chapter? While a clear line cannot be drawn between the two processes because they obviously overlap, generally *dating* is concerned with the particular event and getting to know another person, whereas *courtship* is concerned with mate selection and preparation for marriage. Nye and Berardo point out that dating and courtship differ in terms of intent rather than behavior. They go on to say, "We have defined dating as an activity engaged in for its immediate rewards, courtship can be defined as an activity directed toward marriage" (1973:111).

TYPES OF DATING

Some sociologists divide dating into two types: what Golanty and Harris (1982:115) call recreational dating and attachment-oriented dating and Garrett (1982:85) calls casual and serious dating. *Recreational dating* or *casual dating* involves a relationship that revolves around the event. While the date may involve intimate physical contact, there is no commitment beyond the date. Recreational dating allows young people to be involved with a number of persons of the opposite sex without becoming serious with them.

Attachment-oriented dating or *serious dating* involves some level of commitment. The couple become attached to each other, and dating revolves around their relationship rather than the event. In this type of dating many couples "go steady," that is, they date each other exclusively. Attachment-oriented dating may well move into courtship. It might be argued that once the couple begins to think in terms of marriage the line between dating and courtship has been crossed, see figure 3–1.

Recreational
Dating   →   Attachment-
Oriented Dating   →   Courtship   →   Marriage

Figure 3–1. CONTINUUM OF DATING AND COURTSHIP.

SOCIAL FACTORS IN DEVELOPMENT OF DATING

Dating, at least as most of us have experienced it, is a modern practice. It is generally accepted that dating did not become widespread in the United States until after World War I (Cox 1981:112; Garrett 1982:82; Kephart 1981:257; Orthner 1981:61). Before this time dating was quite formal, limited to circumscribed activities, and generally chaperoned. Orthner (1981:62–63) suggests four social factors that led to the development of modern dating: industrialization, urbanization, increased free time, and the automobile.

Industrialization

The Industrial Revolution had a profound effect on society and social relationships, including marriage and the family. Before the Industrial Revolution most men worked in or around the home. With the advent of industrialization and factories, work moved away from the home, and fathers were absent for most of the day and were not as involved in the lives of their children. During World War I many women joined the labor force and began to strive for greater independence. In 1920, women received the vote—a major step in their emancipation.

Social changes brought about by industrialization tended to weaken traditional family ties and the family's control over its members. Attitudes developed that were conducive to dating. Individual values became more important than family values. The next three social factors may be seen as results or extensions of industrialization.

Urbanization

Industrialization with its factories required large numbers of workers in a concentrated area, and large urban areas developed around industrial centers. Urbanization brought many young people together and exposed them to a large group of potential mates. Urban centers provided a sense of anonymity unknown in small rural communities. A couple could get together in the city without everyone knowing about it. The coeducational school systems in urban areas also fostered contact between the sexes.

Increased Free Time

With the enactment of child-labor laws and compulsory education, the amount of free time increased for many young people. And the development of modern machinery and appliances for farm work and household chores allowed a young person more free time. As Orthner states:

> The increase in potential leisure was accompanied by a decline in family-centered activities and increased dependence on commercial recreation. The cinema, soda fountains, dance halls, speakeasies, and amusements of all descriptions emerged to fill the idle moments of the young. They became the places where young people would congregate and meet others, and they structured their leisure-time activities around them (1981:63).

The Automobile

Perhaps nothing has shaped modern dating more than the automobile. The automobile provided both the mobility to engage in a variety of recreational activities and a place of privacy. In fact, many dating activities began to center around the automobile, such as drive-in theaters and carhop restaurants. While most dates involved attending a concert, movie, dance, or party, they frequently ended in a parked automobile on a "lover's lane." A recent addition to this mobility has been the van, which one writer calls a "mobile bedroom" (Cox 1981:112).

FUNCTIONS OF DATING

Dating serves a number of functions in our society (Green 1978:106–7; Scanzoni and Scanzoni 1981:142–44). One of these functions is recreation. A couple may go out together just to have a good time. They can enjoy an event and each other's company without any further commitment. A second function of dating is achieving status. In many settings a certain status is achieved by having a boyfriend or girlfriend. Waller (1937), in his well-known study "The Dating and Rating Complex," points out that a person can achieve high status among one's peers by the attractiveness, personality, or other prestigious characteristics of his or her date.

The next three functions of dating involve socialization. The third function of dating is to provide young people with the opportunity to learn about the opposite sex and how to behave toward those of the opposite sex. As Scanzoni and Scanzoni put it, "dating can be a way of socializing persons into the 'how' of getting along with persons of the other sex—a way of learning and trying out social skills" (1981:143). A fourth function of dating is that it enables young people to learn more about themselves, to understand better both their personality and gender identity. Dating provides young people with the opportunity to explore their personality and values and to further develop and clarify their gender-role identity. A fifth function of dating is preparatory socialization for marriage and family roles. As Cox states, "One learns something about marital and familial roles by relating with the opposite sex" (1981:113).

A final function of dating is to facilitate mate selection. By dating a number of different people a person can discover the type of person he or she is most comfortable with. Dating allows one to learn about oneself and others, as was pointed out above; this knowledge aids in mate selection. In the American culture, most people meet the person they will eventually marry through the dating process. A couple may have no thoughts of marriage during their early dating, but during the dating process they may discover that they are compatible, share common interests, have similar values, and find they are developing deep feelings for each other. At that point the couple may move beyond dating into courtship.

GOING STEADY

Ken gave Sharon his high school ring, which she wore on a chain around her neck. Ken, who had been given Sharon's ring, wore the smaller ring on the last finger of his left hand. No other boys at school ever asked Sharon out while she wore Ken's ring. Ken did not ask any other girls out while he wore Sharon's ring. The exchange of class rings signified that Ken and Sharon were going steady. The exchange of class rings, "friendship" rings, or other items was quite common in the 50s and 60s as part of going steady.

Going steady may be defined as an arrangement whereby a couple date each other exclusively over a period of time. Some sociologists believe that the practice of going steady is waning (Green 1978:109; Scanzoni and Scanzoni 1981:144). However, from my observations, I would agree with Cox, who says, "Couples still go steady, but . . . the relationship seems less formal, more relaxed and casual" (1981:114). What appears to be waning is many of the older practices associated with going steady, such as the exchange of tokens and a formal commitment. However, exclusive dating appears to continue to be widely practiced.

Reasons for Going Steady

Why do couples choose to go steady, whether or not it is a formal arrangement? One reason for going steady is security. A person is always sure of having a date. One is relieved of the stress of having to ask for a date or waiting to be asked. Going steady also provides security from the competition of the open market (Scanzoni and Scanzoni 1981:144).

Another reason for going steady is status or prestige. In many circles it is considered a status symbol to have a steady boyfriend or girlfriend. As Nye and Berardo point out, "It may be essentially a desired status . . . either in one's own perception or in that of the peer group" (1973:111). Going steady means that someone values the person enough to want to date him or her regularly and exclusively. Also, American culture is still couple oriented, and going steady fits that pattern.

In addition, going steady is often socially reinforced. If a couple begin dating regularly, others will frequently treat them as if they are going steady, whether or not they are. A complaint I frequently hear from women in my classes is that if they go out with a fellow more than twice, other guys stop asking them out.

Gordon (1978:183) has suggested that some couples go steady out of convenience. Some couples find themselves in a *de facto* state of going steady. That is, neither of them may desire an exclusive relationship, but they may find themselves in a situation where there are no other options. A couple may also go steady out of habit; that is, a comfortable relationship has developed and neither is interested in disturbing it.

Problems With Going Steady

There can be problems with going steady. Cox (1981:116) suggests a number of these problems. One is that going steady places sexual pressures on a couple. There is greater probability of becoming involved in premarital sex. Another problem is jealousy and possessiveness. Going steady is an exclusive arrangement, and it is easy for one partner or the other to become jealous of others or to become possessive of the other partner. This can add tension to the relationship.

Still another problem with going steady, especially during early adolescence, is the lack of opportunity to interact with and get to know a variety of persons of the other sex. As Cox says, "The young person who has always gone steady is unlikely to have had enough experience with a broad cross-section of the opposite sex to have developed his or her interpersonal abilities to the fullest"

(1981:116). Also, the young people who have gone steady most of their dating experience may not have had enough experience to make a good mate choice.

An additional problem with going steady during early adolescence is that sociological research indicates that the earlier young people start to go steady, the earlier they tend to marry (Clayton 1979:343; Cox 1981:116). In the next chapter we will see that early marriages have quite a low rate of success. It is important that young people date a number of different persons in their early dating years. During this time, dating should not be considered as much a romantic activity as a recreational activity and an opportunity to meet and get to know other young people.

ATTRACTION

Why do we find some people more attractive than others? How important is physical appearance to attractiveness? Why are some physically less attractive persons socially attractive? Do men and women find the same features in others attractive or are there sex differences? These are some of the questions and issues social scientists are attempting to study.

Physical Attractiveness

Usually, the first thing that attracts or repels us about another person is his or her physical appearance. While "beauty is in the eye of the beholder," there are certain social norms by which physical attractiveness is judged. If this were not so, we would not have beauty contests, fashion models, movie stars, and centerfolds. Our culture generally prefers slender to fat, tall over short, hair to bald, and muscular to skinny. If you took five photographs of different men who varied in physical appearance and asked people to rank them by physical attractiveness, you would not get unanimous agreement, but you would very likely get a high level of agreement. An illustration of how social norms affect our perception of physical attractiveness is men's hair styles. When I was a teen-ager, the most popular hair style was the crew cut (the hair cropped short all over the head), and a man with hair over his ears was considered effeminate. However, in the 1980s the crew cut is considered odd, and many men are wearing longer hair styles with hair over their ears.

The American culture places a heavy emphasis on physical attractiveness. Social research indicates that, all other things being equal, we attribute higher social status to more attractive persons and lower social status to less attractive persons (Belkin and Goodman 1980:109). Several studies have demonstrated that physical attractiveness affects how we react to people. A study done in a traffic court found that attractive defendants were treated more leniently than unattractive defendants (Piehl 1977). Another study, using simulated court cases, found that under identical circumstances, attractive persons received more favorable treatment than unattractive defendants (Stephen and Tully 1977). Even professionals can be biased toward physically attractive people. A study found that clinicians were more likely to find unattractive persons mentally disturbed than attractive persons exhibiting the same behavior (Jones, Hansson, and Phillips 1978).

We tend to attribute favorable characteristics to attractive persons. Physically attractive persons are seen as more romantic and sexual. They are perceived as being more exciting dates. Physically attractive people are also seen as possessing more socially desirable traits than less attractive persons. It is easy to see why physical attractiveness is such an important aspect of interpersonal attraction.

What should be our attitude as Christians toward physical attractiveness in general and these research findings in particular? In the Old Testament, Samuel fell prey to attributing socially desirable characteristics to a physically attractive person. God sent Samuel to Bethlehem to the home of Jesse to anoint a king to replace Saul. When Samuel saw Jesse's oldest son, Eliab, who was tall and good-looking, he thought, "Surely the Lord's anointed stands here . . ." (1 Sam. 16:6). God's reply was, "Do not consider his appearance or his height, for I have rejected him. The Lord does not look at the things man looks at. Man looks at the outward appearance, but the

Lord looks at the heart" (1 Sam. 6:7). The same principle is found in the New Testament. Peter advises Christian wives, "Your beauty should not come from outward adornment, such as braided hair and the wearing of gold jewelry and fine clothes. Instead, it should be that of your inner self, the unfading beauty of a gentle and quiet spirit" (1 Peter 3:3–4).

The Bible teaches us that we should be careful not to be fooled by outward appearances, but to be concerned with inner qualities. While we should attempt to be well groomed and dress attractively, our emphasis should be on developing our inner qualities (Gal. 5:22). Also, we need to be careful not to judge people by their appearance, but rather by their personhood (James 2:1–12). We need to take care that we do not allow the world's emphasis on physical appearance to overshadow the Bible's emphasis on inner qualities.

Sexual Stimulus Value

While physical appearance is a significant aspect of our attraction toward a person of the opposite sex, it is a person's total effect on us that attracts us to that one. Belkin and Goodman (1980:113–18) call this total effect *Sexual Stimulus Value* (SSV). They suggest that in addition to physical appearance there are five key factors that contribute to a person's SSV.

Self-confidence

The first factor in SSV is confidence. Our behavior, as well as others' responses to us, is affected by our self-confidence or lack of it. People are generally more comfortable around self-confident persons. When persons feel good about themselves, others are also more likely to feel good about them. Also, self-confident people make it easier for others to feel good about themselves too.

It is important to distinguish between confidence and conceit. Confidence says, "I'm okay; I like myself." Conceit says, "I'm better than you; you're lucky to have me around." Confidence lifts self up; conceit puts others down. Conceit turns others away whereas confidence attracts others.

Power

The second factor that contributes to SSV is power. A person in a position of power or control usually enjoys a higher level of SSV than he or she would in ordinary circumstances. Both ex-Governor Marvin Mandell of Maryland and Governor Hugh Carey of New York married younger, physically attractive wives. Neither man is particularly physically attractive. Another example is ex-Secretary of State Henry Kissinger. While secretary of state, he dated many beautiful socialites and movie stars. He was constantly seen in the company of beautiful women. Persons in positions of power, despite their personal appearance, frequently find members of the opposite sex attracted to them.

Public Recognition

A third factor in SSV is public recognition. Fame is a "turn-on." John Hinckley attempted to assassinate President Reagan in order to achieve fame to attract movie star Jodie Foster. Each of us can think of music or movie stars that are not particularly physically attractive but have a large following. Belkin and Goodman (1980) cite the example of Tiny Tim, a rock star of the previous generation. Eccentric and repulsive in appearance, he never had a date as a teen-ager; no one wanted to go out with him. When he became a recording star, two body guards were required to protect him from his female fans.

Showing Interest

A fourth factor that contributes to SSV is showing interest in another. Most people find someone who shows an interest in them attractive. We all like to receive attention, and when someone pays attention to us, we generally enjoy being with them. Counseling with married persons who have had an affair often reveals that their initial attraction to the other person was not physical. Often the affair involved a person of the other sex who showed interest in them and gave them the attention they did not receive at home. A person will often explain that at the beginning it was a friendship relationship and then the affair "just happened."

Gentleness

The fifth factor that contributes to SSV is gentleness. Gentleness makes another person feel secure and encourages trust. Gentleness also infers strength. Belkin and Goodman say, "When we encounter gentleness in another, it may actually produce a physical effect" (1980:117).

We have seen that attraction between members of the opposite sex is based on more than physical appearance. There are many factors about another person that may attract us. Many of the SSV factors that attract us to another may be unconscious. That is, we may have a difficult time explaining why we find a person attractive.

Theories of Attraction

Social scientists have speculated on the basis of interpersonal attraction. They have attempted to explain why we are attracted to some people and not to others. The research in this area has led to a number of theories. We will examine two of the more widely cited theories.

Equity Theory

The first of these theories, the equity theory, is based on social exchange. This theory argues that we are most attracted to persons from whom we get at least as much as we give.

Walster and Walster, in their development of equity theory have set forth four basic propositions:

1. We seek pleasure rather than pain.
2. However, we have to be able to give pleasure in order to receive it. The more we give, the more we receive.
3. We are most comfortable when there is a fair balance between what we give and what we receive. Having less than we deserve makes us resentful.
4. If the giving and receiving are out of balance, we will work to restore a balance, either actually or in fantasy, or we will end the relationship (1978:135).

We might look back at the discussion of Sexual Stimulus Value to illustrate this theory. A prominent political figure with both power and public recognition, who was not particularly physically attractive, might enjoy being seen with a physically attractive younger woman. The woman might enjoy the excitement and recognition of being with a prominent political figure. They are attracted to each other because each believes he or she is *receiving* at least as much as *giving to* the relationship. In the next chapter we will again look at the exchange theory as an approach to mate selection.

Attribution Theory

Researchers who hold to the attribution theory postulate that people attribute characteristics, motives, and feelings to others based on their behavior and appearance. They also believe we have expectations of how others will behave in the future based on how they have behaved in the past. People are usually attracted to persons who (1) are attracted to them, (2) have similar values, and (3) provide emotional support (Berscheid and Walster 1969). These characteristics are not directly observable, but are attributed based on behavior and appearance. Based on peoples' behavior and appearance, we attribute traits and characteristics to them, and if these are ones we like, we will be attracted to those persons.

LOVE

Attraction for some people often leads to love. And love, at least in North American culture, is seen as the basis for marriage. Several years ago Frank Sinatra had a hit song with the line, "Love and marriage go together like a horse and carriage; you can't have one without the other." Love is an important aspect of dating, courtship, and marriage.

While most of us have experienced love, we have a hard time defining it. For one thing there are several different types of love. Even if we eliminate the trite types of love, such as love for a car or a type of food, there are still several significant types of love. These include:

1. Neighborly love. This is the care, concern, and respect for other human beings; it is the type of love

the Bible refers to when it says, "Love your neighbor" and "Love your enemies."

2. Friendship love. Sometimes referred to as "brotherly/sisterly love," this is the love between close friends, such as David and Jonathan in the Bible.

3. Familial love. This is the love between a parent and child, between siblings, and between other close family members.

4. Heterosexual love. This is the love between a man and a woman; it is the type of love on which marriage is usually based.

Many attempts to define love involve listing the characteristics or qualities of love. Golanty and Harris define love in terms of four qualities:

1. Love is an emotion, a desire for the person.

2. Love involves a positive attitude toward the person.

3. Love involves affection, feelings of warmth and closeness.

4. Love involves wanting to interact with the loved one (1982:34).

Considering heterosexual love, which is the concern of this chapter, Kephart defines it in terms of three characteristics:

1. A strong emotional attachment toward a person of the opposite sex.

2. The tendency to think of this person in an idealized manner.

3. A marked physical attraction (1972).

Several social scientists have turned to the three Greek words for love—*eros, philia,* and *agape*—to define the various aspects of love (i.e., Cox 1981; Green 1978; Lasswell and Lasswell 1982; Saxton 1980; Scanzoni and Scanzoni 1981). Another who has turned to this approach is Rollo May. He sees *eros* as the human side of love. He points out that while *eros* involves sex, it is more than that:

It is this urge for union with the partner that is the occasion for human tenderness. For eros—not sex as such—is the source of human tenderness. Eros is the longing to establish union. . . . The two persons, longing, as all individuals do, to overcome the separateness and isolation to which we all are heir as individuals, can participate in a relationship that, for the moment, is not made up of two isolated, individual experiences, but a genuine union (1969:75).

May goes on to define *philia* as "brotherly love and friendship" (1969:317). He sees *agape* as an altruistic or self-giving love. He says it is "the concern for the other's welfare beyond any gain that one can get out of it" (1969:319). Both Rollo May (1969:320) and Paul Tillich (1957:114–15) argue that these three types of love, *eros*, *philia*, and *agape*, are not in opposition to each other, but rather are complimentary. They argue that true love combines all three. May calls the combination *authentic love*.

Theories of Love

In their study of love as a behavioral and social phenomena, sociologists and psychologists have developed a number of theories. Two of the more widely accepted theories are the two-factor theory and the wheel theory.

Two-factor Theory

The two-factor theory of love is part of a larger theory for explaining all types of emotions. Basically, this theory argues that our emotions, including love, are a result of physiological changes and our cognitive interpretation of the change and the situation. For example, under romantic circumstances such as a candlelit dinner with an attractive person of the opposite sex, if one became physically aroused, he or she would likely label those feelings as "love."

Belkin and Goodman (1980:121) illustrate this theory with an unpublished study conducted by Belkin and his associates. In this study, male subjects were randomly divided into two groups. One group was told they would receive electric shocks; the control group was not told anything about shocks. The subjects in both groups were introduced to an attractive female. The males who had been aroused by the fear of an electric shock were more attracted to the female than members of the control group.

The study by Belkin and his associates is an interesting demonstration of the two-factor theory. The subjects who were already aroused by the fear of the electric shock interpreted their physiological arousal as attraction when they met the attractive female. The subjects who had not been told about an electric shock were not physiologically aroused before meeting the attractive female. Therefore only the physiological arousal experienced by meeting the female was experienced as attraction. The two-factor theory postulates that emotions are a combination of physiological arousal and the label we apply to the arousal. When people become physiologically aroused, they interpret their arousal by the stimuli present. A physiological arousal in the presence of a rattlesnake might be interpreted as fear; however, in the presence of an attractive person of the opposite sex the same arousal might be interpreted as attraction.

Wheel Theory

One of the most widely cited theories of love is Ira Reiss's Wheel Theory (1980). His theory consists of four interconnected processes: rapport, self-revelation, mutual dependency, and intimacy and need fulfillment. The processes are cyclical, with one running into the next. Reiss pictures the relationship between the processes as a wheel (see figure 3–2).

The love relationship develops and deepens as one moves clockwise through the processes or stages of the wheel. One "falls out of love" by moving counter-clockwise through the stages. We will examine the individual stages briefly and then discuss the whole wheel.

The first stage is *rapport*. In this stage a couple meet and become acquainted. They begin to discover if they have mutual interests and are comfortable with each other. If they find they share some things in common and are able to communicate easily with each other, rapport begins to build. Reiss argues that a couple must first develop rapport before they can move on to the next stage.

The second stage, *self-revelation*, grows out of the first. As a couple becomes comfortable with each other,

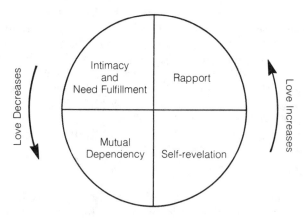

Figure 3-2. REISS'S WHEEL THEORY OF LOVE (Reiss 1980).

their communication will move from more superficial matters to more personal issues. As each reveals intimate information about himself and herself to the other, a feeling of closeness develops. Reiss believes that a couple must have intimate communication and understanding for real love to develop.

Self-revelation leads to *mutual dependency*, the next state. As a couple gets to know each other more intimately, they begin to desire each other. They enjoy being together and begin to develop a lifestyle that involves the other. A mutual dependency begins to form. According to Reiss, it is at this stage that the relationship becomes serious and the love bond begins to form.

The final stage is *intimacy and need fulfillment*. This stage centers around some of our deepest needs—acceptance, trust, support, and love. These needs can be met only in an intimate relationship. Because these needs are so pervasive, most people look for a permanent relationship in which these needs can continue to be met. This is one reason why people marry. It also helps explain why some marriages break up. If a person's needs are not being met in the relationship, dependency weakens and the person begins to withdraw.

Looking at Reiss's Wheel Theory, we can see that he understands love as developing from a social relationship.

At each stage a couple may move backward or forward. If a couple moves forward through the stages, the result will be a paired dependency bond or love. Some people may commit themselves to marriage before moving through all the stages. While they might complete the process after marriage, the probability is that the process will begin to reverse and the marriage will dissolve. A good marriage requires intimacy and mutual need fulfillment. We will look further at the bases for marriage in the next chapter.

Authentic Love Versus Infatuation

Not all romantic attraction is authentic love. It may be only infatuation. We may define *infatuation* as an immature emotional response to a person of the opposite sex based on superficial or idealized characteristics rather than the whole person. Saxton says,

> Infatuation tends to focus on a single aspect of the other, whereas love focuses on the whole person. An infatuated person tends to relate to the other as an *object* to be manipulated, controlled, or used, whereas a person in love tends to identify with the other. Further, this identification tends to be persistent and enduring in love, while infatuation tends to be relatively short-lived (1980:205).

Saxton goes on to contrast love and infatuation as follows:

> Infatuation is self-centered, whereas love is other-centered; that is, infatuation tends to be characterized by preoccupation with oneself and with one's own feelings. The person often feels awkward, constrained, self-conscious, unfulfilled, fragmented, and insecure and may withdraw from sensory experience and contact with others, becoming less and less aware of incoming stimuli (daydreaming, staying away from friends, being unable to eat). On the other hand, a person in love is oriented toward the well-being of the other and tends to be *less* self-conscious or concerned with feelings of difficulty or inadequacy, feeling relatively *more* self-assured, secure, and adequate. The person in love is active and open to sensory experience and feels healthy and keenly alive, delighting in all aspects of the environment—food, friends, sights,

and sounds. A person in love is moved to put dreams into action (1980:205).

How can we tell if we are in love with someone or only infatuated? A number of distinctions between love and infatuation are presented in table 3–1. Perhaps the most important distinction is that love takes time to develop. Contrary to the statements found in some novels and poetry, there is no such thing as "love at first sight" or "falling in love." Authentic love involves the total person, and it takes time to get to know another

TABLE 3–1
THE DIFFERENCE BETWEEN INFATUATION AND AUTHENTIC LOVE

INFATUATION	AUTHENTIC LOVE
1. Infatuation is born at first sight and will conquer all.	1. Authentic love is a developing relationship and deepens with realistically shared experiences.
2. Infatuation demands exclusive attention and devotion and is jealous of outsiders.	2. Authentic love is built on self-acceptance and is shared unselfishly with others.
3. Infatuation is characterized by exploitation and direct need gratification.	3. Authentic love seeks to aid and strengthen the loved one without striving for recompense.
4. Infatuation is built on physical attraction and sexual gratification. Sex often dominates the relationship.	4. Authentic love includes sexual satisfaction, but not to the exclusion of sharing in other areas of life.
5. Infatuation is static and ego centric. Change is sought in the partner in order to satisfy one's own needs and desires.	5. Authentic love is growing and developing reality. Love expands to include the growth and creativity of the loved one.
6. Infatuation is romanticized. The couple does not face reality or is frightened by it.	6. Authentic love enhances reality and makes the partners more complete and adequate persons.
7. Infatuation is irresponsible and fails to consider the future consequences of today's action.	7. Authentic love is responsible and gladly accepts the consequences of mutual involvement.

Source: Adapted from Kelley 1969:212–13.

person. In terms of Reiss's Wheel Theory, infatuation develops at the rapport state, whereas authentic love develops as one moves through all the stages. In the next chapter we will see that short acquaintanceships before marriage produce a higher divorce rate. In all likelihood many of these couples who married after short acquaintanceships thought they were in love but were only infatuated with each other. Before a step as serious as marriage is considered, two people need to be certain their relationship is based on authentic love—not just infatuation.

Biblical Love

The Bible has much to say about love. Not only does it talk about God's love for us and our love for God, it also discusses neighborly love, friendship love, familial love, and heterosexual love. When the Bible speaks of heterosexual love, the topic of this chapter, it generally speaks of it in connection with marriage. The Song of Solomon speaks of the love between a man and a woman and presents the ideal of heterosexual love.

In the New Testament, when Paul tells husbands to love their wives (Eph. 5:25, 28; Col. 3:19), he uses the Greek word *agape*. When most of us think about love, we think of an emotion. *Agape* love is not an emotion; it is an act of the will. In the Bible love is never described in terms of feelings, but in terms of action. Feelings are the by-products of love, not the essence of love. Someone has paraphrased 1 Corinthians 13:4–8 to show how a person in love will act:

> I will be patient with you;
> I will be kind to you;
> I will not envy you;
> I will not boast or proudly elevate myself above you;
> I will not be rude to you;
> I will not exploit you for my own selfish ends;
> I will not be easily angered with you;
> I will keep no record of wrongs;
> I will not delight when you are harmed, or
>   I hear evil concerning you;

I will rejoice with truth;
I will always protect you;
I will always trust you;
I will always hope in you;
I will persevere with you;
I will never fail you.

(Source Unknown)

DISCUSSION QUESTIONS

1. In your opinion, should young people engage in recreational dating with a variety of persons of the opposite sex before starting to date one person seriously? Why?

2. Why do you think exclusive dating has remained popular even as the older practices associated with "going steady" have disappeared?

3. How important do you believe physical attraction is for obtaining a date? Why?

4. Why do you think favorable characteristics are attributed to attractive persons?

5. Which of the theories presented in the chapter best explains attraction? Love? Why?

6. While the Bible does not discuss dating directly, what biblical principles do you believe Christian young people should apply to the dating process?

SUGGESTED READING

C. Stephen Board et al., *HIS Guide to Sex, Singleness, and Marriage* (Downers Grove, Ill.: InterVarsity, 1974). A collection of articles from *HIS* magazine. Topics covered include various aspects of premarital sex and dating, singleness, and preparation for marriage.

John J. Conger, *Adolescence and Youth* (New York: Harper and Row, 1977). A good introduction to adolescent development. Along with physical, cognitive, and social development, this book deals with adolescent sexuality, dating, and peer relationships. It also contains an interesting chapter on moral development and values.

Herbert J. Miles, *The Dating Game* (Grand Rapids: Zondervan, 1975). A Christian perspective on dating. Miles deals with the nature of love, early dating, physical intimacy, parents and dating, as well as courtship. He presents some very interesting ideas about weddings.

H. Norman Wright and Marvin Inmon *Dating, Waiting, and Choosing a Mate* (Irvine, Calif.: Harvest House, 1978). This interesting book deals with all aspects of dating and courtship. It contains an interesting chapter on recreational dating with hundreds of suggestions.

4

Courtship:
The Mate Selection Process

Yes, I chose you.
Out of all the lovely girls I knew,
I chose you.
How marvelous are the women of planet Earth,
    hair flaring in the wind
    rich browns and golds
    a thousand delicious shapes
    girls who laugh saucily
    girls who read Browning
    girls who play sitars
    girls who fix carburetors
Of all those fascinating possibilities,
I chose you.

FROM *"AN ODE TO MARRIAGE"*
HAROLD MYRA (1979:61)

WHILE DATING IS the process of meeting and interacting with persons of the opposite sex, courtship is the process of selecting a specific person and moving toward marriage. Even though there may not be a definite point at which a couple moves from dating to courtship, the two processes can be distinguished by their purpose.

FIELD OF ELIGIBLES

As we consider the mate selection process, think of your own situation. If you are single, is every unmarried person of the opposite sex a potential mate? If you are married, did you consider every unmarried person of the opposite sex before making your selection? Of course not. Most of us did, or will do, our mate selection from a limited group of individuals. Sociologists refer to this group from whom we select our mate as the *field of eligi-*

bles. How is our field of eligibles determined? There are several factors involved that we will examine.

Exogamy

Every society has a culturally defined group within which one may not select a mate. The rule of *exogamy* requires a person to select a mate outside this group. In some societies this may include members of one's clan or extended kin group. For example, among many West African tribes a person may marry cousins of their mother's side of the family but may not marry cousins of their father's side.

In the culture of the United States, the rule of exogamy requires people to marry outside of their close family and sex. All states forbid homosexual marriages as well as marriages between siblings, parents and children, grandparents and grandchildren, and children and their aunts and uncles. Many states forbid marriage between first cousins and half siblings. Some states forbid marriage between stepparents and stepchildren, and some states forbid marriage between a man and his father's former wife or son's former wife. The mating or marrying of a close relative is called *incest.* This will be discussed further in other chapters.

Endogamy

Endogamy requires or encourages mate selection within a culturally defined group. For example, in evangelical circles we practice a rule of endogamy that requires us to select our mate from within the body of believers. Between the forces of exogamy and endogamy lies the field of eligibles (see figure 4–1).

Closely related to endogamy is the concept of *homogamy.* Homogamy is the marriage of two persons who are socially alike, whereas *heterogamy* is the marriage of two persons who are socially different. Most marriages are homogamous; that is, most people marry someone of the same race, social class, and religion, close to the same age. For example, less than one percent of all marriages are interracial (Saxton 1980:254). Approximately two out

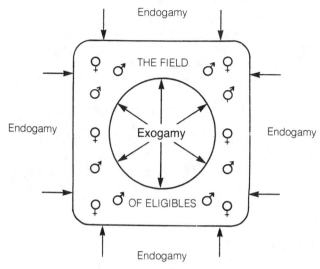

Figure 4-1. THE FIELD OF ELIGIBLES (From *The Individual, Marriage, and the Family*, 5th ed., by Lloyd Saxton. © 1983 by Wadsworth, Inc. Reprinted by permission of Wadsworth Publishing Co., Belmont, CA 94002

of three couples who marry are of the same faith (Saxton 1980:254). In general, homogamous marriages have greater potential for success than do heterogamous marriages, as we shall see later in this chapter.

Propinquity

One of the major factors in mate selection is *propinquity*, the geographical closeness of the other person. If you are living in Chicago, then eligible persons of the opposite sex in New York, Los Angeles, or Atlanta are very unlikely to be selected by you.

Green (1978:113) reports on several studies that demonstrate the effect of propinquity on mate selection. One study found that over half the couples surveyed lived within sixteen blocks of each other during courtship. Another study found that 43 percent of the couples had lived within twenty blocks of each other and that 21 percent lived within five blocks of each other.

Propinquity is a factor in mate selection at Christian colleges. The Christian college brings together hundreds of single young people of marriageable age who share a common faith and many common values. With this propinquity it is not surprising that many young people find their life partner at college. In fact, this is so common that many Bible colleges are jokingly called bridal colleges.

THEORIES OF MATE SELECTION

Even with the field of eligibles narrowed by endogamy, exogamy, and propinquity, why do we select the particular person that we do? Sociologists have suggested several theories to explain mate selection. We will examine a few of the ones that have been the subject of current research.

Role Theory

We have already seen that *role* is one of the foundational concepts in sociology. Role has been defined as the behavior expected of the holder of a particular status. Both "husband" and "wife" are statuses, and each of us has expectations concerning the appropriate behavior or role for each of these statuses. According to role theory, people tend to select their mates from the field of eligibles on the basis of role compatibility.

We need to realize that it is not the roles themselves that are the basis for mate selection, but the degree of agreement between the couple. If both the man and the woman believe that the wife's place is in the home or if both agree the wife has the right to pursue a career, there is role compatibility. As Kephart explains, "As applied to mate selection, persons would tend to choose partners on the basis of courtship and marital role agreement. . . . A compatible couple would be one in which spouses play the expected or agreed upon roles, almost irrespective of what these roles actually are" (1981:242–43).

Value Theory

Value theory suggests that people are more likely to select a mate who shares a similar value orientation. Values are the criteria we use to define what is good or bad, beautiful or ugly, moral or immoral, worthwhile or not worthwhile. Our values are very important to us and form the basis for most of our decisions.

Robert Coombs, who has done extensive research on value theory, explains the theory:

> The thesis is that value consensus fosters mutually rewarding interaction and leads to interpersonal attraction. It is reasoned that sharing of similar values, in effect, is a validation of one's self which promotes emotional satisfaction and enhances communication (1966:166).

Both role theory and value theory are related to homogamy and propinquity. Persons raised in the same neighborhood, the same social class, and the same faith are likely to have similar role expectations and value orientations. Kephart (1981:244) suggests that further research needs to be conducted to determine whether it is the similarity of values that influences mate selection or if mate selection is only a reflection of homogamy or propinquity. He goes on to suggest that the research needs to determine if there is a particular class of values that is involved in mate selection.

Exchange Theory

Imagine you are introduced to a married couple you have never met before. She is a beautiful blonde in her early twenties with bright blue eyes, a flawless complexion, and a nice figure. He is at least fifteen years older, short, overweight, and balding. What is your reaction to this couple?

According to the exchange theory, most people will assume the man is rich, famous, or powerful. That is, they believe that there is a mismatch of physical attractiveness and that the man must be bringing some other assets to the relationship in exchange for the woman's youth and beauty. According to the exchange theory, for a relationship to develop and grow there must be a fairly even exchange among the parties. If a person feels he is giving more than he is gaining from a relationship, that person is likely to discontinue the relationship. Exchange theory postulates that we well select a mate who brings as much to the relationship as we bring. A proponent of the exchange theory, John Edwards states the theory propositionally:

1. Within any collectivity of potential mates, a marriageable person will seek out that individual who is perceived as maximizing his rewards.
2. Individuals with equivalent resources are most likely to maximize each other's rewards (1969:525).

Complementary-needs Theory

We have all heard the phrase "Opposites attract." To a certain extent that may be true in mate selection. While most marriages are homogamous on social factors such as age, race, religion, and social class, the complementary-needs theory suggests that people will select a mate whose psychological needs or personality complements theirs.

The complementary-needs theory was initiated by Robert Winch who states:

> The basic hypothesis of the theory of complementary needs in mate selection is that in mate selection each individual seeks within his or her field of eligibles for that person who gives the greatest promise of providing him or her with maximum need gratification. It is not assumed that this process is totally or even largely conscious.
>
> It follows from the general motivation theory that both the person to whom one is attracted, and the one being attracted, will be registering in behavior their own need patterns. Many second hypotheses follow from the first—that the need pattern of B, the second person or the one to whom the first is attracted, will be complementary rather than similar to the need pattern of A, the first person (1954:242).

Winch illustrates the theory with the following hypothetical anecdote:

> Let us assume that there is a chap by the name of Jonathan, and that Jonathan's most distinguished characteristic is a need to be dominant in interpersonal relationships. We shall assume further that among his acquaintances are two girls, Jean and Jennifer. Jennifer is like Jonathan in being dominant and in being intolerant of differences in viewpoint, whereas Jean does not have strong convictions and

is used to being governed by the judgments and wishes of others. If we are informed that Jonathan is about to marry one of these women, and if on the basis of the information cited above we are asked to guess which one, probably we should agree that Jean would be the more likely choice for Jonathan to make. . . . Thus Jonathan should see Jean as a "truly feminine, tractable, agreeable young lady who knows when and how to help a man," whereas to Jean, Jonathan might well appear as a "vigorous and decisive tower of strength." I should expect further that Jonathan would be repelled by Jennifer and would see her as bossy, unfeminine, and probably shrewish (1958:97).

Some common examples of complimentary needs include:

a. Dominance-Deference. In this type one person has the need to influence and control another while the other needs to have someone lead and make decisions.

b. Nurturance-Succorance. In this type one person needs to give sympathy to or help another while the other needs to be helped, loved, and supported.

c. Achievement-Vicarious. In this type one person needs to accomplish goals and achieve success while the other obtains enjoyment and satisfaction from the other's accomplishments.

While some complementary needs might support a good relationship, other complementary needs are unhealthy. A more obvious example of unhealthy complementary needs are sadist-masochist—one person has a need to hurt another and the other has the need to be hurt. In this situation two unhealthy needs feed on each other. Some instances of spouse abuse fit this pattern. Another unhealthy set of complementary needs is the parent-child pattern—one person needs to "mother" or "father," and the other needs to be "babied."

While the complementary-needs theory seems logical, and each of us can point to cases of couples with complementary needs, some sociologists have challenged the theory. Orthner points out that "the majority of research on married couples has found that the norm in personality needs is similarity" (1981:83). Again, the actual issue may be overgeneralization—in some areas couples are probably similar, in others they are complementary. This has been the case in personality testing I have done with couples in premarital counseling.

Stimulus-Value-Role Theory

The stimulus-value-role theory combines features of some of the other theories we have examined. Developed by Bernard Murstein (1976), this is a stage theory; that is, mate selection proceeds through a series of stages. The first stage is the stimulus stage. A person is drawn to another by the other's physical attractiveness and social attributes. Murstein describes this stage in terms of the exchange theory. One is attracted to another whom he or she perceives as being of equal attraction. For example, a physically attractive woman may be attracted to a less handsome man who has a higher social status, such as a medical doctor or lawyer.

The second stage is that of value comparison. Murstein suggests that if there has been mutual stimulus attraction, the couple will engage in value comparison. If the couple discovers they have similar values, they will move on to the third stage—the role stage.

In the third stage, the couple explore role compatibility. Murstein sees these three stages as filters. Generally, only persons passing through all three filters would be considered potential mates. The stages are diagramed in figure 4–2.

Each of the theories discussed attempts to explain the mate-selection process. While each helps us better understand the process, none of them gives a full explanation of mate selection. This is an ongoing area of sociological research.

PREDICTORS OF MARITAL SUCCESS

Is it possible to know the chances for success of a marriage before a couple marries? Can we predict the possibility for success or failure of the marriage based on characteristics of the couple? These questions are of inter-

Figure 4–2. STIMULUS-VALUE-ROLE THEORY.

est not only to sociologists but also to pastors, marriage counselors, and individuals preparing to marry.

Life insurance companies, basing their projections on a person's age, sex, occupation, lifestyle, place of residence, and other factors, can predict the chance or probability of a person living for thirty more years. For any individual, the prediction may be more or less accurate, but for large numbers of people the predictions are accurate enough for the insurance companies to make a profit. If personal and social characteristics can be used to predict life expectancies with a high level of probability, can they be used to predict marital success?

Dozens of studies have been conducted relating various personal and social factors to marital success. There are three basic measures of marital success. The first, and most commonly used in these studies, is divorce. The assumption is that a nondivorced marriage is more successful than one that ends in divorce. While this may be a crude measure of success, it has the advantage of being objective; either a couple is divorced or they are not. Sociologists usually determine if couples are still married after five years, since they know most divorces take place in the first four years of marriage.

The second type of measure is some sort of marital index. Each couple is given a standard list of questions to answer about their marriage. A standard scoring key and scaling convention are used, and the couple is assigned a score indicating their degree of marital adjustment or "success."

The third type of measure that is used in these studies is the least common because it is the most subjective and more susceptible to bias. This measure consists of the researcher, a marriage counselor, or other observer rating the couple.

William Stephens (1970) examined many of the studies done up to the mid-sixties. Basing his findings on these studies, he has produced seventeen predictors of marital success. He has presented them in order of the strength of the research support, the first one having the strongest research support, the second the next strongest, and so on. We will examine Stephens's seventeen predictors. Research on many of these factors has been done since Stephens surveyed the literature; so we will also look at some of these findings as they relate to Stephens's predictors of marital success.

Age at Marriage

The predictor on the basis of age has the strongest research support, and it shows that age is positively correlated with marital success. The younger a couple is at marriage, the lower their probability of success; the older a couple is at marriage, the greater the probability of success. A more recent study conducted by Robert Schoen (1975) in California examined divorce rates by age at first marriage. He found that 42.5 percent of all first marriages in California end in divorce. However, what is more interesting about his findings is that the percentage of marriages ending in divorce is highly correlated with age at marriage. Schoen found that by the end of thirty-five years, assuming no deaths, two-thirds of the females who married at age sixteen were divorced, almost half of those married at age nineteen were divorced, while only about a quarter of those married at age twenty-seven were divorced (see table 4–1).

TABLE 4–1
PERCENTAGE OF FIRST MARRIAGES ENDED BY DIVORCE
OVER A THIRTY-FIVE YEAR PERIOD (California Females)

YEARS OF MARRIAGE	AGE AT FIRST MARRIAGE			
	16	19	22	27
	(Cumulative Percentage Ended in Divorce)			
1	0.9	0.8	0.4	0.3
5	19.6	11.9	7.5	7.0
10	41.3	25.7	16.3	14.9
15	53.0	34.0	21.8	19.8
20	59.3	40.1	26.3	23.0
25	62.8	43.7	29.8	25.1
30	65.2	46.3	32.1	26.3
35	66.2	47.7	33.2	27.4

Source: Adapted from Schoen 1975:54.

Several research studies show that when both parties are teen-agers, the divorce rate can be up to four times that of marriages begun by couples after age twenty (Eshleman 1981:261). The fact is that teen-age marriages have less than a 50 percent chance of surviving. The probability of marital success becomes much greater in the mid-twenties.

Length of Acquaintanceship

According to Stephens (1970:192), the research unanimously demonstrates a correlation between length of acquaintanceship and marital success. The longer a couple has known each other, the greater the probability of a successful marriage. Cox argues that the problem with a short relationship is that the couple does not have enough time to really get to know each other and that the relationship is based on intense physical contact (1981:135). Stephens (1970:192) suggests that marriages that begin after acquaintanceships of less than a year have a low probability of success.

Premarital Pregnancy

All of the data available indicates that those marriages begun with the bride pregnant have a higher divorce rate than those not involving pregnancy (Eshleman 1981:261). Also, research shows that the earlier in a marriage a child is born, the greater the probability of divorce (Belkin and Goodman 1980:436). Obviously, when the bride is pregnant, a child is born early in the marriage.

It should be apparent from the data that marriage may not be the best solution to a premarital pregnancy. Although, from a biblical perspective, premarital sex is wrong, to attempt to correct one mistake with a second mistake may not be the solution. While I believe both the father-to-be and the mother-to-be should be responsible, marriage may not be the most responsible course of action. If the couple is not ready to marry, perhaps they should share the maternity costs and place the infant with an evangelical adoption agency.

Religious Involvement

Sociologists generally measure religious involvement by measurable factors such as church membership, frequency of attendance, level of stewardship, and hours volunteered in religious service. The research shows a correlation between religious involvement and marital success. The more a couple is involved in religious activity, the greater the probability of marital success. Also, marriages performed by clergy have a lower divorce rate than those performed by a justice of the peace or other civil official.

Similarity of Faith

When we examine religious experience, there is also another factor to consider—interfaith marriages. Interfaith marriage usually refers to marriages between members of America's three major religious groups—Protestant, Catholic, and Jewish. Most studies have found a higher divorce rate among interfaith marriages (Kephart 1981:491; Eshleman 1981:273; Stephens 1970:193). These last two indicators demonstrate the wisdom of the biblical injunction not to be unequally yoked. Although this injunction has specific reference to believer with unbeliever, it certainly has implications for interfaith marriages as well.

Social Class

Generally speaking, the higher the social class, the lower the divorce rate when social class is measured by income or occupation. According to Saxton (1980:388), income is an even more powerful predictor of marital success than occupation.

What about marrying someone of a different social class? Research on social-class heterogamy and marital success indicates that it results in greater marital conflict and divorce (Stephens 1970:193; Eshleman 1981:268–69). Apparently, rich girl marries poor boy and they live happily ever after usually happens only in fairy tales. Actually, it is not difficult to understand why marriages between persons of different social classes are generally not successful. Each social class develops a world view and a value system. When two people bring different perspectives and values, not to mention lifestyles and tastes, to a relationship as intimate as marriage, there is a strong potential for conflict and misunderstanding.

Level of Education

The research results are unanimous in finding that as years of education increase, divorce rates decrease (Stephens 1970:193; Saxton 1980:387). The 1970 census also shows that divorce rates decrease as education increases. In addition, the census data shows that as the years of education increase, the age at marriage increases (U.S. Bureau of the Census 1973). We have already seen that as age increases the divorce rate drops. Also, income rises with education, and we have seen that divorce rates drop as income increases. Therefore, it is difficult to tell how much effect education itself has on marital success, since it is also affected by age at marriage as well as income and occupation.

There is only one exception to these findings, that is, women with graduate training. Men's divorce rates fall with increased education. However, women's divorce rates fall with increased education up to the bachelor's level and then rise with additional education. The divorce rate for women with bachelor's degrees in 1970 was 11 percent. But for women with one year of graduate training it was 15 percent and for women with two years of graduate work it was 19 percent (*Psychology Today* 1980:20). These findings may result from the greater career orientation of women with graduate education as well as their greater potential for financial independence.

Divorced Parents

Children of divorced parents score lower on marital adjustment tests and have greater rates of separation and divorce than young people from intact homes. Effect of parental divorce on marital success of offspring appears to be greater for men than for women (Stephens 1970:193).

Residence

Where a couple chooses to reside also seems to affect divorce rates. Rural areas have lower divorce rates than urban areas (Kephart 1981:483; Stephens 1970:194). Divorce rates also increase as one moves west. New England and the Middle Atlantic States have the lowest divorce rates, the Midwest has intermediate divorce rates, while the West Coast has the highest divorce rates (Golanty and Harris 1982:366; Kephart 1981:483). Divorce rates also increase as one moves from north to south (Saxton 1980:388). West Coast divorce rates are more than double the Middle-Atlantic divorce rates (Kephart 1981:483). The large Catholic populations in New England and the Middle Atlantic States may be part of the explanation, since

Catholics have lower divorce rates than Protestants and Jews.*

Parents' Approval

All of the studies agree that couples with the approval of both sets of parents have the greatest probability of marital success (Stephens 1970:194). Parental support probably helps to stabilize a marriage, however, parental objections may tend to produce self-fulfilling prophecy and undermine the marriage.

Sociability

Persons who are "popular" or have a large circle of friends tend to score high on marital-adjustment tests (Stephens 1970:194). If a person can get along with other people, he or she can probably get along with a mate.

Difference in Age

Several studies have found that marriages between persons with an age difference of greater than five years have higher divorce rates than marriages between persons who are closer in age (Stephens 1970:194).

Siblings

Children from one-child families have less probability of marital success than persons with brothers and sisters (Stephens 1970:194). The most likely explanation for this finding is that individuals with siblings have had to learn to give and take in the home, whereas the others never had that opportunity.

Relationship With Parents

Individuals reporting a great deal of conflict with their parents tend to score low on tests of marital adjustment (Stephens 1970:194).

---

* It should be noted that Evangelicals have lower divorce rates than Catholics.

Relationship Before Marriage

Several studies reveal that couples who fought a great deal during their courtship also fought regularly in marriage (Stephens 1970:194). Again, this is not surprising. If a couple cannot get along before marriage, why should they be expected to do better in marriage?

Mental Health

Several studies found a positive correlation between an index of mental health and an index of marital adjustment (Stephens 1970:194). The more mature and emotionally stable a person is, the better the marriage risk.

Race

A factor not examined by Stephens, but which has been the subject of much research is race. Blacks have a higher divorce rate than whites, the black divorce rate being nearly double the white divorce rate (Eshleman 1981:280). While interracial divorce rates are lower than the black divorce rate, they are higher than the white divorce rate (Eshleman 1981:280). It is generally accepted that the black divorce rate is not related to race, but rather to the fact that blacks, in general, receive less education than whites and have lower incomes than whites—all of which are associated with higher divorce rates.

NEGATIVE REASONS FOR MARRIAGE

Individuals have many reasons for marrying, some of them positive and others negative. If a couple marry for negative or poor reasons, the marriage will have less chance for success. H. Norman Wright suggests several negative reasons for marriage (Wright 1977:20–21).

Pregnancy

Wright points out that in one out of every four weddings the wife is pregnant. He goes on to say that many of these weddings would not have taken place if the bride had not been pregnant (Wright 1977:20). We have already seen the statistics on marital success when the bride is pregnant, and they are not very encouraging. Frequently a couple is pushed into marriage by well-meaning friends and family in order to "legitimize" the child and protect the family's reputation. If a couple is older and had intended to get married before the pregnancy occurred, it might be feasible for the couple to marry because there already was a commitment to marriage. However, a pregnancy, in and of itself, is a negative reason for marrying. In fact, marriage may well only make a bad situation worse.

Rebound

It is not uncommon for a person who has just had an engagement broken or a marriage ended by death or divorce to quickly marry someone else. The person had an emotional attachment to one person, and when that person is no longer available, the emotions are transferred to another person. The problem is that the emotions associated with the first person eventually dissipate, leaving one with no emotional attachment to the second person.

Widowhood, divorce, or a broken engagement result in a loss. The most common emotional reaction to a major loss is grief. It is generally agreed that it takes at least a year to work through the grief of a major loss (Collins 1972:146; Grunlan and Lambrides 1983:116). We have already seen that a year is the minimum period of acquaintanceship for marital success. Therefore, a good rule of thumb would be to consider any marriage occurring less than two years after death, divorce, or broken engagement a rebound marriage.

Rebellion

Rebellion is often a motive for marriage. Young people rebel against their parents' wishes as a means of demonstrating their independence. In fact, parental opposition often pushes a couple closer together. This is called the Romeo and Juliet effect. A group of researchers administered a questionnaire to dating couples that measured the intensity of their love for each other as well as the amount of parental opposition they experienced. The findings indicated that those couples with the greatest parental opposition were the most intensely in love (Drisoll, Davis, and Lipetz 1972:1–10). Again, we have seen earlier that lack of parental support decreases the probability of marital success.

Escape

Some people marry to escape an unhappy or stressful home life or some other intolerable situation. Cox, writing about escape as a basis for marriage, says, "Rather than dealing with a current relationship, many persons run away, hoping a new person or a new environment will be better. A marriage so conceived is often the first of a series of failures"(1981:134).

Loneliness

While marrying for companionship is a positive reason for marriage, marrying to avoid loneliness is a negative one. Cox points out that "if overcoming loneliness is one's only motivation for marriage, chances are high that this reason alone will not sustain a long-lasting relationship" (1981:134). A lonely person will frequently place unreasonable demands on his or her partner, putting a strain on the relationship. Many problems can develop from this type of relationship.

Physical Appearance

There is nothing wrong with finding the one we are considering marrying attractive. The truth is that physical appearance most likely influences everyone to some extent. While physical attraction is a legitimate aspect of a romantic relationship, it should not be the sole basis for a marriage.

One danger of physical attractiveness is what is called the halo effect. Belkin and Goodman (1980:109–10) report on a number of studies that indicate attractive persons have more positive characteristics attributed to them than less attractive persons. Attractive persons are perceived to be more intelligent, more honest, more kind, and to generally have more socially desirable characteristics than less attractive persons. The danger here is that we may attribute characteristics to a physically attractive person that they do not possess.

Some people desire a physically attractive partner to enhance their own prestige. An attractive partner adds to one's value socially. Belkin and Goodman (1980:110) report on a study that found college women who were seen with an attractive man were rated more positively by their peers than they were when seen with an unattractive man. Whether one chooses an attractive mate for one's own gratification or as a status symbol, it is a negative reason for marriage. The Scriptures seem to indicate that as Christians we should be more concerned with inner beauty than with outer beauty (1 Peter 3:3-4).

Social Pressure

Friends, family, and society all extend the same message: "It is normal to get married; there is something wrong with you if you do not marry." Since about 96 percent of all Americans marry (Garrett 1982:150), it is easy to see how marriage has become a cultural expectation. An unmarried adult past thirty years of age will often find himself or herself the object of well-meaning friends' pity or attempts at matchmaking. This can be irritating and insulting to many single persons who have chosen either not to marry or to delay marriage.

Another social pressure to marry is a desire for adult status. Single persons are often not perceived as adults in the same way their married peers are. For example, we speak of a single *girl* and a married *woman* or a play*boy* and a married *man*.

Guilt

Guilt is a powerful motivator, albeit a very negative one. A person may marry another person because of guilt—over shared physical intimacies, over leading the other person on as far as they have, or any number of other reasons. It should be apparent that guilt does not lead to a stable marriage relationship.

Pity

It is easy to confuse pity with love. Pity felt for a person because of a handicap, illness, or a poor lot in life is not a sound foundation on which to build a marriage relationship.

Romance

Every marriage should be romantic. I feel sorry for couples who have let the romance go out of their marriages. However, a marriage needs a lot more than romance to survive. Sitting up all night with a sick child is not very romantic, especially by the third or fourth night. Caring for your mate when he or she has the flu is not romantic. Changing dirty diapers and washing diapers are not at all romantic. There are many aspects to marriage that are not romantic and that require more than infatuation to get through. Romantic love is based on feelings; however, genuine love is based on commitment. It is commitment, not romance, that will carry a couple through the difficult times.

POSITIVE REASONS FOR MARRIAGE

While there are negative reasons for marrying, there are also positive reasons for marrying. God has created us as male and female and has established marriage as the framework within which most of us will spend our adult lives. While a person can live a fulfilled and meaningful life without a partner, we are so created that most of us will find our fulfillment and meaning with another person. Golanty and Harris (1982:84) present several positive reasons for marriage that are consistent with a biblical understanding of marriage. We will briefly examine each of these reasons.

Conformity

While in its "popular" usage most persons do not like to be considered conformist, sociologically, all behavior is either conformist or deviant. That is, one either conforms to social norms or deviates from them. The Scripture teaches that Christians should conform to social norms unless they violate scriptural teachings (Rom. 13:1-7; 1 Cor. 9:19-23; 11:2-16). In our culture it is the norm for a couple desiring to live together to become legally married. A couple who wish to live together should conform to both biblical and social standards by marrying.

Legitimation of Sex

As a couple moves through courtship, there will naturally be a desire for physical union symbolic of their deepening relationship. This physical desire is a normal part of human sexuality. We must remember that it was God who created us male and female. Marriage is the setting for physical union between a man and a woman (1 Cor. 7:3-5, 9; Heb. 13:4).

Love

In the preceding chapter we distinguished between mature and immature love. It was pointed out above that romantic love, based on feelings, is a negative reason to marry. However, mature love, based on commitment and self-giving, is a positive reason for marrying.

Companionship

According to Golanty and Harris (1982:84), companionship may be the most important reason for marriage. Companionship leads to security and stability and meets some of our deepest needs. Marriage is a means of having regular companionship. The writer of Ecclesiastes put it so well when he wrote:

> Two are better than one,
> > because they have a good return for their work:
> If one falls down,
> > his friend can help him up.

But pity the man who falls
   and has no one to help him up!
Also, if two lie down together, they will keep warm.
                      (4:9–11)

Sharing

We all need someone to share ourselves with. We need someone to share our success and failures. Somone to share our dreams and fears. Experiences are more meaningful when we have someone to share them with.

Communication

We also need people to communicate with. God created us as social beings with the ability and need to communicate. Communication is a key to a good marriage. In fact, when communication breaks down then a marriage begins to break down.

Marriage meets many of our needs, and there are many positive reasons for marrying. Taken by itself, any one of the above reasons might not provide a strong foundation for marriage; but taken together, these reasons provide such a foundation for marriage.

BASES FOR MARRIAGE

On the basis of the sociological research and statistics we have examined, it is possible to suggest some criteria for a successful marriage. Personal maturity and a healthy outlook are foundational to a good relationship. Common backgrounds and common interests also increase the probability of a stable marriage. A courtship of sufficient length to get to know one another well, along with family support, also portends a successful marriage.

From a Christians perspective, the primary basis for a marriage is a shared faith (2 Cor. 6:14–16; 1 Cor.7:39). The Scriptures also call for a lifetime commitment (Gen. 2:24; Matt. 19:4–6; 1 Cor. 7:39). A Christian marriage is a couple's commitment both to each other and to God.

DISCUSSION QUESTIONS

1. What is your field of eligibles? How did you delineate the field?

2. Which of the theories presented do you think best explains mate selection? Why?

3. How much consideration should a person give to the predictors of marital success discussed in this chapter? Why?

4. Which of the negative reasons for marrying do you believe would result in the least successful marriages? Why?

5. How important do you think companionship is for marriage? Why?

6. What do you see as the biblical requirements for mate selection?

SUGGESTED READING

David Belgum, *Why Marry?* (Minneapolis: Augsburg, 1972). A discussion of choices in the decision to marry. Written from a Christian perspective, this brief book offers some helpful advice.

Anthony Flori, *Two to Get Ready* (Wheaton, Ill.: Victor, 1978). A popular, easy-to-read primer for individuals and couples considering marriage. This book deals with most of the major issues a couple faces in preparing for marriage. Written from a biblical perspective.

Robert Fryling, *A Handbook for Engaged Couples* (Downers Grove, Ill.: InterVarsity, 1977). As the title says, this is a handbook for engaged couples and is a highly recommended book for use in premarital counseling.

Charlie W. Shedd, *Letters to Karen* (Nashville: Abingdon, 1965) and *Letters to Philip* (Garden City, N.Y.: Doubleday, 1968). These two volumes contain a series of letters a father wrote to his daughter and son-in-law about married life. These are two delightful works that should be read by engaged couples and newlyweds. Shedd is a popular writer with an incisive style.

5

Premarital Intimacy

Engagement was the worst period in our relationship. We experienced frustration when we maintained our moral standards and guilt when we violated them.

A *BIBLE COLLEGE COUPLE*

IN THE LAST two chapters we have looked at dating and courtship. Both of these processes generally involve physical intimacy between the couple. This physical intimacy may involve activities from holding hands to a good-night kiss, from making out to petting, from tongue kissing to sexual intercourse.

Each of us draws the line at various places on what is acceptable physical intimacy at different stages of a relationship. This is an issue that Christians have struggled with in the past and will continue to struggle with. When I was a teen-ager, in many conservative Christian groups it was considered improper for a couple to kiss before they were engaged. Today many Christians would not oppose a good-night kiss after a date.

When Christians turn to the Bible for guidance in this area, they find basically a single principle—a prohibition against sexual intercourse before marriage (i.e., 1 Cor. 6:9–20; 7:1–9; Gal. 5:19–21; Eph. 5:3). But what of holding hands, kissing, and petting? Because dating was unknown in the biblical cultures and courtship was vastly different from modern practices, these are never discussed. For the most part, a couple had little or no physical contact before their wedding. Marriages were often arranged by the couple's families, with the young people having limited choice. Since the Scriptures do not directly address issues such as hand holding and good-night kisses, Christians have sought to draw up guidelines based on what they believed were biblical principles. After examining some current practices and statistics, we will discuss the issue of Christian standards for dating and courtship.

DEGREES OF PREMARITAL INTIMACY

As pointed out above, physical intimacy can range from handholding to sexual intercourse. For purposes of discussion and research, scholars, as well as the general public, have attempted to define and label various degrees of physical intimacy. Acts of physical intimacy have been divided into two major categories: (1) those intimacies that lead up to sexual intercourse and (2) coitus (Orthner 1981:245). Those intimacies that lead up to sexual intercourse are called necking or petting. Kinsey and his associates treat *necking* and *petting* as synonymous terms (1953:227).[1] They go on to define petting as "physical contacts which involve a deliberate attempt to effect erotic arousal . . . . While petting may not always result in arousal, we have considered that the term was applicable if there was an attempt to achieve arousal" (1953:228). Another social scientist defines petting as "a generic term subsuming all possible physical contacts that cause an erotic response" (Saxton 1980:125). Recognizing the wide range of activities covered by the term *petting*, some researchers have divided petting into subcategories. King and his associates (1977:455–59) have devised a scheme for classifying various levels of petting. They place such activities as handholding, lip kissing, and tongue kissing under *light petting*. They say *medium petting* consists of caressing the breasts, and *heavy petting* is manually caressing or orally manipulating the genitals. The progression that petting generally follows in a relationship is described for us:

---

[1]The subculture in which I was raised differentiated between these terms. "Necking" or "making out" referred to extended kissing and hugging, while petting referred to caressing of the breasts and genitals. However, most writers do not distinguish between these terms.

Petting typically proceeds in a fairly uniform pattern in Western society. Hugging and kissing begin the process, and this is followed usually by tongue kissing, stimulation of the woman's breasts, stimulation of her genitals, and then perhaps to stimulation of the man's genitals. This may be followed by the rubbing together of their genitals in simulated intercourse and sometimes by oral-genital contacts, either as a prelude or an alternative to coitus (Orthner 1981:245).

The definitions above clearly show that premarital intimacy refers to much more than sexual intercourse. Premarital intimacy involves everything from holding hands to caressing of the breasts and genitals to sexual intercourse. While there is a vast difference between holding hands and caressing genitals, it may be useful for us to view these activities as various stages of a single process. As Cox says, "In the broadest sense, intimate physical contact of any kind between male and female is sexual behavior" (1981:119).

EXTENT OF PREMARITAL INTIMACY

While any physical contact between males and females may be construed as sexual behavior, the types of behaviors that are generally of concern to both sociologists and the public are heavy petting and coitus. To what extent are these activities taking place among the unmarried? Sociologists have questioned teen-agers and college students about their practices, and we will examine the findings. First, it should be pointed out that the findings are self-reports that may or may not be true. Some individuals may attempt to "cover-up" their behavior, and others may tend to exaggerate or "brag." Many researchers assume that these two groups will tend to cancel each other out. However, as Kephart warns us, "The available figures refer only to *reported* behavior; hence, all statistics on the subject should be regarded as approximations" (1981:288).

A large-scale study, reported in 1977, found that 55.2 percent of the females in the study had engaged in premarital sexual intercourse by age nineteen. It is estimated that the figure approaches 70 percent by the time of marriage (Kephart 1981:289). From current research it is estimated that 85 to 90 percent of males have engaged in sexual intercourse before marriage (Scanzoni and Scanzoni 1981:73).

While the extent of premarital sexual activity in the past decade has risen only slightly for males, it has increased dramatically among females. When we look at the results from surveys conducted by King and his associates (1977) between 1965 and 1975, we find that the percentage of college females engaging in heavy petting and sexual intercourse has nearly doubled (see table 5–1).

TABLE 5–1
PREMARITAL SEXUAL ACTIVITY AMONG COLLEGE STUDENTS

Year	Percentage engaging in heavy petting		Percentage engaging in sexual intercourse	
	Males	Females	Males	Females
1965	71.3	34.3	65.1	28.7
1970	79.3	59.7	65.0	37.3
1975	80.2	72.7	73.9	57.1

Source: Adapted from King et al. 1977:456.

Another study compared female premarital intercourse experience over twenty years, from 1958 to 1978 (Cox 1981:120–21). This research broke down the findings by religion and type of relationship. The study found that Protestant females had higher rates of premarital intercourse than Jewish or Catholic females. (It should be noted that often in social research everyone who is not a Jew or Catholic is lumped under "Protestant.") Also the percentages increased with the type of the relationship (see table 5–2). While the percentage of females engaging in premarital coitus greatly increased during the 1970s, this does not mean that females have become more promiscuous in the sense of "sleeping around." Research indicates that at least half of these females had intercourse only with the man they intended to marry (Duvall 1977:27; Scanzoni and Scanzoni 1981:73). It appears that a large number of females are moving their first sexual intercourse to before the wedding rather than waiting until after. Of interest and concern to us are the reasons for this increase in premarital sexual activity.

TABLE 5–2
PERCENTAGE OF FEMALES HAVING PREMARITAL COITUS,
BY RELATIONSHIP AND RELIGION, 1958–1978

	PROTESTANT		
Year	Dating	Going Steady	Engaged
1958	10	20	38
1968	35	41	67
1978	56	79	88
	CATHOLIC		
Year	Dating	Going Steady	Engaged
1958	8	14	18
1968	15	17	56
1978	46	63	69
	JEWISH		
Year	Dating	Going Steady	Engaged
1958	11	14	20
1968	20	26	40
1978	45	64	69

Source: Adapted from Cox 1981:121.

FACTORS IN THE RISE OF PREMARITAL INTIMACY

We need to realize that premarital sex has long been a social issue. In the Old Testament premarital sex was prohibited and various degrees of punishment, including the death penalty, were prescribed for violators (Exod. 22:16–17; Lev. 19:20–22; Deut. 22:13–29). In the New Testament, Joseph thought Mary had engaged in premarital sexual intercourse and was going to break their engagement until he learned the nature of her pregnancy (Matt. 1:18–25). The apostle Paul also addressed the issues of premarital sex and chastity (i.e., 1 Cor. 6:12–20; 7:1–9).

While premarital sex has long been a social issue, the incidence of coitus before marriage was quite low in American society before World War I (Kephart 1981:275). Since that time, the proportion of the population engaging in premarital sex has steadily increased. What is responsible for this rise in premarital sex?

Changing Attitudes

There are many factors that have probably contributed to the rise in premarital sex. It would be difficult to determine which factor is dominant or antecedent to the others since the factors obviously interact and feed back to each other. One contributing factor is changing attitudes and public opinion. Duvall reminds us, "That attitudes toward sexual activity before marriage have become more permissive in recent years is beyond question" (1977:28).

In one of the more recent national surveys on attitudes toward premarital sex, conducted in 1978, respondents were asked if they thought premarital sexual relations were (1) always wrong, (2) almost always wrong, (3) wrong only sometimes, or (4) not wrong at all. The subjects responded as follows:

Always wrong	29.3%
Almost always wrong	11.7%
Wrong only sometimes	20.3%
Not wrong at all	38.7%

(Kephart 1981:284–85)

It is interesting to note that more people thought premarital sex was never wrong than thought it was always wrong. Also over 70 percent felt premarital sex was all right—at least under certain circumstances.

Perhaps more important than the most current figures is the direction and extent of attitude change during the seventies. If the persons who responded "wrong only sometimes" and "not wrong at all" are combined and labeled permissive, the trend appears to be toward permissiveness according to the figures in table 5–3.

While attitudes among the general public are changing, they are changing even more rapidly among college students. King and his associates surveyed samples of college students in 1965, 1970, and 1975. The results of their surveys are presented in table 5–4.

TABLE 5–3
TREND IN PERMISSIVE ATTITUDES

Year	Percent Permissive
1972	51.6
1974	54.3
1975	56.8
1978	59.0

Source: Kephart 1981:285.

TABLE 5–4
PERCENTAGE OF COLLEGE STUDENTS STRONGLY AGREEING
WITH SPECIFIC STATEMENTS RELATED
TO PREMARITAL SEXUAL INTERCOURSE

Statement and Years	Males	Females
1. I feel that premarital intercourse is immoral.		
1965	33.0	70.0
1970	14.0	34.0
1975	19.5	20.7
1980	17.4	25.3
2. A man who has had sexual intercourse with a great many women is immoral.		
1965	35.0	56.0
1970	15.0	22.0
1975	19.5	30.1
1980	26.5	38.9
3. A woman who has had sexual intercourse with a great many men is immoral.		
1965	42.0	91.0
1970	33.0	54.0
1975	28.5	41.0
1980	41.8	49.6

Source: Adapted from Robinson and Jedlicka 1982:239.

King and his associates summarize the results of their research for us:

Two major changes in the nature of premarital sexual behavior and attitudes were found in this study. First, although a considerable liberalization in premarital sexual behavior and attitudes had taken place in the later 1960's (especially among females) liberalization accelerated in the early 1970's. Second, due to the greater liberalization in female premarital sexual behavior and attitudes, the difference between male and female behavior and attitudes has greatly diminished (1977:458).

Media

A large debate exists over whether the media shape our attitudes or reflect our attitudes. The truth is that probably they do both. However, a number of social scientists believe that the media have played a role in changing sexual attitudes and behavior (e.g., Kephart 1981:287; Belkin and Goodman 1980:151; Strong et al. 1981:25).

We need only to observe current movies and television programing to discover that the treatment of sex outside of marriage is quite permissive. As Kephart states, "Whether the theme is that of adultery or premarital coitus, the persons involved are likely to be portrayed in a sympathetic light, while the activity itself is seen as a more-or-less natural manifestation of man's inexorable nature" (1981:287).

A new application of television is cable television and videocassettes. The August 7, 1981, issue of *Christianity Today* pointed out:

> A major topic at the recent national convention of cable TV operators was whether they should get into X-rated movies; R-rated films are standard fare, the only question being that of "proper" times to broadcast them. Two of the leading promoters of programs featuring nudity, profanity, and violence already have 150,000 subscribers. . . . Concern is certainly not misplaced, if one looks at the booming market for "adult" titles of videocassette films.

As much as movies, television, and novels depict a sexually permissive lifestyle, the greatest influence may come from advertising. There is hardly a product that is not sold with sex. While one might expect toothpaste and perfume to be associated with sex appeal, sex is used to sell everything, from cars to airlines tickets. One of the more suggestive advertisements being seen on television and in magazines at the time this is being written, features a teen-age actress in designer jeans striking various provocative poses. At a minimum, the advertisement communicates that teen-agers should be sexually active.

Strong and his associates address the effect of advertising on sexual attitudes and behavior:

> The economic shift to consumption and the accompanying increase in advertising have had profound effects on the sexual landscape. We are encouraged to consume, to satisfy our every whim, to buy a car that assures masculinity or a perfume that assures femininity. Advertising has put a spotlight on sex, legitimizing it along with consumption (1981:25).

Contraception and Abortion

One factor that often receives the blame for the rise in premarital coitus is modern contraceptives and particularly the "pill." While modern contraceptives and their ready availability have more than likely affected premarital sexual behavior, their effect may not be as great as is often thought. For, as Cox tells us, "despite improved birth control methods, especially birth control pills, premarital pregnancies have continued to increase" (1981:123). From 1950 to 1974 the illegitimate birthrate increased over 170 percent, and during the same period the national birth rate gives only half the picture because a third of all first-born babies were conceived out of wedlock and over half of all babies born to teen-age wives were conceived out of wedlock (Cox 1981:123). Also not included in the illegitimate birth rate are unmarried women who had an abortion. It is estimated that unmarried women had close to three million abortions between 1973 and 1976 (Scanzoni and Scanzoni 1981:543).

If modern contraceptives are so convenient and readily available, how does one explain the large increase in premarital pregnancies? Scanzoni and Scanzoni (1981) suggest that it results from what they call the "nice girl dilemma." They point out that even in our modern, permissive society virtue is still valued. A "nice girl" is not promiscuous; she does not "sleep around." However, a "nice girl" may be swept away by the passion of a moment. This slip would be seen as an exception to her normal virtue. But if a woman uses contraceptives, it is an acknowledgment that she is going to engage in sexual intercourse. Therefore she loses her excuse of being swept away by passion.

Extended Adolescence

A factor that may be as responsible for the increase in premarital sex as any of the others is extended adolescence. Adolescence may be defined as the period between puberty and adulthood. Before the Industrial Revolution adolescence, as we know it today, was virtually nonexistent. Before this century puberty came later and responsible adulthood came earlier, so that the two events tended to be simultaneous. In this century, puberty has come increasingly earlier and responsible adulthood increasingly later, creating the period of time called adolescence.

Data from several northern European countries and the United States show that the average age of menarche (first menstrual flow) for females was seventeen in 1830 and that it had dropped to 12.8 years by the mid 1970s (Dworetzky 1981:497–98). Males reach puberty (able to produce mature sperm), on the average, between thirteen and fourteen years of age. This means that the average adolescent is sexually mature by thirteen or fourteen. However, the legal age for marriage without parental consent in most states is eighteen, but marriages usually take place later, at about twenty-two for females and twenty-four for males, according to current census data. Thus the average adolescent is sexually mature eight to ten years before marriage.

Before the Industrial Revolution, young people married about the time they reached puberty. According to the Talmud (the collection of Jewish law and tradition), people were expected to be married before they were eighteen, and in Roman society a female who was not married by nineteen was considered an "old maid." During the Renaissance in Europe parents considered it a disgrace if their daughters were not married by seventeen. In eighteenth-century England the legal age for marriage was fourteen for males and twelve for females (Koteskey 1981:25).

Koteskey argues that extended adolescence is a major cause for increased premarital sexual activity.

> There is a period of five or more years during which it is impossible for young men and women to get married. While other factors . . . no doubt play a part in the rising incidence of both masturbation and premarital intercourse, it seems to me that postponing marriage for legal and economic reasons is a major cause (1981:27).

LIVING TOGETHER

When premarital sex is discussed, we often tend to think of it as isolated acts. However, much premarital coitus takes place in an arrangement where a couple live together. This arrangement is called *cohabitation*. Duvall defines cohabitation for us as "sharing a bed with someone of the opposite sex to whom one is not married for four or more nights a week for three or four months" (1977:120).

To what extent is cohabitation taking place? According to 1977 U.S. Census Bureau data nearly two million unmarried couples were living together (Scanzoni and Scanzoni 1981:214). In 1978 unmarried couples accounted for 2.3 percent of all couples living together with 24 percent having one or more children (Cox 1981:435). Among college students, research indicates that about one-fourth cohabitate at some point in their college career (Kephart 1981:515). A nationwide random sample of males in the United States between twenty to thirty years of age found that between 1962 and 1972, 18 percent had lived with a woman outside of marriage for at least six months (Scanzoni and Scanzoni 1981:226).

Although a significant number of persons are living together without the benefit of marriage, they are not all doing so for the same reasons or with the same intent. Scanzoni and Scanzoni (1981) suggest that there are three basic categories of cohabitation: trial marriage, common-law marriage, and ad hoc arrangements.

Trial Marriage

Some people believe that with the high rate of divorce, it might be better for couples to live together for a while to discover if they are really compatible and want to make the arrangement permanent. As someone has said, "You would not buy a car without a test drive, so why take a spouse without a test period?" The idea of a trial marriage is not new. It was brought up by Maurice of Saxony in the eighteenth century. Again in 1926, Judge Ben B. Lindsey proposed the idea. Bertrand Russell suggested it for college students in 1929, and Margaret Mead reintroduced the idea in 1966.

While the concept of trial marriage may seem to have a level of logic or reason to some, the social research does not support it. In 1972 researchers interviewed 159 couples applying for marriage licenses in Los Angeles County in California. They found that one-third of the couples had cohabited for at least three months. Four years later they followed up on all the couples. The researchers found that the divorce rate for those couples who had cohabitated was as great as for those couples who had not. Marital satisfaction was equal in both groups, but the couples who had cohabitated had more problems with alcohol, drugs, and marital infidelity (Rubenstein 1981:19). The finding on marital infidelity is consistent with other research that indicates that females who engaged in premarital coitus are more likely to engage in extramarital coitus (Duvall 1977:36). Summarizing other studies on cohabitation and marriage, Cox concludes from the research that there is "little if any relationship between cohabitation and the degree of satisfaction, conflict, emotional closeness, or egalitarianism in later marriage" (1981:439).

Common-Law Marriage

In thirteen American states, Washington, D.C., and the Virgin Islands, a couple may live together without license or ceremony, blood tests or witnesses, and if they consent to be considered husband and wife, the state will recognize their status (Kephart 1981:312–13). This arrangement is known as common-law marriage. The amount of time the couple must live together varies from state to state, but in the thirteen states that recognize common-law marriage, after a prescribed period of time a couple living together can receive legal status.

It needs to be pointed out that common-law marriage is an after-the-fact legality. As Scanzoni and Scanzoni remind us, "Whether or not a union has been a valid marriage according to common-law is something that is determined *after* the union has been entered" (1981:216). In order for common-law marriage to be recognized, a couple must have been cohabitating for a specified period of time.

It also needs to be understood that where common-law marriage does take place, it is as binding as a licensed marriage and can be broken only by divorce or death. If a couple live together in a common-law state and pass themselves off as husband and wife, after a period of time they may, in fact, be considered legally married.

Ad Hoc Arrangements

According to the *Merriam-Webster Dictionary*, the Latin expression *ad hoc* means "concerned with a particular purpose" (1974:27). Couples may cohabitate for a variety of reasons. There are couples who live together and are neither engaging in a "trial marriage" nor a "common-law marriage." There are couples who want to live together for a variety of reasons but are not interested in marriage or being considered married.

CONSEQUENCES OF PREMARITAL INTIMACY

Frank Cox, a secular sociologist, writes, "As American mores have relaxed, the differentiation between premarital and marital sex activities have lessened. However, there are still a number of problems that are clearly related to premarital sex" (1981:123). Cox goes on to suggest at least four problems. We will briefly examine each of these.

Venereal Disease

Many people believe that venereal disease (VD) has been controlled by modern drugs, and for a time there was a dramatic drop in the incidence of VD. However, in the 1980s VD has reached epidemic proportions, and some types of VD have no known cure. After the common cold, gonorrhea and syphilis are the most common infectious diseases in the United States (Cox 1981:284). The U.S. Public Health Service estimated that in 1980 50 percent of all high school students would contract VD before graduation. Over two million people a year are treated for gonorrhea and almost a half-million for syphilis. Over 75 percent of the reported cases occur in persons between fifteen and thirty years of age. Since the statistics are based on reported cases, public health officials believe the actual incidence of VD is much higher.

Venereal diseases can be more than just painful and embarrassing; they can have serious effects. Untreated or improperly treated, they can result in sterility; damage to reproductive organs; brain damage; and, in some cases, death. For a description of the various venereal diseases, their causes, consequences, and treatment see the appendix, p. 339.

Unwanted Pregnancies

As we saw earlier in this chapter, even with the advent of modern birth control techniques and the availability of abortion on demand, the rate of illegitimate births continues to rise. There are over one million pregnancies a year among fifteen- to nineteen-year-old females (Scanzoni and Scanzoni 1981:90).

According to *Newsweek* (January 17, 1983:27) more than one out of every three babies in 1980 was born out of wedlock, and preliminary analysis of the 1981 and 1982 data indicates the rate of illegitimate births is rising. In 1970 about one out of ten babies was born out of wedlock. This means there was a 367 percent increase in the proportion of illegitimate births from 1970 to 1980. Further analysis of the data reveals that 83 percent of births to black teen-agers and 29 percent of births to white teenagers occur out of wedlock.

The three major solutions to premarital pregnancy practiced today are abortion, marriage, and raising the child in a single-parent home. There are over a million teen-age pregnancies a year. Over a third of these pregnancies are terminated by abortion. About one in eight ends in a miscarriage. Almost a fourth result in out-of-wedlock births. One in ten births is made legitimate by marriage (National Center for Health Statistics 1981).

Relatively few children are put up for adoption.[2] Approximately 75 percent of pregnant teen-age girls have no intention of marrying before the child is born. White teen-agers are seven times as likely as black teen-agers to terminate a pregnancy by abortion, whereas, black teen-agers are twice as likely as white teen-agers to keep their illegitimate child (Duvall 1977:106). For those persons who do marry, the prospects are not very good. Roughly half of all marriages that begin when the bride is pregnant end in divorce, and if she is a teen-ager, the divorce rate is closer to 75 percent (Stephens 1970). When a female becomes pregnant out of wedlock, none of the options available to her may be very satisfactory. The woman's sex partner will often disavow any responsibility and leave her with the consequences of their act. Family and friends frequently may be judgmental and attempt to push one solution or another on the pregnant woman.

While as Christians we recognize that premarital intercourse goes against the teachings of Scripture and that sin has its consequences, it is important for us not to be judgmental (Matt. 7:1–2), but rather to support and help the unmarried pregnant woman to find forgiveness and the best solution to her problem (Gal. 6:1–2). We must recognize that premarital sexual relations are always wrong because God's Word teaches us that sexual intimacy is reserved for marriage (Heb. 13:4). Even so, while we cannot overlook sin, we must always reach out and minister to the sinner. The person who has sinned is often aware of his or her failure and certainly does not need our words of condemnation but needs God's message of forgiveness and restoration when there is repentance.

---

[2] I do not see abortion as an option for Christians, but do believe that giving a baby up for adoption by a Christian couple may be the best solution if marriage is not feasible.

Early Commitment and Isolation

When a young couple move into heavy petting and coitus, they often begin isolating themselves from their peers. They tend to want to be alone and have privacy. Because of this tendency, they narrow their social relationships and hence their social development.

Because sex is a powerful force and related to emotions, there is also a tendency for two people involved in heavy petting and premarital coitus to make an early commitment to each other. If they marry, they may discover that their relationship was based primarily on sex.

Particularly during the teen years, young people need to interact with a number of persons and have a variety of social experiences. There is a need to have a wide range of relationships with persons of the opposite sex, as well as same-sex peers, rather than the exclusive relationships that tend to develop when engaged in premarital sex.

Quality of Marital Sex

Premarital sexual experience may affect the quality of marital sex. Cox presents an interesting argument when he hypothesizes

> that early sexual experiences largely set the attitudes that an individual will hold toward sexual intercourse throughout his or her life. If one's early sexual experiences occur premaritally, the chances are that the quality of such experiences will be under less than optimum conditions. As a result, large numbers of our youth may begin their adult sexual life with negative attitudes toward the sexual act (1981:126).

It has also been pointed out in this chapter that those females who engage in premarital sex are more likely to engage in extramarital sex. Because of the nature of premarital sex, it lays the seeds for both guilt and mistrust. There is no evidence that premarital sex enhances marital sex, but there is good reason to believe that premarital sex may adversely affect the quality of marital sex.

Guilt

In addition to the four consequences to premarital sex presented by Cox, a fifth consequence is guilt. While research indicates that many persons experience guilt from premarital intercourse, this problem is particularly acute for the Christian. As we have seen, the Scriptures teach that premarital coitus is a sin. Many Christians would extend the prohibition to heavy petting. When a Christian practices sin and violates his or her conscience and the teachings of God's Word, guilt will result. The Holy Spirit will bring conviction into the life of the believer. If a person does not respond to that guilt with confession and repentance, he or she may be able to suppress it. However, suppressing the guilt does not make it go away. The guilt is only pushed below the surface of consciousness to produce other symptoms, such as anxiety and/or depression (Minirth and Meier 1978:101-3, Grunlan and Lambrides 1983:146).

This discussion has not been intended to "scare" young people out of engaging in premarital sex, but rather to present some of the possible consequences. It is my firm belief that the Christian's motive for obeying God and His Word is not fear but love (John 15:10-14; 1 John 2:5-6). However, we must also understand that the Bible teaches that there are consequences of sin (Gal. 6:7-8).

CHRISTIANS AND PREMARITAL SEX

How Far?

A standard question asked by young people in general and Christians in particular is, "How far can we go?" What expressions of physical intimacy are acceptable before marriage and which ones are restricted to married couples? As we discussed earlier, there was little if any physical contact between couples before marriage in Bible times; therefore, the Scriptures do not deal with kissing and petting but only with sexual intercourse. In modern Western culture, physical contact between couples before marriage is permitted, the only question being that of extent. Differing degrees of physical intimacy at various stages of a relationship are presented in figure 5-1.

While levels 1 to 8 in figure 5-1 show a progression from permissive to conservative degrees of physical intimacy, level 9 portrays the situation faced by many Chris-

DATING AND COURTSHIP

STAGES

Levels	Friendship	Dating	Going Steady	Engaged	Married
1	L T	h H k K fk B			
		SO SI			
2	L T	h H k K fk B	SO SI		
3	L T	h H k K fk	B SO	SI	
4	L T	h H k K	fk B	SO SI	
5	L T	h H k	K fk	B SO	SI
6	L T	h H k	K	fk B	SO SI
7	L T	h H	k K	fk	B SO SI
8	L T	h H	k	K	fk B SO SI
9	L T	h H k K fk			B SO SI

KEY:

    L — Look
    T — Touch
    h — Holding Hands Lightly
    H — Constant Holding Hands
    k — Light Kiss
    K — Strong Kiss
    fk — French Kiss
    B — Fondling of Breasts
  SO — Sexual Organs
  SI — Sexual Intercourse

Figure 5–1. DEGREES OF SEXUAL BEHAVIOR (Wright and Inmon 1978).

tian young people. Early in their dating they have gone as far as they believe is right and they spend the next stages of their relationship frustrated because they maintain their standards, or guilty because they violate them (see quote at beginning of the chapter). While Christian couples may differ in how far they feel it is okay to go, most experience this syndrome.

Level 5 in figure 5–1 illustrates what the literature calls "technical virgin" (Scanzoni and Scanzoni 1981:118). Since the Scriptures only prohibit sexual intercourse before marriage (i.e., Acts 15:28–29; 1 Cor. 6:9–10; Gal. 5:19–21), some Christian young people feel that anything short of coitus is acceptable. However, is a young woman who engages in heavy petting with numerous young men any more virtuous than a young woman who once engaged in coitus with her husband-to-be before her marriage?

Addressing the issue of how far a Christian should go in physical intimacy before marriage, H. Norman Wright suggests to us:

> Given our conviction to refrain from sexual intercourse until marriage, the question remains: How far shall we go, short of sexual intercourse, before marriage?
>
> The answer to this question depends upon how far along you are in your relationship (first date or engaged) and upon your abilities to withstand the very strong temptation to have sexual intercourse.
>
> However, a general principle which we feel applies to everyone is the following: That which has its natural end in sexual intercourse should be held to your wedding night.. . . This means at the very least, that heavy petting, direct stimulation of each other's sexual organs, and mutual masturbation should be out. . . . This also means that you should not engage in any physical activity which will build up the other person's sexual drives to the point of no return (1977:197).

I personally go along with what Wright advocates. In fact, an even slower approach might be advocated. It is not enough to stop only at the right point but also at the right stage of the relationship. As was pointed out earlier, very early in their relationship many Christian couples go as far as they believe right. It is my contention that couples ought to move slowly in the area of physical intimacy. Rather than engage in every permissible behavior early in their relationship, they ought to save various expressions of physical intimacy to celebrate various stages of their relationship. For example, most Christian couples have no new act of physical intimacy left with which to celebrate their engagement. Using the same format as in figure 5–1, figure 5–2 presents a possible progress of physical intimacy for a Christian couple.

Friendship	Dating	Going Steady	Engaged	Married
L T	h H	k K	K fk	B SO SI

Key on figure 4–1.

Figure 5–2. SUGGESTED LEVELS OF INTIMATE ACTIVITIES.

Remember that our sexuality and sex drives are not wrong or sinful. They are not part of our fallen nature but are part of the original creation that God called "good" (Gen. 1:26–28, 31). It is only the misuse and abuse of them that is sinful. When the Christian uses his or her sexuality and sex drive as God intended and directed, it is a beautiful thing, God's gift of life and love.

On a practical level there are several things a couple can do to avoid temptations in the area of sexual behavior. One is to do a lot of "public dating," that is, a couple should spend time in public places such as restaurants and parks rather than in a parked car or alone in a living room. A couple can have all the privacy they need to talk and get to know each other in a public place without the temptations of a secluded setting. Another suggestion is "double dating" or "group dating"; again, there is security in numbers. A couple should also avoid those places and activities that either stimulate sexual desire or provide opportunity for sexual activity. Perhaps the best safeguard for a Christian couple is to have a close walk with the Lord and maintain both a Spirit-filled life and a Spirit-filled relationship. Prayer and Bible study should be a regular part of a couple's relationship.[3]

Masturbation

A few years ago the dean of students at a Christian college told me that the number one source of spiritual problems on his campus was masturbation. Research indicates that 90 percent of males and 60 percent of females have engaged in masturbation by age twenty-four (Strong et al. 1981:236). Research conducted by Miles (1971:174) on a Christian college campus found that 47 percent of the females surveyed had engaged in masturbation. Research I conducted found that 90 percent of the male students and 60 percent of the female students surveyed at a Christian college had engaged in masturbation.

For purposes of our discussion masturbation will be defined "as the deliberate and conscious self-stimulation

---

[3]This does not mean a couple needs to have "devotions" on every date, but they should have some regular pattern of spiritual interaction.

so as to produce sexual excitement with the goal of orgasm" (Seamands 1977:104). It is not achieving an orgasm that defines masturbation, but rather the attempt, whether or not the goal is reached.

The question facing Christian young people is whether or not masturbation is a sin. While hosts of evangelical writers have condemned it as such, in recent years some evangelicals have taught that a limited practice of masturbation for the purpose of self-control in relating to the opposite sex may be permissible (e.g., Dobson 1978; Miles 1971; Seamands 1977; Shedd 1976; White 1977.

In attempting to answer the question of whether masturbation is sinful or not, we must begin by recognizing that the Scriptures do not address the issue directly. There are two passages that some writers have used to condemn masturbation, Genesis 38:8–11 and 1 Corinthians 6:9–10. However, on closer examination it will be seen that they do not address the issue. In Genesis 38:8–11, Onan's sin was not masturbation or even practicing coitus interruptus, but disobeying God's command to raise up seed for his dead brother. In the King James Version the term "abusers of themselves" appears in the Corinthians passage. While some understood this phrase to refer to masturbation, it refers to homosexuality and is so translated in later versions (i.e., NIV; NASB; TEV). Because the Bible does not discuss masturbation directly, it is an issue concerning which Christians may come to different conclusions. It is one of those areas in which we must be careful not to judge others and to be faithful to our own conscience and understanding of God's Word.

While recognizing the right and need of every believer to settle this issue for himself or herself, I would like to share three reasons why I believe that masturbation is a practice best avoided by Christian young people. First, there is no biological necessity for masturbation. Females have no need for a biological release. In mature males the testes continually produce sperm and the prostate gland produces semen. The sperm is deposited in the seminal fluid and stored in the seminal vesicles. When these fill with seminal fluid, there is a need for release. A certain amount of seminal fluid may be drained off during urination. Another mechanism for releasing the seminal fluid is the nocturnal emission. While the male sleeps, the bladder fills and presses against the seminal vesicles. The male has an erection and experiences an ejaculation.[4] God has provided the mechanism for release of seminal fluid.

Second, masturbation is a solo act, and God created us as sexual beings to bring men and women together (Gen. 1:26–28; 2:24–25). Our sexuality was meant to be a coupling mechanism rather than lead to an act conducted in isolation. Masturbation can easily become an emotional substitute for normal interpersonal relationships. It can become a means of avoiding meaningful relationships with members of the opposite sex.

Third, and perhaps the strongest argument against masturbation, is the thought that accompanies the act. Research studies have found that nearly all men and two-thirds of all women fantasize when they masturbate, with the fantasies providing part of the stimulus (Strong et al. 1981:237). While the Scriptures do not directly address the act of masturbation, the Bible does speak to the issue of our thought life (Matt. 5:27–28). Because of this, if the sin does not lie in the act of masturbation, it often does in the thoughts.

For the person who concludes that masturbation is wrong for himself or herself and is trying to control the practice, I would like to offer a few practical suggestions. First, avoid the time and places where masturbation has been practiced. We are all creatures of habit, and a good procedure for breaking a habit is changing your routine. Second, avoid sexual stimuli, whether it be certain types of music, movies, television programs, magazines, or whatever. As the apostle Paul advises, "Whatever is true, whatever is noble, whatever is right, whatever is pure . . . think of these things" (Phil. 4:8). Third, do not fight your thoughts related to masturbation; when you fight them you are thinking about them. Instead you should replace those thoughts with something else. Fourth, take it a day

---

[4]Nocturnal emissions are often accompanied by dreams with sexual content. In some of these dreams the male may be engaging in sexual activity in which he would not engage when conscious. No guilt should be felt over these dreams since one does not have control of unconscious brain activities such as dreams.

at a time. Just try for victory the next time you are tempted. A habit is defeated one step at a time. Fifth, and most important, commit the matter to God in prayer. Get other believers to pray for you—you do not have to tell them specifics. Also spend time in God's Word. As with all sexual temptations, remember the words of James: "Submit yourselves, then, to God. Resist the devil, and he will flee from you. Come near to God and he will come near to you. Wash your hands . . . and purify your hearts" (James 4:7–8).

DISCUSSION QUESTIONS

1. What is your reaction to Cox's assertion that "intimate physical contact of any kind between male and female is sexual behavior"? Why?

2. Do you believe that the media more often reflect current sexual attitudes or shape them? Why?

3. Why do you think more unwed mothers are keeping their babies? Do you believe it is best for an unwed teen-age mother to keep her baby or put it up for adoption? Why?

4. Why do you believe white teen-agers turn to abortion when they become pregnant in much greater numbers than black teen-agers?

5. What is your reaction to the author's suggestion that dating couples practice a "go slow" approach to physical intimacy and save permissible expressions of intimacy to celebrate significant stages of their relationship? Why?

6. In your opinion why does the Bible take such a strong stand against premarital sexual relations?

SUGGESTED READING

Herbert T. Miles, *Sexual Understanding Before Marriage* (Grand Rapids: Zondervan, 1971). This popular book covers the basic biological facts of sex. It also deals with dating, premarital sex, masturbation, and sexual sins. The author presents a biblical case for premarital chastity.

Lewis Smedes, *Sex for Christians* (Grand Rapids: Eerdmans, 1976). The author presents a biblical perspective on human sexuality and behavior. He develops ethical principles for dealing with sex.

Bryan Strong et al., *Human Sexuality: Essentials* (2nd ed.) (St. Paul: West, 1981). A basic introduction of human sexuality. The book presents the biological and social aspects of sex.

John White, *Eros Defiled* (Downers Grove, Ill.: InterVarsity, 1977). This book deals with the Christian and sexual sin. The author covers all aspects of sexual immorality, including premarital sex, adultery, homosexuality, and personal morality. Written from a Christian perspective, this book provides some practical advice.

PART III

MARRIAGE

6

Husband-and-Wife Relationship

The man said, "This is now bone of my bones and flesh of my flesh; she shall be called 'woman,' for she was taken out of man." For this reason a man will leave his father and mother and be united to his wife, and they will become one flesh.

GENESIS 2:23–24

THE INSTITUTION OF marriage has received a good deal of bad publicity in the 1980s. We have all read the accounts of the rising divorce rate and the stories of wife abuse. We are constantly hearing about the demise of the family. All of this negative press may lead us to question the future of marriage. However, while there are serious problems with many marriages in our society, these problems do not seem to have turned people away from marriage. In fact, today a greater percentage of Americans marry than at any other time in history.

EXTENT OF MARRIAGE

Approximately 96 percent of all Americans will eventually marry, according to the U.S. Census Bureau. This means that most of those reading this book either are married or will be married. While the percentage of Americans who eventually marry has risen steadily since the founding of our nation, the age at which first marriages take place has fluctuated. The median age at first marriage in the United States was 26.1 for men and 22.0 for women in 1890. By 1950, the ages had dropped to 22.8 for men and 20.3 for women. However, since 1960 the age has been climbing steadily and by 1978 had reached 24.2 for men and 21.8 for women (see table 6–1).

TABLE 6-1
MEDIAN AGE AT FIRST MARRIAGE

Year	Men	Women
1890	26.1	22.0
1950	22.8	20.3
1960	22.8	20.3
1970	23.2	20.8
1978	24.2	21.8

Source: Adapted from Saxton 1980:279.

Season and day also affect the occurrence of marriage. In the United States twice as many marriages occur in June as in February. After June, the next two most popular months for weddings are August and September. January and March have almost as few weddings as February. It is also interesting to note that age at marriage and season interact. It seems that younger couples prefer June, middle-aged couples prefer December, and older couples choose July (Eshleman 1981:406-7). Nevertheless, no matter the age or season, the most popular day, by far, for getting married is Saturday. Over half of all weddings (55 percent) occur on this day.

MARRIAGE AS A CONTRACT

When we think of marriage, we generally think of "being in love" and of romance. We think of commitment and "becoming one." While marriage may well be all of those things, it is also a legal contract. It is as much a legal contract as a sales agreement, a promissory note, a deed, or a job contract. In fact, it often has aspects of all of these types of contracts. Marriage is a legal contract between two people and between those two people and the state.

We will first consider the contract between the couple and the state. The state controls whom we may marry and under what circumstances. All states have incest laws that prohibit marriage between close blood relatives—parents and children, brother and sister, uncle and niece, aunt and nephew, and grandparents and grandchildren. Many states do no allow marriage between a half brother and sister or between first cousins. Some states prohibit the marriage of second cousins and in-laws. However, every state prohibits polygamy.

The state also determines the minimum age for marriage and whether there is a waiting period for a marriage license and/or a waiting period after the issuing of the license. The state also determines whether or not a blood test is required. State laws are summarized in table 6-2.

The state also addresses the relationship between the husband and the wife. While marriage laws differ from state to state, under the laws of most states the husband is required to support his wife financially, and in return she is required to maintain his home and to have sexual relations with him when he wishes.[1]

State laws often make the husband the head of the home and give him control of both his own and his wife's property. Title 8 of California's Senate Bill 252 is typical of many state laws:

> Husband and wife contract toward each other obligations of mutual respect, fidelity and support.
>
> The husband is the head of the family. He may choose any reasonable place or mode of living, and the wife must conform thereto.
>
> Neither husband nor wife has any interest in the property of the other, but neither can be excluded from the other's dwelling (except under certain circumstances recognized by the court).
>
> The respective interests of the husband and the wife in community property during the continuance of the marriage relations are present, existing and equal interests under the management and control of the husband.

With the rise of the women's movement and the push to pass the Equal Rights Amendment, many states are reexamining their marriage laws. The 1980s may well see the rewriting of marriage laws in many states. If the Equal Rights Amendment were to be passed, it would mandate the changing of most of our present marriage laws.

The state also controls the termination of the marriage contract through divorce laws. These laws prescribe the

---

[1]Some states no longer have the sexual relations requirement. In 1978 an Oregon woman sued her husband for rape.

TABLE 6-2
STATE MARRIAGE REGULATIONS

State or Other Jurisdiction	Age at Which Marriage Can Be Contracted Without Parental Consent		Age at Which Marriage Can Be Contracted With Parental Consent		Maximum Period Between Examination and Issuance of License (Days)	Blood Tests and Other Medical Requirements		
	Male	Female	Male	Female		Scope of Medical Inquiry	Before Issuance of License	After Issuance of License
Alabama	18	18	17(a)	14(a)	30	(b)	...	...
Alaska	18	18	16(c)	16(c)	30	(b)	3 da.	...
Arizona	18	18	16(c)	16(c)	30	(b)	(d)	...
Arkansas	18	18	17(c)	16(c)	30	(b)	3 da.	...
California	18	18	18(a,c)	16(a,c)	30	(b,e,f,g)	...	...
Colorado	18	18	16(c)	16(c)	30	(b,f,h)	...	...
Connecticut	18	18	18(c)	16(c)	35	(b)	4 da.	...
Delaware	18	18	18(c)	16(c)	30	(b)	...	(i)
Florida	18	18	16(a,c)	16(a,c)	30	(b)	3 da.	...
Georgia	18(j)	18(j)	16(c,j)	16(c,j)	30	(b,e)	3 da.(k)	...
Hawaii	18	18	16	16(c)	30	(b,f)	(m)	...
Idaho	18	18	16(c)	16(c)	...	(f)	3 da.	...
Illinois	18	18	16(c)	16(c)	15	(b,e)	3 da.	...
Indiana	18	18	17(c)	17(c)	30	(b,e)	3 da.	...
Iowa	18	18	16	16	20	(b)	3 da.	...
Kansas	18	18	18(c)	18(c)	30	(b)	3 da.	...
Kentucky	18	18	(a,o)	(a,o)	15	(b,e)	3 da.	...
Louisiana	18	18	18(c)	16(c)	10	(b)	...	72 hrs.
Maine	18	18	16(c)	16(c)	60	(b)	5 da.	...
Maryland	18	18	16(c)	16(c)	...	...	48 hrs.	...

Massachusetts	18	18	18(c)	18(c)	30	(b,f)	3 da.	
Michigan	18	18	(r)	16	33	(b)	3 da.	
Minnesota	18	18	18	16(q)			5 da.	
Mississippi	21	21	17(c)	15(c)	30		3 da.	
Missouri	18	18	15(c)	15(c)	15	(b)	3 da.	
Montana	18	18	18(c)	18(c)	20	(b)	5 da.	
Nebraska	19	19	17	17	30	(b,f)	2 da.	3 da.
Nevada	18	18	16(a,c)	16(a,c)				
New Hampshire	18	18	14(q)	13(q)	30(r)	(b)	3 da.	
New Jersey	18	18	16(c)	16(c)	30	(b)	72 hrs.	
New Mexico	18	18	16(c)	16(c)	30	(b)	72 hrs.	
New York	18	18	16	14(s)	30	(b,e)		24 da.(t)
North Carolina	18	18	16	16(c)	30	(b,f,u,v)		
North Dakota	18	18	16	16	30	(b,w)		
Ohio	18	18	18(c)	16(c)	30	(b)	5 da.	
Oklahoma	18	18	16(c)	16(c)	30	(b)	(m)	
Oregon	18	18	17	17	30	(b)		(a,b)
Pennsylvania	18	18	16(c)	16(c)	30	(b,y)	3 da.	
Rhode Island	18	18	18(c)	16(c)	40	(b,f,v)		
South Carolina	18	18	16(c)	14(c)			24 hrs.	
South Dakota	18	18	16(c)	16(c)	20	(b)		
Tennessee	18	18	16(c)	16(c)	30	(b)	3 da.(ab)	
Texas	18	18	14(c)	14(c)	21	(b)		
Utah	18	18	16(a)	14(a)	30	(b)		
Vermont	18	18	16(c)	16(c)	30	(b)		5 da.
Virginia	18	18	16(a,c)	16(a,c)	30	(b)		
Washington	18	18	17(c)	17(c)		(b,r,aa)	3 da.	
West Virginia	18	18	(q)	(o)	30	(b)	3 da.	
Wisconsin	18	18	16	16	20	(b)	5 da.	
Wyoming	19	19	17(c)	16(c)	30	(b)		
Dist. of Col.	18	18	16(a)	16(a)	30	(b)	3 da.	
Puerto Rico	21	21	18(c)	16(c)	10(ab)	(b,aa)		

(a) Parental consent not required if previously married.
(b) Venereal diseases.
(c) Legal procedure for younger persons to obtain license.
(d) Blood test must be on record at least 48 hours before issuance of license.
(e) Sickle cell anemia.
(f) Rubella immunity.
(g) Tay-Sachs disease.
(h) Rh factor.
(i) Residents, 24 hours; nonresidents, 96 hours.
(j) Parental consent is not needed regardless of age in case of pregnancy or when couple has a living child born out of wedlock.
(k) Unless parties are 18 years of age or over, or woman is pregnant, or applicants are the parents of a living child born out of wedlock.
(l) Generally no, but may be recognized for limited purposes, e.g., legitimacy of children, workers' compensation benefits, etc.
(m) Three days if parties are under 18 years of age.
(n) However, contracting such a marriage is a misdemeanor.
(o) No minimum age.

(p) No provision in the law for parental consent for males.
(q) Permission of judge also required.
(r) Maximum period between blood test and date of intended marriage.
(s) If under 16 years of age, consent of family court judge also required.
(t) However, marriage may not be solemnized within 3 days of date on which specimen for blood test was taken.
(u) Mental competence.
(v) Tuberculosis.
(w) Some marriages prohibited if a party is severely retarded.
(x) License valid 3 days after application signed and valid for 30 days thereafter.
(y) Court order needed if party is weakminded, insane, or of unsound mind.
(z) May be waived if certain conditions are met.
(aa) Affidavit of mental competence required. Also, no epilepsy in Puerto Rico.
(ab) Maximum time from blood test to expiration of license.

Source: Reprinted from The Book of the States, *1980-1981, published by the Council of State Governments, Lexington, Kentucky.*

circumstances under which the marriage contract may be terminated. They also direct the distribution of property, the custody of children, and other matters pertaining to the termination of the marriage contract.

While marriage is a contract between a couple and the state, it is also a contract between two individuals. In their marriage vows, a couple make certain promises to each other. The nature of these promises varies from ceremony to ceremony. For example, in the traditional wedding vows the woman promises to "love, honor, and obey" her husband. Modern vows, used by many couples today, usually substitute the phrase "love and cherish." In fact, today many couples write their own vows. Some couples even enter marriage with written contracts stating responsibilities, property distribution, and spelling out other matters. The legality of these contracts, particularly if they are not consistent with state law, is still very much in question.

The thing that is of interest to me is that most people enter a marriage in total ignorance of their state's laws and the specific things they are contracting to perform. Usually a couple's only concern is with minimum ages (if they are young), blood tests, and waiting periods. Most couples think of their marriage as a romantic and religious occasion and are unaware that they are also entering a legal contract with each other and the state.

Frequently, Christians also see marriage as a contract between a couple and God. They view their vows as not only promises to each other but also promises to God. These Christians see God, through His Word, giving responsibilities and principles for the couple to carry out in their life together. I believe that marriage is a commitment made before God and that He has given believers guidelines for living together. Some of these guidelines will be explored in this chapter and others will be examined in later chapters.

SEX ROLES

We have already seen that the concepts of status and role are central to the sociological study of society. Roles are defined as the behavior expected from the person holding a particular status. We saw that ascribed statuses are those assigned to an individual by his or her society. Ascription is generally based on characteristics of birth, such as sex. Thus sex roles are the behaviors expected of persons based on an ascribed status–sex. For example, if we expect little girls to play with dolls and little boys to play with trucks, those are expected sex roles. That is, we expect a behavior based on the person's sex.

Masculinity and Femininity

While our gender, that is maleness and femaleness, is innate, masculinity and femininity are learned. While there are biological differences between males and females (see table 6–3), the ongoing debate concerns the

TABLE 6–3
NORMAL BIOLOGICAL SEX DIFFERENCES

MALE	FEMALE	CHARACTERISTIC
XY sex chromosomes	XX chromosomes	Sex is determined by sperm bearing X or Y chromosome uniting with X bearing ovum
Androgens (testosterone)	Estrogens	Male and female sex hormones
Penis	Clitoris	Erectile genitals
Scrotum	Vulva	Sensitive, soft external genitalia
Testes	Ovaries	Paired gonads producing male and female hormones and germ cells
Spermatozoa	Ovum	Germ cells produced by testes and ovaries
Vas deferens	Fallopian tubes	Tubes for carrying germ cells from gonads
Facial, body, and pubic hair	Pubic hair	Adult characteristics
Strong, heavy muscles	Fatty layer beneath skin over smaller muscles	Adult body development
Narrow hips, broad shoulders	Broad hips, sloping shoulders, developed breasts	Adult body shape

Source: Adapted from Duvall 1977:6.

effect of these differences on behavior. Sandra Bem, a social psychologist, developed a test for measuring masculine and feminine trait characteristics (1977). The test consists of twenty traditionally masculine characteristics and twenty traditionally feminine characteristics. The test also contains twenty neutral characteristics as filler items (see table 6–4 for all the items). American college students rated the items as masculine, feminine, and neutral. Are these characteristics innate or learned?

Sociologists are generally agreed that these characteristics (table 6–4) are primarily learned. One of the strongest evidences supporting this conclusion is that behaviors considered masculine in one culture may be considered feminine in another culture. For example, among the Tchambuli of Indonesia women are dominant and

TABLE 6–4
MASCULINE, FEMININE, AND NEUTRAL ROLES
ON THE BEM SEX-ROLE INVENTORY

Masculine Items	Feminine Items	Neutral Items
Acts as a leader	Affectionate	Adaptable
Aggressive	Cheerful	Conceited
Ambitious	Childlike	Conscientious
Analytical	Compassionate	Conventional
Assertive	Does not use harsh language	Friendly
Athletic	Eager to soothe hurt feelings	Happy
Competitive	Feminine	Helpful
Defends own beliefs	Flatterable	Inefficient
Dominant	Gentle	Jealous
Forceful	Gullible	Likable
Has leadership abilities	Loves children	Moody
Independent	Loyal	Reliable
Individualistic	Sensitive to the needs of others	Secretive
Makes decisions easily	Shy	Sincere
Masculine	Soft spoken	Solemn
Self-reliant	Sympathetic	Tactful
Self-sufficient	Tender	Theatrical
Strong personality	Understanding	Truthful
Willing to take a stand	Warm	Unpredictable
Willing to take risks	Yielding	Unsystematic

Note: Items in each column are listed alphabetically.
Source: Adapted from Bem 1977:208.

impersonal while men are dependent and emotional. In the Marquesas Islands, males are the primary child-care agents because they believe "women are not maternally inclined" (Vander Zanden 1979:330). If gender determined behavior, masculinity and femininity should be the same in every culture. The fact that sex roles vary greatly from culture to culture indicates that most behaviors we consider masculine or feminine are learned.

Sex Role Socialization

We have seen that while gender is determined by birth, masculinity and femininity are learned. We acquire our sex roles by the process of socialization. This process begins at birth. I have two sons and a daughter. When my sons were born, they were wrapped in blue blankets, whereas my daughter was wrapped in a pink blanket. Why was this done? Was it so the hospital personnel would know how to treat them? Researchers have found that caretakers will play rougher with a male infant than with a female infant. On the other hand, they will talk more with a female infant than with a male infant. However, male infants receive more physical contact than female infants (Orthner 1981:170). When my infant sons were brought home from the hospital, friends and relatives gave them trucks and balls. When my daughter arrived home from the hospital, she received dolls and frilly outfits.

Television plays a significant role in the socialization of children. If you observe television programs, and particularly commercials, you will see a great deal of sex-role stereotyping. What different roles do women and men play? As long as children see men fixing cars, driving trucks, and performing surgery and women scrubbing tables, preparing supper, washing clothes, worrying about "static cling," and working as secretaries and nurses, they will be socialized to accept these traditional sex roles.

Parents, teachers, and peers also play important roles in the socialization process. The roles and attitudes of parents have a profound effect on children. Parents are the earliest role models children are exposed to. Teachers also have a profound influence. Research conducted in

1978 found that teachers and guidance counselors, for the most part, still continue to direct students into courses and programs that will prepare them for traditional masculine and feminine roles and occupations (Orthner 1981:172). While sex roles are changing, socialization is the major determiner of the direction and extent of the change.

Traditional Roles

Traditionally, in most cultures, the husband has been responsible for supporting his wife. In return the wife has been expected to keep the home, prepare the meals, and bear and care for children. The working husband and housewife/homemaker roles are still seen by many as the ideal arrangement. Research conducted among college students indicates that many young people still prefer traditional husband-wife roles. The study found that about one-fourth of graduating college males believed women should be homemakers (Duvall 1977:84). Other research found that many women employed outside the home prefer to be only homemakers and that half the women who did not work outside the home had no desire to do so (Saxton 1980:84). As we examine the findings of various researchers, we discover that many Americans, both male and female, are content with traditional family roles.

Traditional husband/wife roles are based on what sociologists call division of labor. In traditional roles, division of labor is highly specialized. That is, certain jobs are considered women's work and certain jobs are considered men's work. Generally, men's work consists of tasks such as maintaining the family car, cutting the grass, shoveling the snow, making major repairs of the house, paying the bills, and being the final decision-maker. Women's tasks consist of primary child care, meal preparation, maintaining the home, and being submissive. The more traditional couples are in their roles, the more specialized the roles become. I know a college professor who will not even load a dishwasher because he believes that it is his wife's responsibility. The next time you are visiting in someone's home observe who prepares and serves the meal and who cleans up after the meal. Is there any discussion of who should do it or does one person automatically assume it is his/her responsibility?

Changing Roles

While many people are content with traditional husband-wife roles, many others are not. They see traditional sex roles as limiting. They would prefer to see marriage as a partnership in which both the husband and wife provide the support and both keep the home and care for the children.

Over the past four years I have administered to my sociology classes the Attitudes Toward Women Scale, a test that indicates a person's attitudes toward the roles of women. Each year the females have indicated significantly more liberated attitudes toward female sex roles, while males have indicated more traditional attitudes. However, on the whole, the attitudes of both males and females have become more liberated each year. It will be interesting to see the types of husband-wife roles that develop as these students begin to marry.

Changing Wife Roles

A Gallup survey conducted in 1980 found that over half of the adult women in America prefer the traditional sex roles of mother and wife. If they work outside the home, it is to supplement the family income rather than to have a career. However, a growing number of women are becoming dissatisfied with traditional sex roles. Further analysis of the research data indicates that it is the older adult women who prefer the traditional roles, while the younger women are indicating more liberated views. For example, only one in six women under twenty-six years of age indicated "strongly agree" to the statement "A woman's place is in the home" (Orthner 1981:183).

The changing roles of wives is most evident in the area of employment outside the home. According to U.S. Department of Labor the percentage of single women in the labor force rose from 48 to 60 percent between 1940 and 1980, while during the same period the percentage of married women rose from 15 to 50 percent. While women made up 24 percent of the labor force in 1940, the U.S. Department of Labor estimates they will make up more than 40 percent of the labor force by 1985. If we look at the statistics of 1978, we find that 45 percent of all married women living with their husbands are employed outside the home. For women with children under six years of age, 55 percent are in the labor force. When the children reach school age, the participation in the labor force for married women jumps to 73 percent. In fact, married women with children are more likely to be employed than married women without children (Horton and Hunt 1980:229).

With the increase of participation in the labor force of married women with children, another role of married women is changing, that of caring for children. While in the traditional role the mother provided primary child care, these responsibilities for employed women are being shared with baby-sitters, child-care workers, camp counselors, and other service personnel and agencies.

A question that may come to your mind is, What effect does a wife's employment outside the home have on the marital relationship? Horton and Hunt surveyed a number of studies on this question. They conclude that the answer is uncertain; however, working wives seem more satisfied with their lives than housewives. They conclude that the happiest wives are those with a husband and children and a job to which they are not totally committed (Horton and Hunt 1980:230).

Changing Husband Roles

As we might expect, changes in the roles of wives has led to changes in the roles of husbands. Orthner (1981:186) tells us that during the 1940s and 1950s it was quite common to find cartoons in magazines like *The Saturday Evening Post* that made fun of men doing housework or engaged in child care. We rarely see that sort of humor today. Humor is often a good reflector of society's values and norms. Society's expectations for men in the areas of housework and child care have changed.

With more and more wives entering the labor force, husbands have had to pick up some of the responsibilities at home. Also, as women have been liberated from their traditional roles, there has been some spillover effect in liberating men from traditional expectations. However, we need to realize that the changes in husbands' roles have not been as drastic and far-reaching as they have in wives' roles. For example, while large numbers of wives are entering the full-time labor market, relatively few men are becoming full-time househusbands. For the most part, husbands still see themselves as the primary breadwinners. Also, while husbands do help their wives with household chores, the major responsibility for household tasks still rests on the wives even if they are employed outside the home.

HUSBAND-AND-WIFE RELATIONSHIP

While the traditional American family was highly patriarchal, research indicates that it has moved toward a more equalitarian model. Duvall (1977:81) reports the results of a national survey conducted in 1975. The survey found that 61 percent of the couples had a "partnership" marriage in which decision making was shared. The other 39 percent had a "macho" marriage—the husband was the main provider and decision-maker and the wives were not employed outside the home unless absolutely necessary.

While attitudes and some areas of the husband-wife relationship have changed in recent years, very few couples have a truly equal marriage. Most marriages still carry over many of the vestiges of traditional marriages. Ellen Goodman catches the subtleness of it for us in an editorial that appeared in the October 30, 1981, issue of the *Minneapolis Tribune:*

> The TV ad is cheerfully maternalistic, a mother and daughter special. In a mere 60 seconds, we see the passing of eternal wisdom from one generation of women to the next.
>
> It begins as we discover that the girl has bought—gasp!—a bargain bleach. This turns out to be more a cause of pity than for censure. Mother, who knows best about washing, explains gently that a bargain is not always a bargain, especially when it is used on a favorite blouse.
>
> By the end of the commercial, the girl has become wise

in the ways of brand-name bleaches, and we have become wise in the ways we really live in our changing families.

The commerical is not more inane than any other, but there is a new character in the advertising soap opera: the commercial geared to the teenage girl as family shopper. The advertising people are hip to something. As more and more mothers go to work, we are looking for more and more help at home . . . from our daughters. . . .

In this laundry-room scene, there is neither father nor brother. Mother and daughter share the laundry and the shopping. It is still women's work . . . and girl's work. . . .

And in that scenario, a great deal more is passed down from mother to daughter than the brand name of a bleach.

Looking at the social research and observing marriages around us, we find that marriages are changing. We conclude that husbands are becoming more involved in household tasks, that more wives are entering the labor force, and that child care is being shared or delegated. However with all these changes, the traditional model of marriage still prevails in American culture. When a husband does household chores or child care, he generally sees himself as helping his wife as opposed to meeting his responsibilities. Many women in the labor force are seen as supplementing the family income rather than pursuing a career. In other words, while a great deal of observable behavior has changed in recent years, it appears that changes in attitudes and beliefs and thus significant role changes are following more slowly.

HUSBAND AND WIFE ROLES AND THE BIBLE

As Christians, we turn to God's Word to find principles to guide us in establishing our norms and values. However, there seems to be a great deal of disagreement among Christians on what the Bible teaches about the husband-wife relationship. Some believers understand the Scriptures to teach a traditional model of family life; others find support for a partnership model of marriage. We will examine both perspectives and their implications.

Traditional Marriage

Those who believe that the Scriptures teach that the traditional marriage is the model for Christians hold a position that sees the husband as the head of the home, the final authority, and the leader, while the wife is to be submissive to that authority and leadership. Larry Christenson explains this position for us:

> God has ordered the family according to the principle of "headship". Each member of the family lives under the authority of the "head" whom God has appointed.
>
> The husband lives under the authority of Christ and is responsible to Christ for the leadership and care of the family. The wife lives under the authority of her husband, and is responsible to him for the way she orders the household and cares for the children. . . . The authority over the children, however, remains essentially one . . . the authority of the mother is a derived authority. She exercises authority over the children on behalf of and in the place of her husband. . . .
>
> Thus God has structured the family along clear-cut lines of authority and responsibility. . . . God has made the well-being and happiness of the family absolutely dependent upon the observance of His divinely appointed order (1970:17–18).

There are a number of Scripture passages that those holding to this position appeal to. We will examine some of them. One of these is Genesis 2:18, "And the Lord God said, It is not good that the man should be alone; I will make him an help meet for him" (AV). It is argued that the husband is in authority both because he was created first and because the woman was created to be his helper (i.e., assistant).

Another verse in Genesis that is appealed to is 3:16,"Your desire will be for your husband, and he will rule over you." This verse is understood as a commandment setting up God's order for family life after the Fall.

The mainstay of the traditionalists' argument from Scripture is Ephesians 5:22–31:

> Wives, submit to your husbands as to the Lord. For the husband is the head of the wife as Christ is head of the church, his body, of which he is the Savior. Now as the church submits to Christ, so also wives should submit to their husbands in everything.
>
> Husbands, love your wives, just as Christ loved the church and gave himself up for her to make her holy,

cleansing her by the washing with water through the word, and to present her to himself as a radiant church, without stain or wrinkle or any other blemish, but holy and blameless. In this same way, husbands ought to love their wives as their own bodies. He who loves his wife loves himself. After all, no one ever hated his own body, but he feeds and cares for it, just as Christ does the church—for we are members of his body. "For this reason a man will leave his father and mother and be united to his wife, and the two will become one flesh." This is a profound mystery—but I am talking about Christ and the church. However, each one of you also must love his wife as he loves himself, and the wife must respect her husband.

Let us see how those that hold to a traditional view of marriage understand these verses. Gene Getz writes:

Though Eve was created as Adam's counterpart, it was God's plan that man was to be the head administrator in the home. Throughout the Old Testament days, this was the pattern for governing family affairs. During the New Testament times, this principle was reaffirmed and illustrated by Christ's relationship to the church (1972:25).

Kenneth Gangel believes that a biblical husband is a ruler. He says, "All arguments regarding the equalization of the sexes fade into nonsense when one looks into the Word of God" (1972:39). He adds, "The quality of 'headship' certainly refers to the deciding voice in the family . . . (1972:40). Henry Brandt and Phil Landrum follow the same line of reasoning. Discussing Ephesians 5:22, they say that in any family decision "the husband has the last word" (1976:98). They go on to say, "It is the husband's duty to see to it that objectives, policies, procedures and rules are set up and carried out" (1976:100).

Those who hold the traditional position argue that while the husband is to be the leader and the final authority in the home this does not mean that he is to be an autocratic dictator or his wife a servant. They point out that this passage teaches that the husband is to exercise his authority in love. Howard Hendricks summarizes this view for us:

The husband is to be the head of the home; he is also to be the heart of the home. It is his leadership which provides authority; it is his heart that provides affection. One without the other always leads to distortion. He is to be a leader; he is to be a lover.

If the husband is a leader without being a lover, he is an autocratic individual; if he is a lover without being a leader, he will be a sentimentalist. If he has leadership with love, no woman in her right mind resists placing herself willingly and submissively under a man who loves as Christ loved the Church (1973:34).

Jack Taylor writes in his book *One Home Under God:*

No organization can function properly without submission. Submission suggests authority. The whole of nature operates on authority and submission. To take these factors away would be to destroy the whole realm of nature. God has ordered the wife to be submissive to her husband, that is to yield to his authority. That is her God given role. Wife, don't try to figure out this matter of submission. Lead with your heart and receive the capacity of submission as a perfect gift from God (1974:24).

Another passage that those with the traditional view hold to is 1 Peter 3:1–7:

Wives, in the same way be submissive to your husbands so that, if any of them do not believe the word, they may be won over without talk by the behavior of their wives, when they see the purity and reverence of your lives. Your beauty should not come from outward adornment, such as braided hair and the wearing of gold jewelry and fine clothes. Instead it should be that of your inner self, the unfading beauty of a gentle and quiet spirit, which is of great worth in God's sight. For this is the way the holy women of the past who put their hope in God used to make themselves beautiful. They were submissive to their own husbands, like Sarah, who obeyed Abraham and called him her master. You are her daughters if you do what is right and do not give way to fear.

Husbands, in the same way be considerate as you live with your wives, and treat them with respect as the weaker partner and as heirs with you of the gracious gift of life, so that nothing will hinder your prayers.

Commenting on this passage as it relates to marriage in our day, Kenneth Gangel reasons as follows:

There is no question that the fifty-fifty marriage makes sense in terms of today's social mores and cultural values.

It remains to be demonstrated, however, that such an emphasis can fit in harmony with the pattern of the Word of God. This is not to say that Scripture suggests that the husband is a brutal dictator in his home. The husband honors his wife as "the weaker vessel", loves her as part of his own body, and her proper response is a regular submission to his leadership (1972:44).

Summarizing the position of those that hold a traditional view of marriage, we see that they understand the Scriptures to teach that it is God's plan for the husband to be the final authority in the home and that the wife is to submit to that authority. While the traditionalists believe that this authority is to be exercised in love, they still see it as final and absolute. Some exponents of the traditional view also associate role behavior with their understanding of this position. They will advocate, for example, that the husband should handle the family finances, since he is the "head" of the home.

On the other hand, when we examine the views of those who hold to a partnership model of marriage, we will discover that they also appeal to the Bible and often to the same passages as the traditionalists.

Partnership Marriage

Those holding to a partnership marriage begin the defense of their position with the creation accounts as do the traditionalists. However, they generally begin with Genesis 1:26–28:

> Then God said, "Let us make man in our image, in our likeness, and let them rule over the fish of the sea and the birds of the air, over the livestock, over all the earth, and over all creatures that move along the ground." So God created man in his own image, in the image of God he created him; male and female he created them. God blessed them and said to them, "Be fruitful and increase in number; fill the earth and subdue it. Rule over the fish of the sea and the birds of the air and over every living creature that moves on the ground."

Believers holding the partnership position note that both men and women are created in the image of God, both are blessed by God, both are given the commission to procreate, and both are given dominion over nature. Pat Gundry, commenting on these verses, points out that "there is no differentiation of power or position, no order or hierarchy established here" (1980:82).

We have seen that those who hold to a traditional view of marriage appeal to the creation account recorded in Genesis 2:18–24. The exponents of partnership marriage counter that this passage in general and verse 18 in particular have been misinterpreted. Gundry helps us understand verse 18 when she writes:

> The words *help* and *meet* in the King James Version translate two Hebrew words, *ezer* and *neged*. The word *ezer* ("help") is never used in the Bible to refer to a subordinate helper but is used in reference to God as our Helper as in Psalms 121:1, 2. The word *neged* is a preposition in Hebrew, but the most accurate way to translate it into English is by giving it a meaning such as "corresponding to". . . . The idea is that Eve was an appropriate, fitting partner for Adam (1977:20).

It is interesting to note that these two Hebrew words are translated *paraclete* in the Septuagint (a Greek translation of the Old Testament in use at the time of Christ). This word, paraclete, is the same word Jesus uses in John 14:16 to speak of the Holy Spirit as a helper.

Looking at the larger context, Scanzoni and Hardesty (1975:26) say that God brought all the animals to Adam, not because He thought the man might find a "helper" among them, but rather to demonstrate to the man that he would never be satisfied with an inferior creature. When the man realized that he would be satisfied only with an equal, God created the woman for him.

Looking at the "one flesh" concept in verse 24, Herbert and Fern Miles write:

> One flesh is a total relationship of the whole person of the husband to the total person of his wife, and the whole person of the wife to the total person of her husband. One flesh affects the whole self of both husband and wife. The two become one, yet they remain two separate individuals. Each and every succeeding act of intercourse continues, maintains, and renews the one-flesh unity. . . .
>
> It is difficult to imagine how the hierarchy doctrine of husband-dominant/wife-submissive relationship could

make any contribution to this sacred act. Equality, on the other hand, tends to encourage sharing and giving, and thereby eliminates problems and discord prevalent where one mate is dominant. The one-flesh unity is in direct conflict with the dominant/subordinate concept (1978:165).

Some traditionalists agree with those holding the partnership view up to this point, but they argue that the Fall brought into being a new order according to Genesis 3:16. Responding to the traditionalists' argument, Prohl explains:

> God is not here issuing a special commandment, "Be thou ruled by him!" or, "Thou shalt not rule!" But here in Genesis 3:16 we have a statement, a prediction, a prophecy, of how man, degenerated by sin, would take advantage of his headship as husband to dominate, lord it over, his wife. Nowhere in the Bible is Genesis 3:16 quoted or referred to as establishing a general subordination of woman to man (1957:39, in Scanzoni and Hardesty 1975:35).

Those holding the partnership view point out that people who use Genesis 3:16 to teach the subordination of women to their husbands never address Genesis 3:18–19 in relation to the use of herbicides, air conditioning, and other devices for overcoming the consequences of the Fall. They feel it is legitimate for people to strive to overcome the consequences of the Fall in certain areas but not in the husband-and-wife relationship.

Next we will turn to Ephesians 5. As we have seen, the traditionalists begin their discussion with verse 22. This is not hard to understand, since some translations begin a new paragraph with verse 22 (i.e., NASB, NIV), and most translations begin a new sentence at that point. Supporters of the partnership position are quick to point out that this is a bias in the translation. In the Greek text the word *submit* is not found in verse 22, for that verse is a subordinate clause without a verb. The translators have added the verb from verse 21, which reads, "Submit to one another out of reverence for Christ." Grammatically, it is very difficult to separate verse 21 from 22. Gundry explains, "Mutual submission was a principle given to guide relationships between all believers. The verses following verse 21 tell how to work it out . . ." (1980:95).

Those interpreting this passage to support partnership marriage appeal to a basic rule of hermeneutics—a passage must be understood in light of its cultural context. Examining the cultural context, we find that:

> Ionia was a conquered province, under sway of Rome, and the law of *Patria Potestas* held the husband responsible for the conduct of his wife; he was amenable for her offenses. . . . Roman law made the husband the sole and absolute head of his wife. His will was her law; from his decision there was no appeal (Starr 1955:246 in Gundry 1977:72).

Commenting on this cultural context, Gundry says:

> If a wife was already subject, why say it to her at all? The answer is in "as to the Lord". . . . The extent of their subjection was already legally established; it was their *manner* Paul was talking about. . . . If the wife imitated the manner of the church in serving Christ, it would be a loving, respectful service without evil motive or hidden barb. . . . The husband was to also work out his mutual submission to his wife by using his absolute legal power over her, not to his own advantage, but as Christ exercises His power over the church, as Savior of the body. Again, it was his manner that would turn his advantage into service and loving protection, not dictatorship or authoritarianism. The "headship" concept expressed here is one of loving service and care, not one of domination (1977:73).

Stewart deals with this passage in the following way:

> Does one interpret this that man is lord of the creation and woman his slave?. . . It is better, I believe, to see in the analogy of the servanthood of Christ, the authority which the male has with his wife. . . . The man does not dominate the woman but ministers to her, as Christ ministers to the church. So the wife may also minister having a stake in leadership. . . . The motive is not power but love, and finds its source in Christ, whose suffering service blots out our sins, our aggrandizement, and our status-seeking (1970:207).

Finally, we will look at 1 Peter 3:1–7 and see how those who hold the partnership position understand this passage. Again, the cultural context needs to be examined. According to 1 Peter 1:1 this epistle is written to those who reside as aliens, "scattered throughout Pontus, Galatia, Cappadocia, Asia and Bithynia." These aliens were Jewish Christians living outside of Palestine in a Greek province with Greek customs, but under Roman law and government. The time is, most likely, after the destruction of Jerusalem (A.D. 70) and the believers are suffering much persecution (1 Peter 1:6; 2:12, 20; 3:17; 4:12–16; 5:10). Apparently they were also being falsely accused of many evil practices (1 Peter 2:12, 20; 4:14–15).

Looking at the passage under consideration, Gundry interprets 1 Peter 3:1–2 as follows:

> Roman law placed women under the complete control of their husbands. Thus, Christian wives were in a position to be easily persecuted and mistreated by unbelieving husbands. A woman might greatly desire to see her husband converted but have little power to influence him in religious matters. Peter says, in effect, "Actions speak louder than words" (1977:82).

In verses 3 to 5, Peter seems to be saying "be as concerned with your personhood as with your appearance." He was telling the women that they should attempt to impress their husbands not so much with their physical appearance as with their personhood. It is suggested that this is the opposite of what is advocated in some works such as *The Total Woman* (Morgan 1973).

Commenting on verse 6, Gundry states:

> The reference to Sarah is unfortunately not translated accurately in most versions, so the import is lost. The word usually rendered "lord" or "master" is better translated "sir," for it was a term of respect, not servitude. Sarah treated her husband with respect and addressed him with respect (1977:82–83).

In verse 7, Peter is saying to husbands that in spite of their physical and legal (in that culture) advantage over their wives they were to treat them as "fellow-heirs." Again, what from a twentieth-century American perspective looks like a teaching of hierarchy, when studied in its cultural context becomes a teaching of husband-wife equality, according to the partnership perspective.

Summarizing the partnership position, we see that those holding this view believe that the Scriptures teach husband-wife equality. They understand the Bible to teach mutual submission as opposed to dominance-submission. They believe that it is God's intention for married couples to live together as partners.

It is important for us to realize that the debate is not between those who accept God's Word as authoritative and those who reject it. Those in both camps believe in the inspiration of Scripture and its authority. The debate does not involve the *authority* of the Bible; it involves the *interpretation* of the Bible. It is my conviction that many in both camps are sincere Christians seeking to follow God's Word.

Equality and Submission

John C. Howell, in a book entitled *Equality and Submission in Marriage* (1979), sees the traditional marriage and the partnership marriage as two ends of a continuum rather than a dichotomy. He says that a couple may be anywhere along that continuum in their relationship (see figure 6–1). He then makes, what I consider to be a significant point. He says:

> Generally couples establish their pattern of relating during the first eighteen months of marriage. Many couples will continue to live out the style of relationship they found satisfactory in those early months. . . . If the relationship has been formed on the independent-dependent style but has retained the essential characteristics of love and respect, the couple can be very happy in the marriage. . . . This marriage is toward the right end of the marital spectrum. If the relationship has been formed on a mutually interdependent style with full affirmation of the equality of the mates in status and role definition, it will be at the left of the spectrum. But many marriages will result in a blending of these styles in such a way that they will not be fully traditional or fully companionship. . . . Its actual position will be subject to some fluctuation based on differing role expectations. The important consideration is that [each of these marriages is] Christian. Under the guidance of the Holy Spirit and in their commitment to building a Christian marriage, couples are free to work out role relationships which meet their own personality needs (1979:129–30).

Figure 6–1. MARITAL SPECTRUM (Howell 1979:129).

Key: X is independent–dependent style marriage.
O is mutually interdependent style marriage.

I appreciate the point that Howell makes. I believe that, as Christians, we should not attempt to force our own personal model of marriage on others. Nor should we question a couple's motives or spirituality based on the position on the spectrum where their marriage is located. My wife and I are a little more to the partnership end of the spectrum. That is the model of marriage that works best for us and that we are most comfortable with. However, I have friends who have a more traditional marriage. They appear to be as happy and satisfied as we are, and they also seem to be fine Christians. The point is that before God we need to develop a model of marriage with our spouse that we believe honors God and meets our needs. True liberation does not consist of moving people from one set of role expectations to another set. That is only exchanging one prison cell for another. True liberation allows people to pick the place on the spectrum where they are most comfortable. In this whole area, Paul's advice in Romans 14:4 is quite appropriate: "Who are you to judge someone else's servant? To his own master he stands or falls. And he will stand, for the Lord is able to make him stand."

At this point I can imagine the frustration that some readers may be experiencing. They may be saying, "Partnership marriage and traditional marriage cannot both be taught in Scripture. If one is right, then the other is wrong." Which one is right? It is my conviction that God gives us more latitude in conducting our lives than we allow ourselves and each other in many cases. I really appreciate Paul's discussion in Romans 14. One man abstains from eating meat whereas another eats meat; in a different case one man observes certain days and another does not. Paul's concern is not with who is right and who is wrong. His concern is with their motivation. If they are doing it to honor the Lord, God will accept it (14:3–6). I am not arguing that the ends justify the means. There are things in the Bible that are clearly wrong, and if they are done God will never honor them. However, in areas where there are sincere differences of interpretation between believers who are faithfully attempting to follow God's Word as they understand it, I believe that even in cases where one view may be in some absolute sense "more correct" than another, God will accept both parties. Rather than being divided on which model of marriage is most accurate, we should be united in the effort of developing and strengthening Christian homes.

DISCUSSION QUESTIONS

1. Why do you think the age of first marriage has been rising since 1960?
2. Do you believe a husband should have to be financially responsible for his wife and the wife should have sexual relations with him when he wishes, as many state laws require? Why?
3. To what extent do you believe television in general and commercials in particular influence sex roles? To what degree do you believe they reflect current values? Why?
4. In your opinion why do college females have more liberated attitudes toward sex roles than college males?
5. How do you account for the fact that today more couples are moving away from the traditional model of marriage toward a partnership model? Is this trend good or bad? Why?
6. What is your understanding of the Bible's teaching on the husband-wife relationship?

SUGGESTED READING

Larry Christenson, *The Christian Family* (Minneapolis: Bethany, 1970). The author presents the traditional position on marriage. The book has sold over a million copies and is generally recognized as a good representation of the traditional view.

Peter DeJong and Donald R. Wilson, *Husband and Wife: The Sexes in Scripture and Society* (Grand Rapids: Zondervan, 1979). Written by evangelical sociologists, the book deals with the biological and social antecedents of sex roles from a Christian perspective. The authors support a partnership model of marriage.

Kenneth Gangel, *The Family First* (Minneapolis: HIS, 1972). This work, by an educator and former college president, also supports the traditional view of marriage.

Patricia Gundry, *Heirs Together* (Grand Rapids: Zondervan, 1980). This book represents the partnership model of marriage. The author explores what she sees as the inadequacies of the traditional position and lays out her arguments for husband-wife equality from a biblical perspective.

John C. Howell, *Equality and Submission in Marriage* (Nashville: Broadman, 1979). The author examines the concepts of equality and submission from a biblical perspective. While he favors the partnership model, he argues for understanding and acceptance among believers over this issue.

7

Human Sexuality

How delightful is your love, my sister, my bride!
How much more pleasing is your love than wine,
and the fragrance of your perfume than any
spice!

You are a garden locked up, my sister, my bride.

Let my love come into his garden
and taste its choice fruits.

SONG OF SONGS 4:10, 12, 16

MARRIAGE IS BOTH a legal and a social relationship, as we saw in the preceding chapter. However, it is more than that; it is also a physical relationship. The Bible says that a husband and wife "become one flesh" (Gen. 2:24). Sex is an important aspect of our humanity and a foundational aspect of marriage. The Bible has a great deal to say about human sexuality in general and sex in marriage in particular. In dealing with a topic such as human sexuality, we need to begin with a biblical perspective.

THE BIBLE AND HUMAN SEXUALITY

We have already seen that God has created us as sexual beings: "Male and female he created them" (Gen. 1:27), and that He ordained sex: "Be fruitful and increase" (Gen. 1:28) and "A man will . . . be united to his wife, and they will become one flesh" (Gen. 2:24). All of these pronouncements were made *before* the Fall. Sex is not a consequence of sin or an accommodation to our sin nature. Sex is part of the original design; it is part of what God declared "very good" (Gen. 1:31). It is true that the Fall and human sinfulness have resulted in the perversion, misuse, and abuse of sex; however, that does not diminish its original purpose. Sex is a physical bonding between a husband and wife; it is a physical act that expresses their spiritual and social unity. Sex is a means for them to give and receive pleasure; it is the most intimate and personal sharing of one another. Speaking of the one-flesh experience, the Penners explain, "The scripture is talking about that mystical union between husband and wife that includes the emotional, physical, and spiritual—*the total person*" (1981:41).

God created us as sexual beings to enjoy and find pleasure in each other as husband and wife. The LaHayes write, "The idea that God designed our sex organs for our enjoyment comes almost as a surprise to some people" (1976:11). The Wheats expand on this point:

> God's plan for our pleasure has never changed, and we realize this even more as we consider how we are "fearfully and wonderfully made" (Psalms 139:14). When we discover the many intricate details of our bodies which provide so many intense, wonderful physical sensations for husbands and wives to enjoy together, we can be sure that He intended for us to experience full satisfaction in the marriage relationship (1977:17).

The Old Testament speaks of the pleasurable nature of sex in Proverbs 5:18–19, "May your fountain be blessed, and may you rejoice in the wife of your youth. A loving doe, a graceful deer—may her breasts satisfy you always, may you ever be captivated by her love." The New Testament has the same emphasis. In 1 Corinthians 7:3–4 Paul writes, "The husband should fulfill his marital duty to his wife, and likewise the wife to her husband. The wife's body does not belong to her alone but also to her husband. In the same way, the husband's body does not belong to him alone but also to his wife." It is interesting to note that both husband and wife have a marital duty to each other, and both are to enjoy each other.

The sanctity of sex in marriage is emphasized in Hebrews 13:4, "Marriage should be honored by all, and the marriage bed kept pure." Commenting on this verse, LaHaye (1976:13) points out that the Greek word for "bed" is *koite* and means "cohabitation by implanting the male sperm." Sex in marriage is God-sanctioned and

God-ordained. Our sexuality and our sexual organs were created by God to unite a man and woman in marriage.

HUMAN REPRODUCTIVE ANATOMY

As we have seen, God created us as sexual creatures. Foundational to understanding our sexuality and the role of sex in marriage is a basic understanding of our reproductive systems. Also, a grasp of proper medical terminology will facilitate later discussions.

The Male Reproductive System

The male reproductive system consists of the male genitals, the penis and the scrotum; and internal glands, the testicles and the prostate gland. Each of these organs will be briefly described and their functions explained. See figure 7–1 for a cross-sectional view of the male reproductive system.

Figure 7–1. CROSS SECTION OF THE MALE REPRODUCTIVE SYSTEM.

Penis

The *penis* contains three columns or tubes of spongy erectile tissue. Two larger tubes, the *corpora cavernosa*, set astride the third, the *corpus spongiosum*. The *urethra* runs through the corpus spongiosum. When a male is sexually aroused, these three columns fill with blood from the many arteries that permeate the penis. At the same time, the veins in the penis constrict, trapping the blood in the columns and causing the penis to become erect. While the size of flaccid or unstimulated penises varies significantly, erect penises are usually about the same size, approximately six inches in length (Strong 1981:42). God created males with the capacity for erection of the penis to permit penetration of the vagina during sexual relations.

Externally the penis consists of two distinct parts. The first is the *shaft* that is covered by loose skin that permits expansion during an erection. The second is the *glans* or the head of the penis. The glans contains many nerve endings and is very sensitive to tactile stimuli. It is the focal point of sexual stimulation. At birth, all males have a fold of skin that extends from the shaft over the glans. This fold of skin is called the *prepuce* or foreskin. A surgical procedure, known as circumcision, is used to remove the prepuce. Over 90 percent of male infants born in American hospitals are circumcised (Strong 1981:42).

The Old Testament Hebrews practiced circumcision as a sign of their covenant relationship with God (Gen. 17:9–14). God commanded that the circumcision be performed on the eighth day after birth. Ed Wheat, a medical doctor, has made the interesting observation that the eighth day is "the very day when blood-clotting and infection-prevention factors are the most favorable they will ever be in a baby's life" (Wheat and Wheat 1977:66).

In our culture, circumcision is generally not practiced as a religious ritual, except by Jews, but for hygienic purposes. In an uncircumcised male, *smegma*, a curdlike substance, accumulates beneath the foreskin. If an uncircumcized males does not frequently pull back the foreskin and wash the area, smegma will build up and develop a foul odor. Smegma can also cause irritations and infections of the glans. Some preliminary statistical studies indicate that uncircumcized males are more prone to cancer of the glans. Also, females with uncircumcized male sex partners have higher incidences of cervical cancer (Strong 1981:42).

Scrotum

The *scrotum* is a pouch, divided into a double sac, that hangs behind the penis. The scrotum consists of wrinkled, elastic skin. The function of the scrotum is to carry the testicles.

Testicles

The *testicles* are the primary male reproductive organs. The testicles are egg-shaped and one and a half to two inches long in an adult male. In firmness they are similar to a flexed muscle. Testicles produce sperm, the male reproductive cells. Each testicle contains a mass of tiny tubes called *seminiferous tubules* where the sperm ure produced. A pair of testicles can produce over one hundred million sperm cells each day. The testicles continuously produce sperm cells, not just when a male is sexually stimulated. The seminiferous tubules of each testicle deposit their sperm into a duct called the *epididymis.* The epididymis, which is folded back and forth against itself, straightens into a tube called the *vas deferens.* With one from each testicle, the vas diferens ascend into the abdomen and loop over the bladder and form the *ampullae,* a series of ducts. These lead to the *seminal vesicles* where the sperm are combined with a lubricating secreation. From the seminal vesicles, the ampulae then enter the prostate gland.

Prostate Gland

The *prostate gland* is located between the bladder and the base of the penis and surrounds the urinary passage from the bladder to the penis. The prostate gland is about the size and shape of a large walnut.

One function of the prostate gland is to produce semen, a milky and slightly gelatinous fluid that is primarily protein. A typical *ejaculation,* the forceful discharge of about a teaspoon of semen from the penis, contains 250 to 500 million sperm cells. Another function of the prostate gland is to close off the urinary duct from the bladder during sexual intercourse. The urinary duct from the bladder joins the ducts from the seminal vesicles to form the *urethra,* a single tube running from the prostate gland through the penis. The urethra is used both for the elimination of urine and the discharge of semen. When a male becomes sexually aroused and has an erection, the prostate gland closes off the duct from the bladder.

Just below the prostate gland are located a pair of glands called *Cowper's glands.* About the size of a pea, these glands produce a clear, sticky fluid. This fluid is secreted prior to ejaculation and oozes from the erect penis. This fluid neutralizes acids in the penis and vagina that might affect the sperm. The fluid also functions as a lubricant for intercourse. The fluid from the Cowper's glands contains thousands of sperm cells—one of the reasons the withdrawal method of birth control is less effective. Fertilization may result even if the penis is withdrawn before ejaculation.

The Female Reproductive System

Like the male reproductive system, the female reproductive system consists of both external genitals and internal organs. We will begin our discussion with the external female genitals, collectively called the *vulva* (see figure 7–2), and then deal with the internal female organs (see figure 7–3).

Mons Veneris

Located about six inches below the navel is a fatty mound known as the *mons veneris,* Latin for "Mount of Venus." In postpubic females the mons veneris is covered by a triangular growth of pubic hair. This fatty mound functions as a shock absorber to protect the genital area.

Labia Majora

The *labia majora,* Latin for "major lips," are two mounds of flesh, running parallel with each other from the mons veneris, along the midline between the legs, to the anus. They normally join over the vaginal opening to provide protection for the other organs. When a woman is

Figure 7-2. EXTERNAL FEMALE GENITALIA.

Figure 7-3. CROSS SECTION OF THE FEMALE REPRODUCTIVE SYSTEM.

sexually aroused, the lips pull back from the vaginal opening and flatten.

Labia Minora

Latin for "minor lips," the *labia minora* are two folds of hairless, smooth, soft tissue within the fold of the labia majora. They connect to the hood over the clitoris and run parallel on either side of the vaginal opening. When a woman becomes sexually aroused, the labia minora become engorged with blood, swell to two or three times their normal size, and protrude from the labia majora. Nerve endings in the labia minora are connected to pleasure centers in the brain and stimulation produces sexual enjoyment in most women.

Clitoris

The *clitoris* has been called the trigger for female sexual arousal. The unaroused clitoris is partially hidden by a hood of flesh, called the prepuce, which is located at the peak of the labia minora. The clitoris consists of two corpora cavernosa that fill with blood when sexually aroused. In some women the clitoris will become noticeably enlarged, in others it will not. The clitoris is generally between a quarter of an inch and an inch in length. The tip of the clitoris, called the *glans clitoris* contains a high concentration of touch-sensitive nerves. As far as current medical and biological researchers have ascertained, the only function of the clitoris is sexual stimulation and the triggering of the orgasm. Based on this finding, some Christian scholars have suggested that this is evidence that God intended sex not only for reproduction, but also for pleasure (Penner and Penner 1981:59–60).

Urethral Meatus

While not part of the reproductive system, the *urethral meatus* is part of the vulva. Located between the clitoris and the vaginal orifice, the sole function of the urethral meatus is the elimination of urine.

Vaginal Orifice

Located at the rear juncture of the labia minora, the *vaginal orifice* is the opening of the vagina. The vaginal orifice may be partially closed by a membrane named the *hymen*, after the mythical god of marriage. The lack of an intact hymen is not necessarily a sign of loss of virginity. It may be stretched or torn under a variety of circumstances, including strenuous physical activities and accidents. Two small glands, called *Bartholin's glands*, are located on either side of the vaginal opening. These glands produce a secretion during sexual arousal.

Inner Vagina

The first of the internal female reproductive organs to be discussed is the *vagina*, Latin for "sheath." An elastic, tubular canal, the vagina extends up and back in the abdomen. The inner walls of the vagina consist of folds of elastic mucous tissue. Normally three to five inches long, the vagina can expand both to receive the penis and to allow the passage of a baby during childbirth. Glands in the folds of this tissue produce secretions during sexual arousal to lubricate the vagina for sexual intercourse.

Uterus

Firm, muscular, and about the size and shape of a pear, the *uterus* is located behind the bladder at the upper end of the vagina. The small end of the uterus, called the *cervix*, extends into the upper end of the vagina. The *os*, a narrow opening in the cervix, joins the uterus and the vagina. The uterus is elastic as well as muscular and can expand to accommodate up to six babies (sextuplets).

The inner lining of the uterus, called the *endometrium*, consists of red, velvety tissue permeated by tiny blood vessels. When fertilization occurs, the embryo is implanted in the endometrium, which provides nourishment for it. When a woman does not become pregnant, the endometrium, which has been thickening in readiness for the possible arrival of an embryo, degenerates, resulting in monthly periods of menstrual flow consisting of endometrial blood and tissue. We will discuss the menstrual cycle in more detail later in this chapter.

Ovaries

The *ovaries* are the primary female reproductive organs. They produce *ova* (eggs) as well as the female hormones *estrogen* and *progesterone*. Each ovary is about the size and shape of a robin's egg. The two ovaries are located on either side of the uterus, one on the left and the other in the right. Females are born with about two hundred thousand follicles in each ovary. Each follicle contains an immature egg, or ovum, which is the female reproductive cell. Every month, after a female reaches puberty, one ovary or the other releases a mature ovum. Occasionally more than one ovum may be released. If all the ova are fertilized, multiple births (twins, triplets, etc.) will result. The ovum is released from the ovary about midway through the monthly menstrual cycle. The releasing of the mature ovum is called *ovulation*. A woman will ovulate about four hundred ova during her fertile years.

Fallopian Tubes

The *Fallopian tubes*, or *oviducts*, provide the passage for the ova from the ovaries to the uterus. Made primarily of muscle, each tube is approximately four inches long and resembles a miniature saxophone. Contractions of the muscles in the Fallopian tubes move the ova down to the uterus. Fertilization takes place in the Fallopian tubes, and the fertilized ova is deposited in the uterus.

Menstrual Cycle

As we have seen, each month the endometrium of the uterus thickens in preparation to receive a fertilized ovum. If fertilization does not occur, this lining is shed and the cycle begins again. The menstrual cycle is calculated from the first day of menstrual flow, which is considered day one.[1] On the first day of menstrual flow the endometrium is twice as thick as it is at the end of the flow. Menstrual flow generally lasts for four or five days. During this time, the typical flow amounts to two to three liquid ounces. Ovulation occurs approximately ten days after the cessation of menstrual flow. About fourteen days later the next menstrual cycle begins (see figure 7–4).

---

[1]The days of the menstrual cycle given here are for an average cycle. A normal female may have a cycle that varies from this. An average consists of shorter and longer cycles.

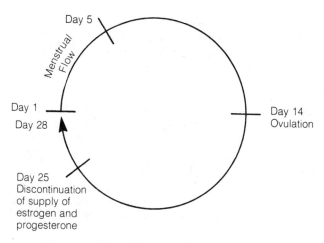

Figure 7–4. FEMALE MENSTRUAL CYCLE.

If an ovum is not fertilized by the time it reaches the uterus, the secretion of two hormones, estrogen and progesterone, is discontinued. Within two or three days the network of blood vessels in the endometrium begin to contract. With the loss of nourishment, the surrounding tissue begins to shed and the weakened blood vessels open. When the tissue has been shed, the blood vessels return to normal size and are sealed.

SEXUAL RESPONSE

A widely accepted scheme for understanding human sexual response has been developed by Masters and Johnson (1966). They have divided the sexual response pattern into four segments or phases. We need to understand that this division is somewhat arbitrary and the phases flow into each other. However, this division is a useful model for studying human sexual response patterns. We should also recognize that the phases are generalizations from which individual deviations are normal and expected. The four phases are the excitement phase, the plateau phase, the orgasmic phase, and the resolution phase (see figure 7–5). We will look at each of these phases individually.

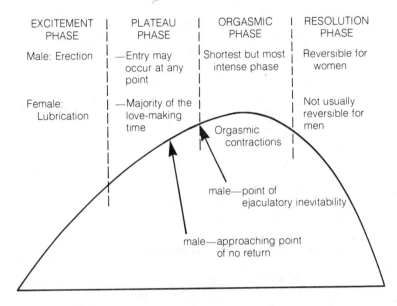

Figure 7–5. PHASES OF SEXUAL RESPONSE (Adapted from Masters and Johnson, *Human Sexual Response* [Boston: Little Brown, & Co., 1966]).

Masters and Johnson's Phases of Sexual Response

Excitement Phase

A person may become sexually stimulated by various sensory inputs, such as the sight of one's sex partner, a touch, a kiss, the words of another, music, even certain odors such as a particular perfume. While one may be sexually stimulated through any of the senses, the most basic and direct means of sexual stimulation is touch (Strong 1981:55). Areas of the body that produce a sexual response when touched are called *erogenous zones*. Some of these responses are *subcortical*—that is, the stimulus does not pass through the brain but responses are produced in both primary and secondary sex organs without the individual being conscious of being sexually stimulated—however, most sexual responses involve awareness.

With the onset of sexual arousal, the changes that occur in the primary sex organs result from the process of *vasocongestion.* Vasocongestion is the engorgement of sex organ tissues with an increased supply of blood. The physiological changes that take place in the primary sex organs of males and females when they are sexually aroused have been discussed above. During the excitement phase, a woman's breasts may enlarge and the nipples may become erect and increase slightly in diameter.

Plateau Phase

The excitement phase merges into the plateau phase, which is a more highly aroused state of sexual stimulation. In this phase penile erection reaches its maximum. The glans swells and darkens. The Cowper's glands begin their secretion, and a few drops may flow from the urethra. The vagina continues to lengthen and balloons into a saclike receptacle for the seminal fluid at the base of the cervix.

During this phase increased *foreplay*, stimulation of the erogenous zones, takes place. This is a period of heightened excitement and enjoyment. It is also during this phase that penile penetration of the vagina takes place, and genital stimulation continues as the couple move rhythmically. As the level of excitement increases, both heart rate and breathing become more rapid, vasocongestion increases, and sexual sensitivity becomes more intense.

Orgasmic Phase

In many ways the orgasmic response is similar for both men and women (Green 1978:86; Strong 1981:57). Orgasm is characterized by a series of contractions of the pelvic muscles accompanied by pleasurable sensations of release, usually lasting five to fifteen seconds. In the male, orgasm begins with contractions of the seminal vesicles, the vas deferens, and the prostate gland, which compresses the seminal fluid behind the sphincter muscle surrounding the urethra. The male experiences a sensation, lasting two or three seconds, in which he knows ejaculation is about to take place, but over which he has no control. Next the sphincter muscle opens the urethra, and the semen is pumped out by contractions of muscles at the base of the penis. These contractions occur less than a second apart and are pleasurable. Most of the semen is ejaculated in the first three contractions, but the male may have a dozen contractions with lesser amounts of semen ejaculated with each contraction.

The female experiences reactions similar to those of the male. However, her contractions may last longer, up to thirty seconds. Her contractions occur simultaneously in the muscles surrounding the vagina and the muscles surrounding the uterus, resulting in a sensation of total pelvic contraction. In both men and women there is a rapid increase in blood pressure and heart rate.

Resolution Phase

Following orgasm, men enter a *refractory period*, which lasts at least five to ten minutes for younger men and longer for older men. During the refractory stage, men are incapable of restimulation and an erection. On the other hand, females do not have a refractory lapse and are capable of immediate rearousal to orgasm. With continued stimulation, most women are capable of multiple orgasms in rapid succession.

In the resolution phase, following orgasm, the physiological characteristics of sexual arousal generally recede more quickly in males than females. If the female has not achieved orgasm, the resolution phase can last as long as two hours before the genitals return fully to a prearoused state. The resolution phase has been called the *afterglow*. It should be a time of intimacy for a married couple.

Kaplan's Model

Masters and Johnson's research was conducted in the sixties. More recent research on human sexual response has been carried out by Helen Singer Kaplan (1974). Kaplan views the human sexual response as a two-phase process. Her first phase, *vasocongestive reaction*, involves the erection of the penis and the lubrication of the vagina. The second phase, *reflex muscular contractions* or orgasmic phase, involves the sensations of orgasm in both sexes. While Kaplan's model contributes little to our understanding of the physiological aspects of human sexual response, it has significant implications for the psychological aspects. Research indicates that inability to achieve an erection is a common occasional problem among males, whereas inability to lubricate is relatively rare among females. However, once a male achieves an erection, it is rare not to achieve orgasm. On the other hand, it is common for a female to achieve vasocongestion without achieving an orgasm. Therefore, Kaplan concludes that psychological factors play a greater role for males during the vasocongestive phase and for females during the orgasmic phase.

SEXUAL DYSFUNCTIONS

The term *sexual dysfunction* refers to problems in giving or receiving sexual satisfaction. While the majority of sexual dysfunctions result from psychological factors, there are also physical causes. Diseases such as prostatitis, hepatitis, cirrhosis, diabetes, and epilepsy may interfere with sexual functioning. Spinal cord abnormalities and multiple sclerosis may also interfere by damaging neural reflex reactions. Sexual dysfunctions may also result from hormonal deficiencies. However, these physical causes account for only a small proportion of sexual dysfunctions (Strong 1981:62). We will discuss some more common male and female sexual dysfunctions and then examine some of the common psychological causes of these dysfunctions.

Male Sexual Dysfunctions

Impotence

The inability of a male to achieve and maintain an erection during sexual intercourse is referred to as *impotence*. This is a common problem, experienced by most married men at one time or another. As an isolated occurrence, it is not serious. However, when a man has experienced impotence several times in succession, it can become more serious. Frequently a cyclical effect develops. The male becomes anxious about not achieving an erection, and the anxiety blocks the sexual response needed for an erection, resulting in further anxiety and further blocking.

Impotence is usually classified into two types. The first type, *primary impotence,* refers to a man's never having experienced an erection. The second type, *secondary impotence,* refers to a man's temporary inability to have an erection though he has experienced erections in the past.

Ejaculatory Dysfunctions

There are two ejaculatory dysfunctions: *premature ejaculation* and *retarded ejaculation.* The most common complaint of men receiving sexual therapy is premature ejaculation (Strong: 1981:268). Premature ejaculation refers to a male's inability to delay orgasm until his partner has achieved orgasm. That is, the male ejaculates and the penis becomes flaccid before his partner has been sufficiently aroused to experience orgasm. Therapeutic techniques have been developed to help a man learn to control his ejaculatory response until his partner has been aroused.

Less common than premature ejaculation, but sill occurring with some frequency is retarded ejaculation. In this condition a male achieves and maintains an erection, but is unable to ejaculate. This problem tends to be transitory.

Female Sexual Dysfunctions

General Sexual Dysfunction

The term *frigid* has widely been used to label sexually unresponsive women. Because of its negative connotations and accusative nature, this term is not clinically accepted. Kaplan (1974) has introduced the term *general sexual dysfunction* to replace it. This term has been generally accepted in the social sciences. General sexual dysfunction refers to both a lack of sexual feelings and stimulation and the lack of physical response such as vasocongestion and lubrication. The cause of general sexual dysfunction is usually psychological, often resulting from learning a negative view of sex.

Female Orgasmic Dysfunction

Some women who are able to become sexually aroused and experience vasocongestion and lubrication never achieve orgasm. Wheat (1977:103) refers to such women as preorgasmic. He feels this is a healthier term because it implies the potential for orgasm. As with the male problem of premature ejaculation, therapeutic techniques have been developed to assist a woman in achieving orgasm.

Vaginismus

The involuntary spasmatic contraction of the muscles around the vaginal opening when the penis attempts to penetrate the vagina is called *vaginismus*. The reaction precludes the possibility of intercourse. A female may experience vaginismus as the result of a traumatic experience such as rape. It may also develop from strong inhibitions toward sexual intercourse formed from a repressive upbringing marked by excessive prohibitions. Vaginismus may also result from a woman's strong feelings of anger or resentment toward her partner. Again we see that many of the causes of sexual dysfunctions are psychological.

Psychological Causes

There are many psychological causes of sexual dysfunctions. We will examine a few of the more common causes in this section.

Stress

"Long term stress can contribute to lowered sexual drive and responsiveness" (Strong 1981:259). Stress related to family matters, health, one's job, or other areas of life may adversely affect one's sexual functioning. The problem often compounds itself because when persons are under stress, they need closeness and intimacy. However, if a person is not able to function sexually, he or she may become upset and experience additional stress. When one partner is under stress, the other partner may need to provide closeness and intimacy that does not demand sexual functioning.

Faulty Learning

Many people have been taught false or misleading ideas about sex. A number of women have been taught when they were young that sex is basically evil, or that it is a man's "pleasure" and a woman's "duty." Some women have been taught that only "bad girls" enjoy sex, while "good girls" endure it. Some men have been taught that sex is something you do to a woman instead of with a woman. They have learned only to satisfy themselves. Many men have been led to believe that a "real" man should always be ready to perform and should be able to please a woman every time.

People bring many false and misleading ideas into marriage. Some of these ideas can be quite destructive and rob a couple of the sexual pleasure and oneness God intended for them to experience. This is why it is so important for parents to provide a healthy, proper, accurate, and biblical view of sex for their children.

Sexual Anxiety

A common male myth is that a man should be able to function sexually anytime and anywhere. When a man—because of stress, physical exhaustion, or other causes—experiences impotence, he may become anxious about it, and that anxiety may inhibit future functioning. Until recently, women were not under as much pressure to perform, since their function is more passive. However, with the current proliferation of sex manuals and sex research, women are experiencing pressure to be "complete women" by experiencing orgasm each time they engage in intercourse. This pressure is described by a wife interviewed in the Hite study:

> I resent the pressure placed on me and other women to have orgasms. Every time I read a survey that says Masters and Johnson or other researchers have found that X percent of women almost always have orgasms, I feel psychologically inadequate (1976:117).

Anxiety about the inability to function sexually in one instance may inhibit functioning in another instance, generating further anxiety and further inhibition. The physiological effect of anxiety on sexual performance is explained by Strong:

> The autonomic nervous system is composed of sympathetic and parasympathetic subsystems. The sympathetic

subsystem controls the release of adrenalin which stimu-
lates our "fight or flee" behavior, preparing us for danger
or adversity. Among men, it controls the physiological responses involved in ejaculation; with women, the sympathetic nervous system governs the motor aspects of orgasm. The parasympathetic subsystem governs not only
sleep, digestion, and relaxation, but erection, vaginal lubrication, and vasocongestion, as well as erotic sensations
accompanying orgasm (1981:260).

Marital Problems

Various problems in marriage may result in sexual
dysfunction. Kaplan (1974) has suggested that there are
six areas of marital problems that are common causes of
sexual dysfunctions. The first of these problems is *trans-
ferences*. It is common for us to transfer feelings about one
person to another person, particularly if these persons are
significant in our lives. Generally, a man transfers some of
the feelings he had for his mother to his wife, and a
woman transfers some feelings she had for her father to
her husband. To some extent this is normal and healthy.
However, when the feelings that are transferred are negative or when the transference is so extensive that one's
partner is confused with one's parent, sexual dysfunctions may result.

A seond problem is *lack of trust*. Marriage is based on
trust. When a man and woman trust each other, they can
expose themselves to each other emotionally, psychologically, and physically. Emotional intimacy is intricately
related to physical intimacy. When trust is broken, emotional intimacy is destroyed, and physical intimacy is affected.

Kaplan's third problem area is *power struggles*. When
a man and woman are struggling for dominance in a relationship, they usually resort to whatever weapons are
needed to win. The power struggle itself may thwart one
or the other partner's sexual drive, and performance or sex
itself may become a weapon in the power struggle. This
may happen unconsciously. One partner may not respond
sexually to the other, unconsciously seeking revenge or
concessions.

The fourth problem area is called *contractual disap-*

pointments. Everyone enters marriage with assumptions and expectations; these are often unspoken, and sometimes unconscious. Each partner believes the other partner has agreed to these unstated expectations by entering the marriage. For example, he expects her to come to bed at night all made up in a flimsy negligee, and she comes to bed in flannel pajamas with curlers in her hair. On the other hand, she expects romantic evenings together, and he hides behind the newspaper. Then they wonder why the other partner is not sexually responsive.

Another problem is *sexual sabotage*. This occurs when one partner demands sex in a manner, at a time, or in a situation that the other partner is not responsive to. This behavior may be due to insensitivity or it may be unconscious. In either case, it has an adverse effect on the person's sexual functioning.

The final problem area, and the most important area, is *communication failure*. Marriage partners are not mind readers. One's partner cannot know what is arousing and what is annoying without being told. Even in our enlightened age, many people are inhibited about discussing sexual matters. However, if a husband and wife want to have a fulfilling and satisfying sex life, they need to discuss it. In therapeutic settings, many sexual dysfunctions are cleared up through communication between the partners. We will examine the area of sexual communication to see how it can enrich a couple's relationship.

SEXUAL COMMUNICATION

"Communication is the means by which relating takes place. . . . Good communication is the ability to transmit and receive meanings; it is the instrument for achieving that mutual understanding which is at the heart of marital intimacy" (Clinebell and Clinebell 1970:87). However good their communication may be in other areas, many couples have a difficult time communicating about sex—particularly their needs and desires. Someone has said, "While a couple may have good sex without having a good marriage, they cannot have a good marriage without good sex" (source unknown). Whether that is entirely true or not, we recognize that sex is an important aspect of marriage; therefore, good communication in this area is essential for marriage to be all it can be.

Communication takes place on two levels, verbal and nonverbal. Nonverbal communication includes touch, facial expressions, tone of voice, posture, any means of communicating beyond words. Verbal communication, of course, is communication by means of words. There is potential for miscommunication at both levels.

Communication in marriage will be discussed in chapter 9, and many of the principles discussed there also apply to sexual communication. In addition, there are some practical things a couple can do to increase their ability to communicate in this area. First, they need to understand human reproductive physiology and the correct medical terminology for the various organs. One reason couples are afraid to discuss sexual matters is ignorance and the lack of adequate vocabulary. Second, they need to talk in terms of their needs and desires and not in terms of accusations. For example, a wife should not say to her husband, "You don't satisfy me," but rather, "I need more satisfaction from our relationship." The one response creates defensiveness, the other openness. Third, a couple should read together some good books on the sexual side of marriage (see Suggested Reading). One partner may want to try a variation but be afraid to mention it, thinking the other will consider it "weird." But when they discover a new technique in a book, they can discuss it, since the book raised the topic. There are many other ways a book on sex can help a couple communicate about sex.

Sex in marriage can be all God intended it to be, or it can be a source of frustration, embarrassment, and contention. If couples want their sex life to be all it can be, they need to live in accordance with God's principles for marriage and sex, maintain open and honest communication, and be willing to seek competent help when needed. Sexual dysfunctions should be discussed, and medical and/or psychological assistance sought. We need to remember that one of God's purposes for sex is to draw a couple together into an intimacy that can only be expressed as "one flesh."

DISCUSSION QUESTIONS

1. What do you believe the biblical phrase "one flesh" means? Why?
2. In your opinion why are so many people embarrassed and afraid to discuss sexual matters?
3. Why do we need to understand sex as more than just a biological function?
4. What similarities do you see between the male and female reproductive systems?
5. Why do you think males have more sexual dysfunctions during Kaplan's vasocongestive phase and females during Kaplan's orgasmic phase?
6. What do you see as the main truths being taught in Proverbs 5:15–19?

SUGGESTED READING

Tim and Beverly LaHaye, *The Act of Marriage* (Grand Rapids: Zondervan, 1976); Clifford and Joyce Penner, *The Gift of Sex* (Waco: Word, 1981); Ed and Gaye Wheat, *Intended for Pleasure* (Old Tappan, N.J.: Revell, 1977). A trio of Christian sex manuals. All three deal with the basics of human sexuality, sexual response, sexual dysfunction, and sexual techniques. They have contributed to a new and healthy openness about sex in marriage among Christians.

Kevin Leman, *Sex Begins in the Kitchen* (Ventura: Regal, 1981); Rusty and Linda Wright, *Dynamic Sex* (San Bernardino: Here's Life, 1979). These two books deal with the emotional and psychological aspects of sex in marriage. They point out that sex is a twenty-four-hour activity, not just a thirty-minute exercise in bed at night.

Lewis Smedes, *Sex for Christians* (Grand Rapids: Eerdmans, 1976). A scholarly work by a noted theologian dealing with theological and ethical issues related to human sexuality. This book attempts to develop an integrated Christian philosophy of human sexuality.

Bryan Strong et al., *Human Sexuality: Essentials* (2nd ed.) (St. Paul: West, 1981). A secular text on human sexuality, well written and tastefully handled. Besides covering the topics in this chapter in fuller detail, it deals with venereal diseases, sexual development and identity, and social issues concerning sex.

8

Economics

I have learned to be content whatever the circumstances. I know what it is to be in need, and I
know what it is to have plenty. I have learned the
secret of being content in any and every situation,
whether well fed or hungry, whether living in
plenty or in want. I can do everything through him
who gives me strength.

PAUL IN HIS LETTER TO THE CHURCH
AT PHILIPPI (4:11–13)

BOTH DAVE AND GWEN have full-time jobs and earn
approximately the same amount of money. They have just
bought a new house and are in the process of furnishing
it. Dave feels they can get by with the hand-me-down
furniture they had in their previous apartment and that
shades are all they need for the windows at this time. He
wants to wait and save for new furnishings. On the other
hand, Gwen wants to charge new furniture and drapes.
She argues that they should enjoy their new home completely. She points out that they are both working, that
the payments will fit their budget, and that inflation will
raise the cost of the furnishings faster than their money
will earn interest.

Dave says he can enjoy the new house without new
furnishings, and anyway, his parents always saved for
major purchases. The only thing they ever borrowed for
was a mortgage. Gwen argues that she is working and
contributing equally to the budget and that she should be
able to enjoy "the fruits of her labor."

Both Dave and Gwen had been willing to work hard
and save for the down payment on the new house, but
now they disagree on how to handle their finances. They

find themselves constantly arguing with each other. Their disagreement over spending seems to be spreading to other areas of their marriage.

Marriage counselors report that the problems most frequently mentioned by couples seeking help involve money (Lasswell and Lasswell 1982:503). Summarizing current research, Saxton concludes, "All recent studies indicate that married couples quarrel over money more than anything else, that economic factors are closely related to marital stability and critical to marital adjustment, and that economic stress is a major cause of marital failure (1980:547). Typical of these studies is a national survey conducted by Yankelovich et al. (1975). This survey revealed that 54 percent of the families surveyed frequently argued about money. The percentage of couples who argued about various specific areas of finances in his study are presented in table 8–1. It is apparent from the studies discussed above that money plays an important part in marriage and the family. Earlier in this book we saw the relationship between income and divorce; as income increases, the rate of divorce decreases. However, conflicts over money often cannot be reduced to dollars and cents. Money has many meanings in our society.

TABLE 8–1
ARGUMENTS ABOUT FINANCES: PERCENTAGE BY AREA

Subject	Percentage
Money in general	59
Need for family to economize	47
Wasting money	42
Unpaid bills	38
Keeping track of where money goes	33
Saving for future	25
Borrowing money	17
Bad investment	10
Lending money	8

Source: General Mills American Family Report 1974–75, "A Study of the American Family and Money." Copyright 1975 General Mills, Inc., 9200 Wayzata Boulevard, Minneapolis, MN 55440. Used by permission.

THE MEANING OF MONEY

Money is defined as "something accepted as a medium of exchange" (*Merriam-Webster Dictionary*

1974:452). However, we are all aware that money is more than just a medium of exchange; it has many meanings. On a monetary level, a twenty-dollar bill is just twenty dollars; its exchange value is the same for everyone in our society. However, to a five-year-old boy from a lower-class family it may be a small fortune, whereas to an upper-class business executive it may be only pocket change. Let us look at some of the common meanings money has in our society. Belkin and Goodman (1980) suggest that, beyond its exchange value, money represents at least three things: power, love, and status.

Money as Power

We are all familiar with expressions such as "Money talks" or "Everyone has a price." While we are all aware of the power of money in society in general, we may not be as aware of its power in marriage. After examining a number of current studies, Orthner (1981) comes to a number of conclusions about the power of money in marriage. One conclusion is that a husband's power over his wife increases with his income. In effect, he buys the right to make decisions. On the other hand, a wife's power increases as the share she contributes to the budget increases. Another finding was that employed women are more likely to influence family financial matters and to share in all major decisions in the family. Parents also use money as a means of control over their children.

Because money is power, marital disputes over money may in fact not be over dollars and cents—but over power. Many times a couple will fight over how money should be spent, not so much because either one really cares that much for the thing they are arguing for, but to see who will control the spending. When a family's financial situation changes because a wife enters or leaves the work force or either husband or wife receives a major raise, the balance of power frequently is tipped and a period of tension often follows. This tension will continue until the power relationship is back in balance.

Ideally, in a Christian family money should not be a source of power, but rather a shared resource. However, in reality, even in Christian families, money becomes a source of power and therefore, of problems. As a couple becomes aware that money is often seen as power and used to control others, they can begin to deal with the problem in their marriage.

Money as Love

One of the ways we show we love a person is by giving presents. Parents give their children presents as tokens of their love. When I am out of town on business, I always buy little presents to bring home to my children because I love them. In dating and courtship, a man and woman frequently give presents to each other. In marriage, husbands and wives give presents to each other. These presents, of course, cost money. The presents, which cost money or even consist of money, become associated with love. Therefore, the withholding of something may be seen as a withholding of love.

In our opening anecdote, Gwen may accuse Dave of not loving her anymore, since he does not want to get the new furnishings at this time. Gwen may interpret Dave's position not so much as a monetary policy but as a lack of concern and love for her. She may feel that if he really loved her, he would want her to be happy. Even the Bible recognizes the relationship between love and money. Jesus told a parable about a money lender who had two debtors, one owed the equivalent of two years' wages and the other the equivalent of two months' wages. The money lender forgave them both, in essence giving them the money. Jesus said the one who was given the most would love the most (Luke 7:41–43). What we do with our money reveals what we love. Jesus said, "For where your treasure is, there your heart will be also" (Matt. 6:21).

Money as Status

In the first chapter *status* was defined as a place or position in a social system with its rights and duties. The statuses in a social system are generally ranked. That is, some are seen as higher, and others are lower. For example, we see the president of a bank as having a higher status than a teller in the bank. The ranking of statuses is known as *stratification*. Sociologists, in studying stratification, use a concept called *socioeconomic status* (SES). A person's SES is determined by an index that includes education, occupation, and income (see figure 8–1). Of these three indicators, income is most important. In fact, a person's SES is often calculated solely on the basis of income.

One marriage counselor writes that money "is an instrument used in our society to calibrate the individual's

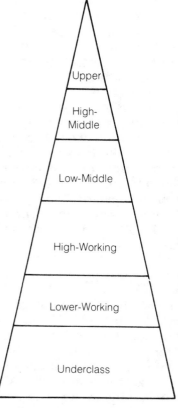

Upper stratum. Family incomes or net assets in excess of $100,000. Typically college graduates. Includes very high occupational status.

High-Middle. College-educated managers and owners, with incomes between $50,000 and $90,000.

Low-Middle. Other white-collar employees, with salaries between $30,000 and $50,000; or college teachers and other low-paid, high-prestige jobholders.

High Working. Skilled blue-collar workers (electrician, plumber, and so on); storekeepers; clerical and factory workers earning between $15,000 and $30,000 per year.

Lower Working. Semiskilled and unskilled workers, in low-status occupations earning between $8,000 and $15,000.

Underclass. Underemployed and unemployed low-skill workers with incomes below the poverty level ($6,600 for a family of four).

Figure 8-1. SIX-PART STRATIFICATION OF SOICAL CLASS BASED ON SOCIOECONOMIC STATUS (Adapted from Hess et al. 1982:175)

character and functioning while at the same time shaping the person's self-perception of adequacy and worth-whileness" (Feldman 1976:3). A sociologist writes, "In our society people are often judged by how much money they have. Thus, one's self-esteem can be tied in with one's finances" (Belkin and Goodman 1980:382).

Since we do not wear our financial statement or bank account on our sleeves, we generally communicate our financial status by things we purchase. These things are called *status symbols*. Common status symbols are cars, home, and clothes. Status symbols also include member-ship in a country club or even the "right" church. Because how a couple spends their income communicates their status, many disagreements over money are really dis-agreements over status. The husband wants to spend extra money on an expensive car to increase his status, whereas the wife wants to spend the extra money on more expensive furniture to increase her status.

As we have seen, money is more than a medium of exchange. It represents power, love, status, and many other things such as security, confirmation of one's worth, and opportunities for oneself and one's family. It is no wonder that finances are such a source of problems in marriage. That is why two people, somewhere in the process of becoming a couple, need to explore the topic of money in depth. It also helps us understand why, all other things being equal, the closer in SES partners are, the greater the potential for a successful marriage.

BIBLICAL VIEW OF MONEY

It is interesting to notice that half the parables of Jesus, recorded in the Gospels, dealt with money and pos-sessions. In fact, Jesus said more about money than about heaven and hell combined. There are about five hundred verses in the Bible dealing with prayer and about five hundred verses on faith, whereas there are over two thousand verses in the Bible concerning money and pos-sessions (Dayton 1971:10).

The Bible teaches that God is the One who provides for our needs (Deut. 8:18; Matt. 6:31–33; Luke 12:30–31; 1 Cor. 4:7). It also teaches we are to be good stewards of what God provides (Gen. 1:28; Ps. 8:6; 1 Cor. 4:2). The Bible addresses debt and how to handle it (Ps. 37:21; Prov. 3:27–28; 22:7; Matt. 5:25–26; Rom. 13:8). The Scriptures even discuss cosigning loans (Prov. 6:1–5; 17:18; 22:26–27). God's Word discusses the acquisition of money by work (Prov. 6:6–9; 13:4; 1 Thess. 2:9; 1 Tim. 4:14; 2 Peter 1:10). It also teaches that we are to be ethical in our financial dealings (Deut. 5:19–21; Prov. 10:2; 11:18; 20:10, 23; 28:12; 29:14; Isa. 33:15; Zech. 8:16–17; Matt. 7:12; Luke 12:15; Rom. 13:9–10). Scripture discusses saving (Prov. 21:20; 30:24–25), investing (Prov. 21:5; Matt. 25:14–29; Luke 19:12–24), and inheritances (Num. 27:8–11; Prov. 13:22). It also instructs us in giving to God (Gen. 28:22; Mal. 3:8–10); Matt. 23:23–25; 1 Cor. 16:2; 2 Cor. 8:3) and to others (Deut. 18:1–5; Prov. 28:27; Rom. 12:13; 1 Tim. 5:17–18).

However, the basic concern of the Bible seems to be with our attitude toward money. Greed and the love of money are particularly addressed. Paul warns Timothy that "the love of money is a root of all kinds of evil" (1 Tim. 6:10). In his letters to the Ephesians and the Colossians, Paul equates greed with idolatry (Eph. 5:5; Col. 3:5). In the story of the rich young ruler we see that the ruler's love of money stood in the way of his following Christ (Matt. 19:16–22). And Jesus taught, "Be on your guard against all kinds of greed; a man's life does not consist in the abundance of his possessions" (Luke 12:14). Jesus went on to teach:

> Do not worry about your life, what you will eat; or about your body, what you will wear. Life is more than food, and the body more than clothes. . . . And do not set your heart on what you will eat or drink; do not worry about it . . . your Father knows that you need them. But seek his kingdom, and these things will be given to you as well. . . . For where your treasure is, there your heart will be also (Luke 12:22, 29–31, 34).

The society we live in has a much more complicated economic system than the societies had in Bible times. However, the principles of Scripture are just as applicable today. As we go on to discuss budgeting, credit, insurance, savings, and wills, we need to keep these principles in mind.

BUDGETING

There is something about the very mention of the word *budget* that sounds restrictive and limiting. A budget is something that everyone says a couple should have—but no one wants to have. Why does the thought of a plan for using money bring up negative reactions in most people? I believe it is because most of us do not want to be restricted and limited in the use of our money. However, that is exactly what a budget should *not* do. It should free us to get the most for our money. A budget is not a master that no couple can faithfully serve, but a budget is a servant every couple should have.

If a couple allows their budget to control them, it will never work. But, if it allows them to control their money, it will work. Let me illustrate. Suppose my wife and I have fifty dollars a week budgeted for groceries and ten dollars a week for entertainment. Let us further suppose we learn of a concert we both want to attend this week, and two tickets cost twenty dollars. Now if our budget is our master, it will only allow us ten dollars for entertainment, and we cannot go to the concert. However, if it is our servant, we can take ten dollars from the grocery money, go to the concert, and have soup and crackers for supper a couple of evenings. When the budget is our servant, it allows us to make trade-offs. But we know what we are trading off. Without a budget, couples also make trade-offs. But they may end up with the least desirable option.

What exactly is a *budget?* Basically, it is a flexible, workable plan for spending money that channels a couple's cash flow into areas that provide the greatest benefit to them. Notice that the two key aspects of the plan are *flexible* and *workable*. It must be flexible. If not, it quickly becomes a master rather than a servant. The plan must also be workable. The best budget in the world is no good if it does not meet a couple's needs. The basic test of a budget is how it performs, and the basic function is to help people get the most for their money.

Purpose of a Budget

Green (1978) suggests at least four purposes or values to budgeting for couples. They point out that a budget

(1) maximizes income, (2) provides a realistic view of financial status, (3) opens communication, and (4) reduces tensions. Let us examine each of these purposes.

Maximizes Income

A well-planned budget helps a couple get the most for their income. A couple has a given income. Without a budget, they find their money is leaking away, and they have no idea where it has gone. Most of us are familiar with families that have about the same income, and yet one family has a significantly higher standard of living than the other. A budget allows a couple to invest in those things they value most.

Provides a Realistic View of Financial Status

A budget supplies a couple with a realistic view of their income and outgo and lets them know where they are and where they are going. In addition, it can help keep a couple out of debt and aid them in developing a program of saving and investment. Frequently couples wake up one day to discover that their bills have become larger than their income. A budget allows them to always be aware of their financial status.

Opens Communication

Developing a budget encourages a couple to discuss their financial plans. It allows them to discuss their goals, desires, and needs. Together they can decide on a lifestyle and their financial future. A budget provides the basis for communicating about their values, for it is basically a statement of values. Figure 8–2 presents a questionnaire that is useful in uncovering one's financial values.

Reduces Tensions

We have already seen that finances are the number-one cause of tension in marriage. Couples fight about money more than any other topic. As we saw above, a budget allows a couple to discuss how they want to spend their money. It aids them in developing a financial plan together. Then once a financial plan acceptable to both of them has been developed, they can work together toward that common goal. A marriage should be a partnership,

Circle the letter that describes how you feel about the following:
(L = Luxury,   D = Desirable,   U = Useful,   N = Necessity)

Life insurance	L	D	U	N
A color TV	L	D	U	N
New furniture	L	D	U	N
A will	L	D	U	N
A stereo	L	D	U	N
A car	L	D	U	N
A second car	L	D	U	N
Owning your own home within five years	L	D	U	N
Tithing	L	D	U	N
Owning stock	L	D	U	N
Pets	L	D	U	N
Vacation once a year	L	D	U	N
Retirement plan	L	D	U	N
Credit cards	L	D	U	N
Going out together once a week	L	D	U	N
Life insurance on husband	L	D	U	N
Life insurance on wife	L	D	U	N
Hobbies	L	D	U	N
Medical insurance	L	D	U	N
New clothes (current fashion)	L	D	U	N
Snack food	L	D	U	N
Stereo tapes	L	D	U	N

Figure 8–2. FINANCIAL VALUES QUESTIONNAIRE (Adapted from Wright 1977a:201).

not an adversarial relationship. A budget helps a couple function as partners.

Developing a Budget

Developing a budget is relatively simple. There are three basic steps. The first is to determine your monthly income. This includes wages (minus regular deductions such as taxes and social security), royalties, dividends, interest, and any other sources. The second step is to determine your fixed or nondiscretionary expenses. These include items such as rent or mortgage payment, car payments, installment loan payments, utilities, insurance, stewardship, and other fixed items. The third step is to list variable or discretionary expenses. These include items such as food, clothing, furnishings, entertainment, savings, and personal allowances. The difference between your income and your fixed expenses is the money you can allot to discretionary spending. A sample budget form for following these steps is presented in figure 8–3.

It should be noted that the term *fixed expenses* is only relative. If a couple wants more money for discretionary expenses and cannot increase their income, they can lower their fixed expenses. They could find less expensive housing, drive a less expensive car, or do without some item on their fixed-expenses list. That is the value of a budget; it allows a couple to make rational decisions about how they want to spend their money.

A question I am frequently asked when discussing budgeting is what percentage of a person's income should be spent on housing or food or other categories. While this has to be an individual decision and will vary from person to person and situation to situation, there are some guidelines we can follow. Howard Dayton offers the following suggested breakdown for a budget:

CATEGORY	PERCENT OF INCOME (after taxes and stewardship)	
Shelter	20–35	
Food	15–25	
Transportation	10–15	
Clothing	4–8	
Insurance	3–5	
Medical	3–5	
Entertainment and recreation	3–5	
Debts (credit purchases)	0–10	
Savings	5–10	
Miscellaneous	3–5	(1979:88–89)

CREDIT

What is credit? We may define *credit* as goods or services received with payment deferred. Or simply put, it is possess now and pay later. Credit is widely used and is an integral part of the American economy. Americans have over 300 million retail credit cards for such stores as Sears, Wards, and Penneys; 133 million gasoline credit cards; and 93 million bank credit cards such as VISA and Mastercard (Lasswell and Lasswell 1982:519). Half of all retail purchases in the United States are made on credit

SOURCES OF MONTHLY INCOME   AMOUNT

Wages $_____
Interest   _____
Dividends   _____
Other: _____
       _____
       _____

                 Total monthly income: $_____

FIXED EXPENSES   AMOUNT

Housing (rent or mortgage) $_____
Utilities (monthly average)   _____
Insurance   _____
Automobile payments   _____
Automobile operating expenses   _____
Installment payments   _____
Stewardship   _____
Medical and dental (average)   _____
Other: _____   _____
       _____   _____
       _____   _____

            Total monthly fixed expenses: $_____

DISCRETIONARY EXPENSES   AMOUNT

Groceries $_____
Household items   _____
Furnishings   _____
Clothing   _____
Entertainment   _____
Savings   _____
Personal allowances   _____
Other: _____   _____
       _____   _____
       _____   _____

            Total discretionary expenses: $_____

Figure 8-3. SAMPLE BUDGET FORM.

(Lasswell and Lasswell 1982:519). Over 200 billion dollars worth of consumer credit is extended to Americans each year. Over one-third of all households use either VISA or Mastercard or both. Seven out of ten bankcard users do not pay off their balance in full each month but pay a minimum payment plus finance charges on the balance (Green 1978:195). The number of VISA credit card holders who file for bankruptcy increased fivefold in 1980 (Lasswell and Lasswell 1982:521).

Types of Credit

Saxton (1980) classifies credit into three categories: open credit, profit-making credit, and nonprofit-making credit. We will examine each of these types of credit.

Open Credit

By *open credit* Saxton is referring to credit advanced with no finance charge. Common examples of open credit include medical and dental treatment for which we are billed at the end of the month; newspaper delivery for which we pay at the end of the week; and utilities, which bill us monthly for the amount of service used. In these cases we utilize the service or product and then pay for it later.

Most department stores, gasoline, and bank credit cards also extend open credit. That is, we may make a purchase today, and if we pay the balance in full within thirty days of being billed, we will not be charged interest. In other words, the store, oil company, or bank is lending us the amount of the purchase without interest if we pay in full when billed.

There are several advantages to using open credit. One of these is the elimination of the necessity of carrying around large amounts of cash. Another is that the charge slip or bill provides a convenient receipt, especially when dealing with tax-deductible items. A third advantage of open credit is that it gives us leverage with the seller if the product is faulty. When we pay in cash, the seller may not be anxious to make the purchase right. But if we have not yet paid, the seller may be more willing to correct the situation. Under recent federal legislation, this is even true for bank credit cards. Still another advantage of open credit is that it allows us to take advantage of sales. If I need something that I already had budgeted to take out of next week's paycheck and it goes on sale for this week only, at half price, I can take advantage of that savings.

A final advantage of open credit is that our money can be drawing interest in savings or other short-term investments while we use the retailer's or bank's money interest-free to make our purchase. For example, if I want to buy a washer and dryer from a major department store chain for $700, it would be best to use my credit card for the purchase even though I have the cash. The bill would come approximately fifteen days later[1] and would need to be paid within thirty days of the billing. That means I can use the store's money for about forty-five days interest free. If I put $700 in a money-market fund paying 12 percent annual interest, I could make $10.50 in interest for those forty-five days.

While there are obvious advantages to open credit, there are also pitfalls. The major pitfall is spending money we do not have. If I operate on a cash basis, then, when I see something I want, I can get it only if I have the money in hand. But if I have a credit card, I can purchase something without the means to pay it off in full. Open credit should be used only for planned and budgeted purchases. If a bill cannot be paid in full, we cease to have open credit because we will be paying a finance charge which generally ranges from 16 to 24 percent annually.

Profit-making Credit

Saxton considers a loan or an extension of credit to be *profit-making credit* if the return on the use of the credit will equal or exceed the interest paid. For example, I buy a lawn mower on credit and use the mower to start a lawn-cutting business. If the profit from my lawn cutting exceeds the interest paid on the lawn mower loan, it would be profit-making credit. Saxton considers educational loans as profit-making credit because education increases

---

[1]A usual billing cycle is thirty days. Purchases made early in the cycle give you more time; purchases made later in the cycle provide less time.

one's earning power. Also, loans to start a business, purchase tools for a trade, or other income-producing causes would fall into this category. A home mortgage might also fall into this classification if the tax advantages and increasing value of the home offset the interest payments.

Non–profit-making Credit

The interest paid exceeds the monetary value of the purchase in *non–profit-making credit*. An example of this type of credit is taking out a two-year loan to finance a vacation to Europe. Saxton does not argue that one should not use credit in this way, but only that there is no monetary profit to this type of purchase. This type of credit allows people to enjoy something now rather than waiting to save.

Non–profit-making credit may also save a couple money in some instances. By way of example, a couple decides they would like a new refrigerator that will cost $500. They decide to save $50 a month for ten months in order to purchase it. The next week the refrigerator goes on sale for $400. If they buy the refrigerator for $400 and finance it at 18 percent interest for ten months, the interest would be $22 if they paid $40 on the principle each month. Therefore, their total cost would be $422 as opposed to $500.

There are some basic rules a couple or individual should keep in mind if they want to use credit wisely and stay out of financial trouble. These include:

1. Do not make impulse purchases on credit. If you see something you really would like to have, wait thirty days and see if you still feel the same way.
2. Use credit cards only for planned or budgeted purchases. Leave credit cards at home except when making a planned purchase.
3. Make sure the monthly payment on a credit purchase will fit the family budget.
4. When possible, save for an item rather than purchasing on credit.
5. Make sure that the value of an item is always greater than the amount owed on the item.

INSURANCE

Insurance is a program for pooled risk. In the case of automobile insurance, a group of car owners contribute to a pool of funds generally handled by an insurance company, and if any of them is involved in an accident, that one is reimbursed from the pool. Insurance is basically a means of sharing risks. There are many types of insurance. Anything from automobiles to lives to business ventures can be insured. We will look at three areas of insurance that are important for all families: life, health, and property.

Life Insurance

Life insurance provides funds in the event a member of the family dies. Generally these funds are used to replace the income or services that had been provided by that family member. It is usual for the breadwinner in a family to have enough life insurance so that, in the case of death, the income can be replaced for a given period of time. There are many factors that go into determining the amount of coverage a breadwinner should have. These include number and ages of children, social security, other sources of income, and financial goals.

There are two basic types of life insurance, term and whole life. *Whole life insurance*, which is also referred to as ordinary life or straight life, is a lifetime policy with a fixed premium. That is, if a husband purchases a fifty-thousand-dollar whole-life policy, he pays a fixed premium until his death (or on some policies until age sixty-five or some other age), and at death his beneficiaries will collect fifty thousand dollars. Most whole life policies have a *cash value* based on interest paid on premiums. This interest is paid on only part of the premium and is generally a low rate, 2 to 5 percent. If the policy is cancelled by the policyholder, the accumulated cash value is refunded. The policyholder may also borrow money from the policy, up to the accumulated cash value, at reasonable interest rates. For some people, whole life insurance functions both as insurance protection and a forced savings plan.

While whole life insures a person from the time the policy is bought until death, *term insurance* covers a person for only a specific period of time. Term insurance generally is issued for terms of five, ten, or twenty years, although some policies can be written for any term desired. Since only a period of a person's life is insured, there is a probability that the person will not die during the term, and the insurance company will not have to pay. On the other hand, the insurance company knows it will have to pay sooner or later on a whole-life policy. Since the insurance company will not have to pay on all term policies, term insurance is significantly less expensive. The value of term insurance, besides cost, is that insurance needs vary throughout the life cycle. When children are young, more protection is needed; when they are grown and just the couple are home, less protection is needed. During the young years when the most coverage is needed, the probability of death is lower, so greater coverage at lower cost is available through term insurance.

Which is the best buy—whole life or term? While every individual's and family's needs vary and there is not an absolute rule to cover everyone, for most people term insurance is the best buy. I have a friend who sold life insurance, and he says factitiously, "Only two people profit from whole life, the insurance salesman and the stockholders in the insurance company." The reason term insurance is less expensive is that you pay only for the risk factor for your age bracket. But does not the cash value feature of whole life offset the premium savings of term insurance? In most instances the answer is no. To demonstrate the difference, let us suppose one thirty-year-old male buys a $50,000 whole-life policy and another thirty-year-old male buys five-year renewable term insurance and both die at age sixty-five. Table 8–2 shows their premiums with the difference invested at 10 percent interest compounded annually. When the man with whole life dies, his beneficiaries will collect $50,000 plus the $27,300 cash value for a total of $77,300. When the man with renewable term dies, his beneficiaries will collect $50,000 from the insurance company plus have $134,599 in investments for a total of $184,599. That is a difference of $107,299.

TABLE 8–2
COMPARISON OF BUYING WHOLE LIFE OR TERM INSURANCE
AND INVESTING THE DIFFERENCE

Age	Annual Premium[1] for Renewable Term Insurance	Annual Premium[1] Whole Life $50,000*	Annual Difference in Premiums	Accumulated Savings During Five-Year Period at 10% Annually	Total Savings Plus 10% Compounded Annually
30–34	$ 192	$ 750	$ 558	$ 3,747	$ 0,000
35–39	215	750	535	3,592	9,627
40–44	279	750	471	3,160	18,661
45–49	392	750	358	2,402	32,452
50–54	579	750	171	1,146	53,408
55–59	877	750	– 127	– 635	83,573*†
60–64	1,216	750	– 466	– 2,330	134,599*†

[1]Premiums and cash value (†) from Saxton 1980:586–87.

*Cash value at age sixty-five will be $27,300.

†Accumulated principle plus interest minus premium difference.

For most people five-year renewable term insurance is the best buy. Such a policy insures your life for five years at a time with renewal guaranteed. That allows you to pay the lowest rate at any given period. It also pays to shop around for insurance; the rates vary widely. Saxton (1980:585) found that for a thirty-year-old white male, the premiums varied from $3.85 to over $8.00 for each $1,000 of coverage. Many times lower rates can be obtained through professional associations or other groups. Also, some companies offer lower rates to nondrinkers and/or nonsmokers.

While most people think of life insurance for the primary breadwinner (traditionally the husband), life insurance for the rest of the family is often considered a luxury. However, life insurance for every family member is a practical idea. When a wife is employed outside the home, what would happen to the family's lifestyle if her income was lost? Whether or not the wife is employed outside the home, how will the services she provides in child care, housecleaning, laundry, and other domestic services be replaced? Domestic help costs between six and ten dollars an hour. If a wife dies from a lingering illness, what about medical bills not covered by health insurance? What about burial expenses? It becomes readily apparent that life insurance for a wife and mother is a necessity.

Life insurance for children is also a good idea. Again, if a child suffers a lingering illness, there will be medical expenses. When a child dies, burial expenses are the same as for an adult. The death of a child involves enough grief and emotional distress without adding indebtedness. Another advantage of insuring children is that you can also insure their insurability. Most children's policies have a conversion feature whereby, when the child reaches a certain age, usually nineteen or twenty-one, the young person can purchase up to a specified amount of life insurance regardless of his insurability. That is, even if young people have cancer, heart problems, or any other medical difficulty that would normally prevent them from being issued a policy, they can convert their policy at the current rates for their age group. A policy with a face value of ten thousand dollars and convertibility up to fifty thousand dollars has annual premiums of only about thirty-six dollars for a year-old child.

Health Insurance

Hospital and medical expenses have been rising much faster than the general rate of inflation. In 1975 the average daily cost of hospitalization was $228 a day (Green 1978:193). By 1981 it had risen to over $400 (Orthner 1981:289). Medical expenses are such that a serious illness would bankrupt all but the wealthiest families. Many people receive medical insurance as part of a benefit package where they are employed. It is important to ascertain if the plan covers one's family as well. For individuals who do not have medical coverage through their employer, it is important to purchase a private plan.

Major medical

A popular form of personal insurance is major medical. It is often referred to as "tragedy" insurance. Major medical is coverage that takes over where regular health coverages end. It is designed to cover serious accidents and prolonged illnesses. Frequently there is a deductible, ranging from a hundred to a thousand dollars. After the deductible is satisfied, major medical will provide benefits to as much as a hundred thousand dollars depending on the policy.

Property Insurance

Property insurance is insurance that covers one's property against damage or theft. The two most common types are collision and comprehensive insurance on automobiles and home-owners insurance on a house. Collision insurance on a car provides for repair or replacement of the car in case of accident, regardless of who is at fault. Comprehensive insurance covers theft, storm damage, vandalism, and other hazards. Home-owners insurance covers a house from loss due to fire, storm, vandalism, or other sources of damage. It also covers the contents of the home from theft and damage. Home-owners insurance usually provides liability coverage also. That is, if a person is injured on one's property or in one's home, the insurance will cover the costs.

Many renters do not have property insurance. They believe that the building owner has insurance. While that is usually true, the insurance covers only the building. The personal property of the renter is not covered. The cost of replacing the wardrobes and furnishings of a typical couple can easily run over ten thousand dollars. Also, if someone is injured in an apartment, the renter—not the owner—is liable. *Renter insurance* is available at very reasonable rates and will cover these risks. It is important for families to have their property insured, since most are not in a position to replace items stolen or damaged.

WILLS

Each year about two million Americans die and over half of them do not have a will (Dayton 1979:66). Many people put off making out a will, thinking they will do it when they are closer to death. However, over one-third of all Americans die before age sixty-five. Others argue that they own little or nothing and so a will is not important. However, there are several important reasons for couples to have a will.

Perhaps the most important reason to have a will, if a couple has children, is to designate who will raise the children in the event that both mother and father should die. If a couple does not have a will, the courts will decide who receives custody of their children. A couple may think that everyone in the family is agreed on what will happen if they die, but as many lawyers can tell us, strange things happen in families after a death. A will insures that one's children will be cared for as one desires in the event of death.

Even if a couple does not have children, a will insures that the surviving spouse has access to communal property in the event the other dies. In many states, when a person dies, checking and savings accounts are impounded and personal property placed under court control. If there is a will, it can usually be speedily probated and funds and property released.

Death is enough of a trauma without leaving the survivor with legal problems as well. That is why every couple should have a will. In the case of simple estates, a will is relatively inexpensive. As with any other product, shop around for lawyers' services. Some lawyers are much more reasonable than others.

STEWARDSHIP

The Bible clearly teaches that the material blessings God gives us are not merely for our personal benefit. They are a stewardship to be used for furthering His kingdom and benefiting His children. The Bible teaches that we should have a regular pattern of stewardship: "On the first day of every week, each one of you should set aside a sum of money in keeping with his income" (1 Cor. 16:2). The Bible also addresses the attitude with which we should give: "Each man should give what he has decided in his heart to give, not reluctantly or under compulsion, for God loves a cheerful giver" (2 Cor. 9:7).

How much should one give? This is a matter of some controversy. I personally believe the tithe, which is 10 percent, should be the starting point. The tithe is mentioned in Scripture before the law of Moses was given (Gen. 14:20; 28:22). The tithe is, of course, an integral part of the Mosaic Law (Lev. 27:30; Deut. 14:22; 26:12). Tithing is also mentioned in the New Testament (Matt. 23:23; Luke 11:42;18:12; Heb. 7:8–9). It was also commended by Jesus (Matt. 23:23). Nowhere in the New Testament is the tithe done away with, but proportional giving is encouraged (1 Cor. 16:2). The main problem I have with tithing is not the basic concept, but that many people who tithe feel they have done their part. They believe 10 percent is God's and 90 percent is theirs. It is all God's. The tithe should be the beginning point of stewardship—not the end.

Regardless of whether one agrees with my views on tithing or not, I think we can all agree that stewardship should be a prominent part of family financial planning. As God blesses us we should be sharing with others. The Bible teaches that the use of our money is a good indicator of our spiritual condition. Our material resources are given to us in trust. We are stewards of what we possess.

DISCUSSION QUESTIONS

1. What else do you think money might represent in addition to love, power, and status?

2. In your opinion why are there so many biblical references to money?

3. Do you see life insurance for a newly married couple as a necessity or a luxury? Why?

4. Why do you believe so many people have trouble making and keeping a budget?

5. In the opening anecdote, who do you side with—Dave or Gwen? Why?

6. What do you see as the major biblical principles for guiding a couple in financial decisions?

SUGGESTED READING

Howard L. Dayton, *Your Money: Frustration or Freedom* (Wheaton, Ill.: Tyndale, 1979). A Christian perspective on personal finances. This work contains a great deal of biblical research on financial matters. While dealing with such areas as budgeting, insurance, investing, etc., it has a strong emphasis on stewardship.

George Fooshee, *You Can Be Financially Free* (Old Tappan, N.J.: Revell, 1976). Written by the head of a credit agency, this book deals with some of the common financial pitfalls and how to avoid them. Written from a Christian perspective, it offers some practical advice.

Malcom MacGregor and Stanley G. Baldwin, *Your Money Matters* (Minneapolis: Bethany, 1977). This book emphasizes the spiritual dimension of stewardship and personal finances. It contains many helpful suggestions.

Harold A. Wolf, *Personal Finance* (Boston: Allyn and Bacon, 1975). A secular text on personal finances. A comprehensive treatment covering budgeting, credit, checking, saving, insurance, retirement, investing, home ownership, and taxes.

9

Living and Growing Together

*It is not love that sustains
the marriage, but from now on,
the marriage that sustains your love.*

DIETRICH BONHOEFFER

OVER 90 PERCENT of all Americans will marry, and 38 percent of those marriages will end in divorce. On the other hand, 62 percent of all first marriages will survive until the death of a spouse. What is the difference between the 62 percent who make their marriages work and the 38 percent who do not? In chapter 4 we looked at courtship and saw that a number of demographic factors, such as age and social status, are good predictors of marital success. Yet we all know of couples whose marriages defy all the predictors. The predictors indicate only the situations under which divorce is more likely. They do not tell us why some marriages are successful while others fail under similar conditions.

Lasswell and Lasswell report on a study they did with 130 strong, cohesive, and functional families (1982:18–19). While there were many differences among these families, six qualities clearly stood out in all of them. The first quality was that *the family members appreciated each other.* They supported each other and made each other feel good about themselves. Criticism was generally absent in these homes. Rather, the members showed appreciation for each other and enjoyed being together.

The second quality that characterized these successful families was that *the members arranged their personal schedules so they had time to be together as a family.* While these families had spontaneous times together, they made a strong effort to have planned times together.

They were willing to make an effort to be together.

A third quality of these 130 families was *positive communication patterns*. This involved openness, honesty, patience, respect, concern, and a willingness to discuss differences. The objective is not necessarily the quantity of communication, although it must be adequate, but the *quality* of communication. The family members in the study talked to each other, not at each other. They listened to hear what the other person was saying and feeling. The family members worked on the quality of their communication.

A *high level of commitment to their family* was a fourth quality that characterized these family members. The family is a small group, and in the study families, there was positive group dynamics. There was a cohesiveness, a sense of belonging, a feeling of being part of a team. The members were willing to invest time and energy in the family.

Another quality of the families was a *spiritual orientation*. This does not mean they were religious and regular church attenders, although many were. Rather, this refers to value or morals associated with religion or spiritual experiences. Strong families have a value system or a moral base to which they can turn and on which they build their lives.

The final quality that characterized these strong families was *their ability to deal positively with crises*. First of all, they were able to face their problems realistically. They did not engage in denial or repression. Second, they were adaptable and able to nurture and care for each other during crises. Crises pulled them together, rather than apart.

It is obvious that these six qualities are not isolated characteristics, but are interrelated. They fit together like a mosaic, supporting and complementing each other. In this chapter we will look more closely at some of these qualities and how they can be developed and maintained.

COMMUNICATION:
KEY TO A GROWING RELATIONSHIP

Marriage counselors are generally agreed that communication is the key to a successful marriage and that a lack of communication is one of the major problems in marriages that are failing (Black 1982; Clinebell and Clinebell 1970; Lee 1976; Sanford 1982; Sperry 1978; Wright 1974). Communication involves both the sending and receiving of messages. Of these two, receiving may be the more important. James advises us, "Everyone should be quick to listen, slow to speak" (1:19). The Book of Proverbs also speaks of the importance of listening (12:15; 21:28). Listening is a particularly important skill for marriage partners.

Keys to Effective Listening

There are a number of skills that we can develop to become better listeners. While these suggestions may be applicable to many different types of communication settings, we will apply them to communication in marriage. The first characteristic of effective listening is to *establish eye contact and assume a posture that clearly indicates the other person has your complete attention.*

I do a lot of reading, and in every spare minute I have my nose in a book or magazine. When my wife and I were first married, she would speak to me while I was reading, and I would stop reading to listen. However, I kept the book or magazine in front of me with my eyes on the page. My wife interpreted that as lack of attention and concern for her. I had to learn to put down my reading material, turn, and look at her. That little action has done a great deal to improve our communication. The cartoons showing the husband at the breakfast table with his face in the newspaper is not a joke. Nonverbal communication is at least as important as the words spoken. By establishing eye contact and good posture, we are communicating that we are listening, are interested, and care.

A second characteristic of effective listening is to *pay attention to non-verbal cues,* as well as verbal communication. Imagine a husband coming home from work late and his wife greeting him with the words "I've been waiting for you." How do we interpret her words? We have to look at the nonverbal cues. Is she crying? If so, she may be indicating worry and concern, possibly fear he had been in an accident. Is she scowling? In that case she may be indicating anger and displeasure, possibly upset he did not call, saying he would be late. Is she smiling and warm? Then she may be indicating affection. Possibly she has missed him and is glad he is home. Attention to non-verbal cues is critical to effective communication.

Reflective listening is another skill that enhances effective listening. Reflective listening involves hearing the other person's meanings and feelings and reflecting them back to the other person. There are two values to reflective listening. One is that it lets the other person know we have heard and understood what he or she is feeling. The other value to reflective listening is that the other person can correct our understanding if it is inaccurate. By the way of an example, I arrive home from work one evening and my wife says, "My mother is just impossible." A reflective response might be, "It sounds like your mother has been giving you a hard time about something." If that is the case, it lets my wife know I understand. If it is not the case, she can correct my incorrect impression.

Another skill, which is related to reflective listening, is learning to give *open responses*. Open responses reflect the other person's feelings and allow him or her to continue to discuss the issue. Unfortunately, many of us frequently use closed responses that are judgmental or instructive and lead to conflict. Returning to the example of my wife and her mother when she tells me, "My mother is just impossible," I can give an open or a closed response. An example of a closed response would be, "How many times have I told you to put your foot down with your mother and not let her interfere in our home!" That response is judgmental and will bring a defensive response from my wife, and soon we will be involved in a heated disagreement. On the other hand, an open response such as, "Your mother must have done something to really upset you," allows my wife to discuss the matter. She can tell me what her mother did and what happened. As long as I continue to practice reflective listening and give open responses, she can discuss the situation with me as an ally rather than an adversary.

An additional characteristic of effective listening is to *allow the other person to resolve the problem*. Probably the greatest temptation we face is to immediately offer a solution, especially if a solution appears obvious to us. We need to avoid that temptation and help the other person think through the alternatives. If the other person comes up with the solution, he or she will be more likely to follow through on it. Again, returning to the example of my wife and her mother, the fact may be that she needs to stand up to her mother. But if I impose that solution, she is not likely to follow through. However, if I can help her come to that conclusion, she most likely will follow through. After using reflective listening and open responses to help her talk out the situation, I should not offer a solution, but rather say something like, "What do you think we can do about this problem?" Now it is the two of us against the problem rather than the two of us against each other. As we practice these listening skills, we will find that our communication improves.

Keys to Effective Sharing

As we have seen, there are two aspects to the communication process—sending the message and receiving the message. We have already examined the listening process, but what about the sending process? Norm Wright has presented a number of biblical principles of communication:

1. Be a ready listener and do not answer until the other person has finished talking (Prov. 18:13; James 1:19).
2. Be slow to speak. Think first. Don't be hasty in your words. Speak in such a way that the other person can understand and accept what you say (Prov. 15:23, 28; 21:23; 29:20; James 1:19).
3. Speak the truth always, but do it in love. Do not exaggerate (Eph. 4:15, 25; Col. 3:9).
4. Do not use silence to frustrate the other person. Explain why you are hesitant to talk at this time.
5. Do not become involved in quarrels. It is possible to disagree without quarreling (Prov. 17:14; 20:3; Rom. 13:13; Eph. 4:31).
6. Do not respond in anger. Use a soft and kind response (Prov. 14:29; 15:1; 24:14; 29:11; Eph. 4:26, 31).
7. When you are in the wrong, admit it and ask for forgiveness (James 5:16). When someone confesses to you, tell him you forgive him. Be sure it is forgotten

and not brought up to the person (Prov. 17:9; Eph. 4:32; Col. 3:13; 1 Peter 4:8).

8. Avoid nagging (Prov. 10:19; 17:9).

9. Do not blame or criticize the other but restore him, encourage him, and edify him (Rom. 14:13; Gal. 6:1; 1 Thess. 5:11). If someone verbally attacks, criticizes, or blames you, do not respond in the same manner (Rom. 12:17, 21; 1 Peter 2:23; 3:9).

10. Try to understand the other person's opinion. Make allowances for differences. Be concerned about their interests (Phil. 2:1–4; Eph. 4:2) (1976:188–89).

In addition to these practical suggestions, there are a few other points on sharing that are worth considering. One of these is the finding that American women use more nonverbal communication than American men. That is, women load more of the message into the tone of voice, facial expression, gestures, and body movement; however, men put more of the message into the words. The result is that a woman may believe that she has clearly communicated something to her husband, and he has missed the point.

When we were first married, my wife and I had some disagreements because she had sent me a message primarily with nonverbal communication. I missed the message and did not respond as she desired. She thought I did not respond because I did not care, and she became upset. We have both worked on this. She has made an effort to put more of the message into words, and I have made an effort to pay better attention to her nonverbal cues.

Problems can arise also when one message is given verbally and another is given nonverbally. We used to have a dog that would both wag its tail and growl at the same time when strangers came to the house. People did not know which end of the dog to believe (actually he was honest; he loved to bite people). We need to be certain that we send the same message verbally and nonverbally.

Good communication also involves knowing when to be quiet and when to bring things up. It is generally unwise to raise important topics just before going to bed or just before leaving the house. If there is an important matter to be discussed, a couple should set aside time to deal with it. *When* something is said may be as critical as *what* is said. If a couple can develop patterns of open and honest communication, practice effective listening, and be sensitive in their sharing, they have the basis for dealing with any problem.

HANDLING CONFLICT IN MARRIAGE

In a relationship as intimate as marriage, conflict is bound to arise. Two normal, healthy persons cannot live together without having some areas of disagreement. This is true for Christian couples as well as non-Christian couples. When Christian couples claim to have a conflict-free marriage, I like the response of a friend who said, "When a married couple tells me they have a conflict-free relationship, I can tell you one of three things is true of them: either they are liars, one's an idiot, or the other is dead." The fact is each of us is a unique person and that very uniqueness will lead to conflicts in a relationship. Conflict in marriage is not wrong, necessarily bad, or a sin. The critical issue is how the conflict is handled. Conflict may destroy a marriage or it may strengthen a marriage. A number of writers have presented useful suggestions for handling conflict in marriage (Bach and Wyden 1968; Dale and Dale 1978: Scanzoni 1979; Shedd 1968; Wright 1977b). Many of the suggestions of these writers overlap each other. Therefore, these ideas will be combined and summarized so we can discuss them.

Timing

One suggestion made by all the writers is that *timing* is critical to constructive resolution of conflicts. As Bach and Wyden write:

> Far too many fights become needlessly aggravated because the complaint opens fire when his partner really is in an inappropriate frame of mind or is trying to dash off to work or trying to concentrate on some long-delayed chore that he has finally buckled down to. Indeed there are times when failure to delay—or to advance—the timing of a fight can have cataclysmic consequences (1968:70).

While emergencies may arise that need to be dealt with at the moment, most conflicts have developed over time. These conflicts usually do not require an immediate resolution but can be temporarily put off until there is adequate time to deal with them. This is regularly done in business, at church, on committees, and in most other settings. It can also be done in a marriage.

A basic rule related to timing in handling conflict is not to raise controversial issues "just before." Conflicts should not be raised just before going to bed, just before sex, just before leaving the house, or just before anything that will not allow adequate time to deal with the issue.

Communication

One of the basic purposes of conflict is to improve communication. It is for partners to let each other know how they feel and think about an issue. Part of communication is listening. The principles of effective listening discussed earlier are especially critical in handling conflict. Yet, when dealing with conflict, it is often most difficult to apply the principles of effective listening. In most cases, while one party is talking, the other is not listening carefully but is thinking about how to respond. An exercise, which sounds tedious but in practice is quite effective, is to have one party have his or her say. Then the other party has to repeat back to the first party what was said. The first party then either acknowledges that the second party has it correct or corrects any misunderstandings. Only when both parties agree the second party fully understands what the first party said, does the second party get his or her say, and the process is repeated.

Stick to the Issue

A woman complained that her husband became historical every time they had an argument. Her friend corrected her by saying, "You mean he becomes hysterical." "No," replied the woman, "I mean *historical*. Whenever we have an argument, he brings up every related problem since we have been married."

All the writers agree that it is important to stick to the issue at hand. When other issues are brought into the discussion, it hampers resolution of the current conflict. It also opens old wounds and confuses the issue. Bach and Wyden recommend that couples:

> Keep all arguments not only fair but up-to-date so that the books on a marriage can be balanced daily, much as banks keep their debits and credits current by clearing all checks with other banks before closing down for business every evening. Couples who fight regularly and constructively need not carry gunny sacks full of grievances . . . or [drag] the totally irrevelant past into the argument (1968:19).

Fight Fair

The object of conflict is not to win but to resolve the problem. Marriage is meant to be a cooperative effort not a competitive sport. When there is a problem, the goal is not to find fault or assess blame, but to find a solution. The attitude of partners should not be a win/lose approach; that is, every solution involving a winner and a loser. Rather, the attitude of partners should be a win/win approach. The couple faces the problem together and when a solution is found, they both win.

When a couple has a win/lose approach to conflict resolution, they will often resort to unfair tactics in order to win. Unfair tactics may involve anything from emotional outbursts to the withholding of sexual intimacy. Unfair tactics may also involve setting power traps. It is important to remember that the one who "wins" the argument may be advocating the least advantageous solution to a problem. The ability to "win" an argument does not necessarily make one right. When winning and losing become more important than finding the best solution to a problem, regardless of whose idea it is, then both partners become losers in the long run. Unfair tactics are necessary only when the concern is with winning.

Compromise Is Not a Dirty Word

It is rare that in a given situation one party is entirely wrong and the other party is completely correct. Usually the truth lies somewhere in between. Even if a compromise is not the "best" solution, if it works and both parties can live with the compromise, it is a successful solution. The willingness to give in, modify, and negotiate is the secret to successful solutions.

Scanzoni sees negotiation as the key to compromise. He defines compromise as "a process of give and take between two parties, aimed at arriving at a solution or compromise in which each gets something, but not all, that each originally wanted" (1979:28–29). Negotiation involves both partners placing their desires on the table and attempting to harmonize them in a way that both receive as much as possible. By way of example, a wife may want to go out for an evening to a concert that is rather expensive. Her husband may feel they cannot afford to attend the concert. The wife may offer to give up something else to save money to pay for the concert, or the husband may offer to take her out to a less expensive activity. In either case, both are seeking a compromise.

One word of caution needs to be made about compromises. Individuals sometimes use compromise in place of admitting they are wrong. For example, if my wife and I are in disagreement over a discipline matter with one of our children, I may begin to realize that she is right and I am wrong. Rather than admitting I am wrong, I may exploit the use of compromise. That is, I could say, "Okay, I am willing to give in this time, but remember, you owe me one." What I should do is admit she is correct. I should say, "As we have been discussing this, I have realized my approach is not too wise. I think we should try what you have been suggesting." It is important that compromise be used honestly.

DIFFERENCES

When a couple marry, it is like the meeting of two cultures. Each brings values, norms, traditions, and expectations to the marriage. The partners have been raised in different homes with different ways of family living. They bring different personalities to the marriage. In fact, they bring many differences to the relationship and how they are handled will have an important bearing on the success of the marriage.

Types of Differences

While the areas of difference between a couple are limitless, they can be categorized into five types—those related to taste, habits, values, thinking, and temperament.

Taste

We all have our likes and dislikes, our preferences —what we call our tastes. We have tastes in food, music, dress, and many other areas. Frequently in dating and courtship, a man and a woman either are not aware of each other's tastes or do not recognize the implications of those differences for marriage. Even in areas such as food, differences may not be recognized. While dating and courting, when they went out to eat, he ordered steak and potatoes every time while she ordered quiche one time, crepes another, enjoying a variety of dishes. As long as each ordered his or her own meal, their differences of tastes in food did not matter. But after marriage, when they both have to eat the same dinner, it can be critical. He came from a home where dinner meant meat and potatoes. She came from a home where her mother was always experimenting with new recipes.

Frequently in the flush of the romance of dating and courtship, people are willing to "put up" with differences in taste. They may even find the differences interesting when they are encountered occasionally. However, in the day-to-day living of marriage their differences in taste can become annoying and be sources of irritation.

Habits

Do you squeeze the toothpaste tube in the middle or roll it from the end? Do you unroll the toilet paper from the top or bottom? Do you sleep with the bedroom window open or shut? Do you shower at night or in the morning? Do you drink from the bottle or can instead of using a glass? Habits, many developed over a dozen or more years, are such an integral part of us that we are not even aware of them most of the time. Yet habits control most of our routine behaviors. Because they do, we notice when something interferes with our habits.

While many habits are readily apparent, there are three areas of habits that a courting couple may not be exposed to that can have a significant impact on married life. One area is habits related to *hygiene.* Does a woman wash and set her hair before she goes to bed? A man may never see his wife in curlers before marriage. Does he gargle and spit into the sink? She may find that disgusting. Another area of habits where differences may create problems is *diet*—not only what is eaten, but when it is eaten and how. The third area is *sleep habits.* Most people sleep by themselves before they get married. Unless a couple has cohabitated before marriage, they are unlikely to be aware of each other's sleep habits. Should the bedroom door be open or shut? Should the room be perfectly dark or should there be some light? Who sleeps nearest the door or window? Do you go to sleep with music or with quiet? These and many more sleep habits may be deeply ingrained in a person.

Values

One writer defines values as ideas, persons, objects, principles, or behaviors we prize or desire (Elder 1976:36). Another writer says, "Values are whatever an individual within a group considers of importance. In each automatic or consciously made decision some value underlies the choice of one thing over against another" (Mayers 1976:148). In essence, our values determine our priorities. Our values are revealed by our behavior. A person may claim to put God first in his or her life. However, if he or she rarely reads God's Word, frequently engages in recreation rather than attending church, and participates in questionable activities, one would have to conclude that person did not highly value God. Perhaps the two best measures of people's values are what they spend their money on and how they spend their time. As someone said, "Show me a man's checkbook and his datebook and I will tell you what kind of man he is."

While differences in values in some areas may be easily overcome, differences in values in other areas are more difficult to resolve. That is why couples with similar religious and social backgrounds have more successful marriages. Values in the area of religion and finances are concerned with central areas of life.

Thinking

Not everyone thinks in the same way. Different people use different cognitive processes. For instance, some people think dichotomistically, dividing problems up into parts and solving the problem by dealing with the parts. Other people think holistically, treating a problem as a unit. Some people use logical reasoning, while others use intuitive reasoning.

Our culture appears to encourage males and females to think differently. Boys are taught to think analytically, whereas girls are pushed to think conceptually. While there are no differences between the *total* scores of males and females on IQ tests, college entrance exams, and Graduate Record Exams, males score higher than females on the arithmetic component of these tests and females score higher than males on the verbal component (Mischel 1981:361–62). Since marriage involves a male and a female, two people who have been encouraged to think in different ways have to deal with each other.

In thinking about cognitive activity we need to distinguish between *process* and *outcome*. For example, if I ask you how many apples would be in a basket if five boys each placed five apples in the basket, you could add five plus five plus five plus five plus five or you could multiply five times five. Both processes would produce the same answer—twenty-five. One process treats the problem by parts, the other treats it as a whole, but both produce the same outcome. It is not uncommon to see couples have conflicts over thinking processes when their concern should be over outcomes. One may arrive at a solution one way, the other a different way, but if both processes produce similar outcomes, then there really is no difficulty.

Temperament

Ron says the glass is half full; Joan says it is half empty. They are looking at the same glass. Both acknowledge the content level is 50 percent. However, Ron focuses on the occupied part of the glass, Joan on the empty part. This may result from differences in temperament. Temperament is basically a predisposition to behave in a particular way.

While early temperament theories saw temperament as inherited and totally biologically based, current theory understands temperament as a product of heredity and the environment (Schultz 1981:358–59). Heredity provides the potential, and the environment determines the extent of development. One recent theory postulates four temperaments: emotionality, sociability, activity, and impulsivity. These are seen as the building blocks of personality. People's personalities are composed of differing amounts of each of these temperaments (Schultz 1981:358).

Each person has a unique personality. Some are more optimistic, some more pessimistic, some more outgoing, some more introspective, some more cheerful, some more easily despondent. When two people come together in a marriage, each brings to the marriage his or her own unique personality. There are bound to be differences. Some of these differences may not come to light until the couple has been married for several years. Also, people's personalities change, so new areas of difference may recur in a marriage.

Handling Differences

Differences generally do not destroy a marriage. It is *how* these differences are handled that determines the outcome of the marriage. Dan Lambrides, a marriage and family therapist, had suggested five steps for dealing with differences (1982).

Awareness

The first step is to be aware of differences. The more aware a couple is of their differences before they marry, the better the chances are for developing strategies for dealing with those differences. Most marriage counselors use a battery of tests in premarital counseling. These tests are designed to uncover and highlight many of these differences. This allows couples to deal with these differences before they cause problems.

It is common for couples not to be aware of differences. They recognize that there is tension and conflict in their relationship but seem unable to put their fingers on the source. Couples need to be aware of their differences before they can deal with them.

Acknowledgment

Not only must a couple be aware of their differences, they must acknowledge them. There are couples who are aware of their differences but will not acknowledge them. The husband and wife have conspired to ignore and suppress the differences. They see the differences as the problem, when it is how they handle the differences that is the problem. The couple thinks that if they ignore their differences, maybe the problem will go away. Of course it will not; the problem will only get worse. A couple needs to acknowledge their differences to deal with them.

Acceptance

Awareness and acknowledgment are important first steps, but they are not enough. There must also be acceptance, but acceptance does not necessarily mean approval. It does mean accepting reality as it is. Acceptance recognizes what cannot be changed as well as what can be changed and is willing to live with differences. It is saying differences can be okay. We do not need to be mirror images of each other. We can each be ourselves.

Adaptation

Acceptance is the beginning of change. When we are willing to accept things, we can begin adapting. When I can say it is okay for me to be more concerned with time and my wife to be more concerned with people, then we can begin to adapt to each other.

Appreciation

The step of appreciation may be the key to dealing with differences. Rather than seeing my wife's differences as a source of irritation and problems, I need to see them as opportunities for my enrichment. Before I married her, I saw the world through only one set of eyes, thought about things with one cognitive process. In other words, I had a limited perspective. She provides me with a second set of eyes, with another way of thinking through issues, with a broader perspective. Differences can divide or they can unite. A couple's differences can be assets and enrich their relationship. It is how differences are dealt with that is important, not the differences.

SPIRITUAL DIMENSION

Howard and Charlotte Clinebell write, "Intimacy on the horizontal, person-to-person plane and intimacy on the vertical or spiritual plane complement and reinforce each other" (1970:180). They add, "Growth-producing intimacy is difficult if not impossible without a spiritual center and source" (1970:181). It is obvious that non-Christians can have good marriages. We are all familiar with non-Christian couples that have what certainly appear to be good, happy, and successful marriages. Nevertheless, it is my conviction that those marriages would be better with a spiritual dimension.

A marriage is a relationship between two people; the spiritual dimension of that relationship can be no stronger than the spiritual lives of the individuals. It is obvious that as a couple draws nearer to God, they will draw nearer to each other (see figure 9–1). As we have already seen, research demonstrates that the more "religious" a couple is, the more successful their marriage will be.

Scripture

A husband and wife need to look to the Word of God for guidance in their marriage. They need to study the Bible together to discover God's principles for living together, raising children, and other areas of family life, and the children be included in their times of Bible study. They must use the Word of God as a marriage manual as well as a guide to general living.

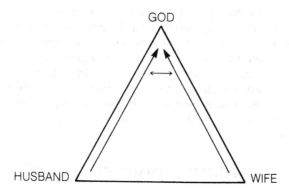

Figure 9–1. A COUPLE'S RELATIONSHIP WITH GOD AFFECTS THEIR RELATIONSHIP WITH EACH OTHER.

Prayer

A couple should pray together—and for each other. Prayer should be a regular part of their relationship, not an exercise to be engaged in when crises strike. A couple should pray about their relationship as a whole and each aspect of it specifically. They need to pray about decisions, about spending—about every area of life. The saying "The family that prays together, stays together" is true.

Values and Ethics

A couple and a family must have a value system to live by. They must have a set of ethics to apply to the various situations that arise in family living. The values and the ethics of a family result from the spiritual lives of the members of that family, individually and collectively. Their values and ethics are forged out of their individual time with the Lord and their family time with the Lord. A family needs to take time to read the Bible and pray together and to discuss the implications of the Scripture they have shared together. How does it apply in their lives individually and as a family? A family needs to develop a biblical value system and a biblical set of ethics. Values and ethics are best transmitted in the home. Parents have a responsibility to help each other and their children develop a Christian philosophy of life.

Worship

A couple should also worship together. While it is good and proper for them to structure private worship experiences for themselves as a couple, it is also important for them to participate in corporate worship. They need to find a church in the area where they are living in which they can become involved and have fellowship with other believers.

Service

Another aspect of the spiritual dimension is service. Serving the Lord together can be growth-producing as well as a togetherness activity. Some of the best experiences my wife and I have had were in Christian service. We have served as youth sponsors and children's church leaders, co-taught Sunday school, and served as missionaries together.

When children are born into the family, the whole family can serve the Lord together. For example, my wife, our three children, and I prepare and send packages to missionaries as a family. The whole family is involved in Christian service.

In each of these areas, we should attempt to make Christ the center of the home. A Christ-centered home will be one of joy, peace, and comfort. It will be a place where family members can come for renewal. Without the spiritual dimension a home can never be complete. For a couple to live and grow together, they must emphasize the spiritual dimension.

DISCUSSION QUESTIONS

1. Which of the six qualities of strong marriages, presented by Lasswell and Lasswell, do you believe is the most vital? Why?

2. Which of the keys to effective listening do you see as most essential? Why?

3. Why do you believe men and women differ in their use of nonverbal communication?

4. Suggest some unfair tactics people use in disagreements. Why are they unfair?

5. In your opinion, what is the explanation for the differences in arithmetic and verbal test scores between males and females? Why?

6. Why is the spiritual dimension important to marriage? Can you think of any additional aspects to the spiritual dimension of marriage other than those mentioned? How would they apply?

SUGGESTED READING

George R. Bach and Peter Wyden, *The Intimate Enemy: How to Fight Fair in Love and Marriage* (New York: Avon, 1968). A well-written book dealing with conflict in marriage. Written in a popular style, this book illustrates its points with case studies. This is a widely referred-to work.

Howard and Charlotte H. Clinebell, *The Intimate Marriage* (New York: Harper & Row, 1970). Written by a seminary professor and marriage counselor, a husband-wife team, this practical work deals with many areas of marital intimacy. It covers both barriers to intimacy and keys to developing intimacy. The spiritual dimension is emphasized in this helpful book.

Gary R. Collins (ed.), *Make More of Your Marriage* (Waco: Word, 1976). A collection of articles by Christian writers. Articles cover sex roles, communication, marriage enrichment, and conflict resolution.

John Scanzoni, *Love and Negotiate: Creative Conflict in Marriage* (Waco: Word, 1979). Written from a biblical perspective, this book deals with resolving conflicts in marriage. The emphasis is on the negotiation process. The author uses case studies to illustrate his points.

H. Norman Wright, *Communication: Key to Your Marriage* (Glendale, Calif.: Regal, 1974). A how-to-do-it manual and workbook for couples. Written by a popular and well-known marriage counselor, this book offers practical suggestions for improving communication. Principles are undergirded with Scripture.

PART IV

LIFE CYCLE OF THE FAMILY

10

Childbearing

Behold, children are a gift of the Lord;
The fruit of the womb is a reward.
Like arrows in the hand of a warrior,
So are the children of one's youth.
How blessed is the man whose quiver is full of
them;
They shall not be ashamed,
When they speak with their enemies in the gate.

PSALM 127:3−5 (NASB)

THE PSALMIST WRITES that children are a gift from God, but they are a gift placed within the mother and father. A couple has the potential to produce dozens of children. How are children conceived? How does a couple decide how many children they want? Should they decide? How can conception be controlled? What about couples who want to have children and are unable to conceive? These are some of the questions that will be dealt with in this chapter.

CONCEPTION

Fertilization or conception takes place in the woman's fallopian tube or oviduct. Each month, when a woman ovulates, one or more eggs are released. The egg then travels down the fallopian tube. If the woman engages in sexual intercourse within seventy-two hours before or after ovulation, it is likely that sperm will be present in the fallopian tube when the egg is there. During ejaculation the seminal fluid, containing millions of sperm, is deposited at the base of the vagina near the cervix. These sperm swim up the cervix, through the uterus, and into the fallopian tubes. The sperm can survive in the fallopian tubes for up to seventy-two hours. Of the millions of sperm ejaculated, generally only several dozen make it all the way to the fallopian tubes.

Of the dozens of sperm present in the fallopian tubes, only one will impregnate the egg. That sperm will penetrate the egg, and as it does so, it loses its tail. Then the head proceeds through the food-rich substance to the nucleus of the egg. When one sperm has penetrated the egg, the egg then rejects all other sperm.

All human cells contain twenty-three *pairs* of chromosomes except germ cells—the sperm and the egg. Germ cells contain twenty-three chromosomes. When fertilization takes place, the twenty-three chromosomes in the egg and the twenty-three chromosomes in the sperm pair up to form the genetic heredity of the new child. The twenty-third pair of chromosomes determines the sex of the child. While eggs always have an X chromosome, sperm may have either an X or Y chromosome. If the sperm containing an X chromosome fertilizes the egg, the child will be a female. If the sperm has a Y chromosome, the child will be a male.

PRENATAL DEVELOPMENT

If newborns could remember and speak, they would emerge from the womb carrying tales as wondrous as Homer's. They would describe the fury of conception and the sinuous choreography of nerve cells, billions of them dancing pas de deux to make connections that infuse mere matter with consciousness. They would recount how the amorphous glob of an arm bud grows into the fine structure of fingers agile enough to play a polonaise. They would tell of cells swarming out of the nascent spinal cord to colonize far reaches of the embryo, helping to form face, head and glands. The explosion of such complexity and order—a heart that beats, legs that run and a brain powerful enough to contemplate its own origins—seem like a miracle. It is as if a single dab of white paint turned into the multicolored splendor of the Sistine ceiling (Begley and Carey 1982:38).

The Bible describes the process this way: "For you created my inmost being; you knit me together in my mother's womb. I praise you because I am fearfully and wonderfully made" (Ps. 139:13–14). Both the authors above and the psalmist describe prenatal development in a literary fashion. The creation of a person is a miracle—fearful and wonderful. Because we can describe it biologically does not mean we can explain it. However, we can study the process. Prenatal development is generally divided into three stages: *germinal, embryonic,* and *fetal.* (see table 10–1).

Germinal Stage

Cell division begins about twelve hours after fertilization. The fertilized egg, called a zygote at this stage, continues dividing as it travels toward the uterus. By the time the zygote reaches the uterus (about seventy-two hours following fertilization), it consists of about thirty-six cells. The cells form into two layers. The outer layer called the *trophoblast* attaches the zygote to the uterine wall and eventually develops into the placenta, umbilical cord, and amniotic sac. The inner cells, called the *blastocyst,* divide into three layers. The outer layer, the *ectoderm,* will develop into skin, hair, and nerve endings. The middle layer, the *mesoderm,* will become sex glands, kidneys, blood, bone, and muscle. The inner layer, the *endoderm,* will develop into the inner body organs. The *germinal* stage lasts approximately two weeks, ending when the zygote is attached to the uterine wall and is drawing nourishment from the mother.

Embryonic Stage

During the *embryonic stage* the developing child is called an *embryo.* This stage lasts about six weeks. During this time rapid cell division continues and cell specialization appears. After two weeks a tiny vessel, which will eventually become the heart, begins to pump. At this time the embryo is not bigger than an adult's thumbnail.

By the end of the embryonic stage (eight weeks) the embryo is approximately an inch long and resembles a human being. The nervous system as well as many of the internal organs have begun to function.

TABLE 10–1
PRENATAL DEVELOPMENT

Stage	Time	Characteristics
Germinal		Sperm penetrates egg.
	12 hours	The division of the fertilized egg begins.
	72 hours	The zygote reaches the uterus.
Embryonic	2 weeks	The zygote/embryo is implanted in the uterine wall and is drawing nourishment.
	4 weeks	The embryo is approximately one-fifth inch in length. A primitive heart is beating. The head and the tail are established. The mouth, liver, and intestines begin to take shape.
Fetal	8 weeks	The embryo/fetus is now about one inch in length. For the first time it begins to resemble a human being. Facial features, limbs, hands, feet, fingers, and toes become apparent. The nervous system is responsive, and many of the internal organs begin to function.
	12 weeks	The fetus is now three inches long and weighs almost one ounce. The muscles begin to develop and sex organs are formed. Eyelids, fingernails, and toenails are being formed. Spontaneous movements of the trunk can occasionally be seen.
	16 weeks	The fetus is now approximately five inches long. Blinking, grasping, and mouth motions can be observed. Hair appears on the head and body.
	20 weeks	The fetus now weighs about one half pound and is approximately ten inches long. Sweat glands develop and the external skin is no longer transparent.
	24 weeks	The fetus is able to inhale or exhale, and could make a crying sound. The eyes are completed and taste buds have developed on the tongue.
	28 weeks	The fetus is usually capable by this time of living outside the womb, but would be considered immature at birth.
	38 weeks	The end of the normal gestation period. The fetus is now prepared to live in the outside world.

Adapted from Dworetzky 1981:126.

During the embryonic stage there is a high rate of spontaneous abortions or miscarriages. It is estimated that one-fourth to one-third of all pregnancies are terminated by spontaneous abortions (Dworetzky 1981:127). Many women, not even aware they are pregnant, experiencing a spontaneous abortion, may believe they are only having an unusually heavy menstrual flow.

Fetal Stage

The *fetal stage* is the third and longest stage, lasting thirty weeks in the case of a full-term pregnancy. During this period the developing child is called a *fetus*. Cell specialization continues, with the muscular and nervous systems forming rapidly. By the twentieth week of pregnancy the mother is able to feel fetal movement. At about twenty-eight weeks after fertilization, prenatal development has reached a point where survival, in case of premature birth, is possible. The final weeks of this stage involve weight gain. A full-term pregnancy ends with childbirth at thirty-eight weeks.

TO HAVE OR NOT TO HAVE

Biologically healthy couples are capable of producing one child after another. Throughout most of human history this, in fact, has been the case. Married women have gone from one pregnancy to the next until they died or reached menopause. While, at least in theory, a woman could bear a child each year, there is a biological mechanism that tends to space children. In societies where women subsist on low fat diets (which includes most primitive societies), while a woman is lactating, she will not usually ovulate. This mechanism functions as natural birth control, preventing pregnancy and the birth of another child until the previous one is weaned. However, in societies with higher fat diets, such as North America, this biological mechanism is overridden.

While a healthy woman is capable of bearing many children, throughout history couples have attempted to control the number and timing of their children. Modern birth-control methods have given couples significant control over their fertility. We will examine the issue of controlling the timing and number of children next; in this section we want to deal with the issue of whether or not to have children at all.

Until recently, it was expected that a married couple would have children, and it was considered a tragedy for a couple to be childless. However, in the past twenty-five years that attitude has changed. Today, couples are deciding not to have children. For example, I am personally acquainted with a couple who have decided not to have children. The husband has had a vasectomy. They believe that they will be better able to serve God if they are not tied down with children.

The number of couples who choose to be childless is steadily increasing. A survey of married women in 1977 revealed that over 5 percent expected to remain childless (Lasswell and Lasswell 1982:248). One interesting finding in this study is that education has a significant effect on the responses, with increased education increasing the desire for childlessness (see table 10–2). Organizations for couples choosing not to have children have begun to spring up. One of the better known is the National Organization for Non-Parents (NON). They advocate the use of the term *child-free* rather than *childless,* which they view as having negative connotations.

TABLE 10–2
PERCENT OF MARRIED WOMEN
WHO EXPECT TO REMAIN CHILDLESS

EDUCATION	PERCENT
Graduate school	14.3
College graduate	7.5
1–3 years of college	7.3
High school graduate	4.9
Non–high school graduate	2.6

Adapted from Lasswell and Lasswell 1982:249.

Obviously, the decision to remain childless has many ramifications. We live in a society that is still family oriented, with children considered an integral part of the family. Parents of childless couples may apply pressure in a desire for grandchildren. A childless couple may find they have less in common with their peers as other couples begin having children and center their lives around the home. The decision to have children or not to have children is a major one for a couple. Table 10–3 suggests some questions a couple should discuss in contemplating the decision to have children.

TABLE 10–3
PARENTHOOD CONTEMPLATION QUESTIONS

1. Do you like children—not just cuddly infants but also cranky two-year-olds, curious eight-year-olds, and anxious teen-agers?
2. Do you view parenthood as a burden or as an enriching experience?
3. Do you feel your marriage is strong enough for you to take on the responsibility of nuturing another person?
4. Are you willing to let go of your childhood and really become an adult?
5. Can you give love without needing an equal amount in return?
6. Do you respond well to helplessness in others?
7. Do you have unrealistic expectations about parenthood? Do you believe, for example, that having a child will automatically ensure solace in your old age? Or save a troubled marriage?
8. Are you prepared for the profound changes parenthood will bring to your lifestyle—in terms of money, time, and professional goals?
9. Are your prepared to work out the necessary compromises regarding child care (particularly in a dual-career situation)?
10. Are you prepared to let a child develop according to his or her bent, rather than according to your predetermined plan?
11. Are you prepared to depend more heavily on family and friends, as is usually necessary when a couple has a child?
12. Do you believe that it is consistent with God's leading in your life to have children?

HOW MANY AND WHEN?

Even when a couple decides that they do not want to have children, there are still decisions to be made. How many children would they like to have? When do they want to have them? What about spacing? Do they want two in diapers at the same time?

Social research has produced some useful findings that should be considered by a couple making a decision concerning parenthood.

We have already seen the results of research that indicates the earlier in a marriage a child is born, the greater the probability of divorce (Belkin and Goodman 1980: 436). How long should a couple be married before having their first child? While many factors will influence the decision, one authority suggests waiting at least "three years after marriage to get the marriage on solid ground emotionally and financially" (Lasswell 1974:242 in Belkin and Goodman 1980:436).

A significant amount of research has been done on birth order, spacing, and number of children. This research indicates that family size and spacing affect the intellectual development of children (Zajonc 1975:37–43; Steelman and Mercy 1980:571–82). What this research found was that children who are closely spaced score lower on IQ tests than children with greater spacing between siblings. The research also found that as the number of siblings in a family increases, the average IQ score decreases. One study (see figure 10–1) found a difference of ten IQ points between the scores of children with one sibling and children with eight siblings (Zajonc

This figure shows the relationship between birth order, family size, and IQ. Each line represents a family of a given size and each dot represents the IQ of a particular child's birth order in a family of that size. It should be noted that the range for average IQ scores is 90 to 110.

Figure 10–1. THE RELATIONSHIP BETWEEN BIRTH ORDER, FAMILY SIZE, AND IQ (Adapted from Zanjonc 1975:43).

1975:43). A leading researcher in this area suggests that if the intellectual development of their children is important to a couple, they should limit their family to two children with at least two years between them (Zajonc 1975: 39–43).

Social research shows us the relationship between various factors such as the timing of the first child and divorce rate or number of children and intellectual development. However, we must keep in mind that these are correlational studies and statistical averages. There are always exceptions to these generalizations. A couple should not make family planning decisions based solely on the results of social research. There are many factors a couple should consider in family planning. Nevertheless, the results of this research should aid a couple in the decision process. The more information they have, the better the possibilities for making a wise decision.

BIRTH CONTROL AND THE CHRISTIAN

A number of Protestant scholars (i.e., Grunlan and Mayers 1979:152; Hulme 1962:34–35; Hughes 1969:100–101; Waltke 1969:20) agree that human sexuality has two functions from a biblical perspective. Sex is God's gift of life and love of humans. One of the functions of sex is to propagate the race (Gen. 1:27–28). Grunlan and Mayers explain the other function:

> Although sex serves a reproductive function in all of the animal kingdom, it serves a second function among humans. It reinforces the relationship between a man and a woman (Gen. 2:24; Prov. 5:18–19; Eph. 5:22–31). Sex is a sharing of each other, a physical intimacy that expresses the spiritual intimacy between two people. Sex is God-ordained. It is not just for reproduction but also for the expression of love between a husband and wife (1979:152).

The task facing a Christian couple is that of harmonizing these two functions of sex. Pregnancy is the natural result of regular sexual activity. The issue is, should a couple continuously produce children as a result of maintaining a one-flesh relationship? William Hulme says:

"Be fruitful and multiply" still means that the Creator expects children to come out of marriage, and "subdue the earth" still means that man is to exercise dominion over the forces of nature. . . . In birth control the theological issue is not whether things work out any better because of conception limitation, but whether conception control is not man's responsibility under God as a part of his elevated status above all other creatures (Hulme 1962:37–38).

Some argue that birth control is interfering with God. They argue that a couple should engage in sexual intercourse and leave the results to God. They say that we are putting ourselves in the place of God when we use birth control and claim a couple should trust God since He knows what is good for them and will bring about what is best for them. As humans we should submit to God. Responding to this type of reasoning, Donald MacKay writes:

The general attitude they express is, I fear, a false humility. It is more akin to the pagan fear of nature . . . than to fear of God in the positive sense that the Bible gives to that phrase . . . it is simply bad theology to conclude from this that God places an embargo on taking our share of responsibility for the way things turn out next.

The distinction we need here is between creation (which is God's prerogative) and procreation (which is man's responsibility) . . . the process within our created spacetime by which human beings bring other human beings into the world. . . . The sovereignty of God does not at all imply that every aspect of the future is inevitable-for-us. On the contrary, the biblical doctrine is that we are accountable for those decisions and actions that are up to us, precisely because He has made us the determinants of them (1979:57–59).

Basically, the issue is not whether or not we are going to "interfere" with nature or not, but to what extent. Every time we visit a physician or dentist, every time we take a drug, every time we build a dam, every time we water a lawn—we are tampering with nature. Most of us do not say when we get a headache, "This must be God's will. When He is ready, He will take it away." Rather, we take an aspirin. The fact is that all of us subdue nature in some way or other every day. The real question is, has

God given us the means and responsibility to subdue nature? If He has, we are responsible to do so. As Hulme argues:

> Christianity is no nature cult. We are to subdue nature, not worship it. Instead of submitting helplessly to the processes of nature, the Christian as a worker together with the Creator channels and subdues these processes to serve the purposes for which God has created and redeemed us. The birth control controversy . . . is a theological conflict over whether there is not a higher source for the revelation of God's will than the processes of nature (1962:39–40).

METHODS OF BIRTH CONTROL

Methods of birth control may be divided into four major categories: (1) natural methods, (2) mechanical methods, (3) chemical methods, and (4) surgical methods. We will examine the basic methods in each category. The advantages and disadvantages of each method will also be discussed. I will not recommend any method. Each couple must weigh the advantages and disadvantages of each method for themselves.

Natural Methods

The methods in this category are called natural because they center around natural processes rather than utilizing some form of interference as do the methods in the other categories. The three natural methods we will discuss are the rhythm method, coitus interuptus, and abstinence.

Rhythm Method

The rhythm method is based on the fact that a woman ovulates only once a month. The egg lives in the fallopian tube for only forty-eight to seventy-two hours, and sperm are not capable of living more than forty-eight to seventy-two hours in the fallopian tube. Theoretically, therefore, conception can occur only during four to six days of any menstrual cycle. The secret to the successful use of this method is determining when a woman ovulates and then avoiding intercourse for seventy-two hours before and after that time.

There are three common techniques for determining when a woman ovulates. One is the calendar technique. This technique is based on the fact that women with regular cycles ovulate fourteen days, plus or minus two days, before the onset of menses, regardless of the length of the cycle. To use this technique, a woman charts the length of her cycles for at least six months. She can then calculate her fertile days by subtracting eighteen days from her shortest cycle to determine the first unsafe day and subtracting eleven from the number of days in her longest cycle to determine her last unsafe day. For example, if a woman's shortest cycle is twenty-five days and her longest cycle is thirty-two days, her unsafe period extends from the seventh day $(25-18=7)$ following the onset of menses to the twenty-first day $(32-11=21)$. She needs to avoid sexual intercourse during those two weeks $(21-7=14$ days) to be safe. Obviously, the more regular a woman's cycles, the shorter the unsafe period will be, while the more irregular the longer the unsafe period will be.

The second technique for determining the time of ovulation is the basal temperature technique. Following ovulation, progesterone is produced that results in an elevation of a woman's temperature .4 to .8 degrees. Using this method, a woman takes her temperature each morning immediately upon wakening and before getting out of bed. A special thermometer, called a basal thermometer, which records small changes in temperature, is used. If a woman has regular cycles, a pattern may develop that allows her to calculate when she will ovulate.

The third means of determining ovulation is the vaginal mucus technique. Just before ovulation, glands in the cervix secrete mucus. The mucus has the appearance and consistency of the white of a raw egg. The woman performs daily self-examinations, feeling the cervix for the onset of mucus secretion. Frequently, two or more of these techniques are used in combination in determining the time of ovulation.

The advantages of the rhythm method are that little or no cost is involved, neither a physician's services nor prescriptions are required, and there are no medical side effects. There are also several disadvantages to this method. A major disadvantage is that only about 60 percent of women have menstrual cycles that are regular enough for this method to work successfully. Another disadvantage is that it requires discipline in application involving keeping track of dates, regularly taking one's temperature, and/or engaging in daily self-examinations. A significant disadvantage is that it restricts sex to certain periods of time and forbids sex during a time when many women experience heightened sexual desire (ovulation).

Coitus Interruptus

The method called coitus interruptus which is also referred to as the *withdrawal method*, requires the male partner to withdraw his penis from the vagina just before ejaculation. Emission of the sperm should take place away from the vagina and external genitalia of the woman. This is an ancient technique and is probably referred to in Genesis 38:9, where it is said of Onan that "he spilled his seed on the ground." Onan was punished by God, not for practicing coitus interruptus, but, for failing to obey God's command to raise up children for his brother as the Old Testament levirate law required (Deut. 25:5).

The advantages of coitus interruptus include the following: there is no cost involved, no physician's service or prescriptions are needed, and there are no medical side effects. There are also disadvantages to this method. One disadvantage is that it requires significant discipline on the part of the male partner. Another disadvantage is that it takes away from sexual enjoyment. The natural tendency for a male is to thrust at the time of ejaculation. Also simultaneous orgasms are not possible, and the couple is not able to abandon themselves to the act, but must be monitoring their reactions. The greatest disadvantage to coitus interruptus is that it is not foolproof. A few drops of semen are secreted from the penis before ejaculation. While that semen generally does not contain enough sperm to impregnate a woman, there are always exceptions. Also, if withdrawal is not timed right, the ejaculation may begin before withdrawal is completed, and the first few drops of semen ejaculated at orgasm have the highest concentration of sperm.

Abstinence

Abstaining from sexual intercourse, of course, prevents pregnancy. One form of abstinence, the post-partum sex taboo, is widely practiced in primitive societies. The post-partum sex taboo is a rule prohibiting a woman from having sexual relations with her husband, or any man, for a specified period of time following childbirth. In a study of fifty-six cultures, researchers found that half of them had a post-partum sex taboo that lasted for at least a year (Otterbein 1977:176). The long post-partum sex taboo, according to Otterbein (1977:176–77), is associated with three factors. The first is polygyny. Since the husband has other wives, a long post-partum sex taboo does not deny his sexual gratification. The second factor is clan organization. The spacing of children is important where women must contribute to a group larger than a nuclear family, such as an extended-family household. The third factor is a protein deficiency in the diet, which frequently occurs in tropical areas. Women living in these climates need to space their children in order for their milk to remain rich in protein.

In technological Western societies, where monogamy is practiced, abstinence is not an attractive birth-control method. With a variety of birth control methods readily available, most couples are not willing to forego sexual intimacy. In my opinion there is only one group of people for whom abstinence should be the birth control method of first choice, that is single persons.

Mechanical Methods

The methods in this category are called mechanical because they either place a mechanical barrier between the sperm and the egg or they mechanically prevent the fertilized egg from implanting in the uterine wall. The methods to be discussed under this category are the condom, the diaphragm, and the intrauterine device.

Condom

The condom is a thin sheath made of latex rubber, lamb membrane, or similar material. It is fitted over the erect penis and collects the ejaculated semen so that it is not deposited in the vagina. Other common names for condoms are *prophylactics, safes, rubbers, skins,* and *Trojans* (the name of a popular brand). The condom is applied just before the penile penetration of the vagina. It is unrolled over the erect penis. Many condoms have a receptacle at the end to catch the sperm. When using a condom without a receptacle, a little space should be left between the end of the condom and the penis for catching the semen (see figure 10–2). The penis should be withdrawn from the vagina soon after the ejaculation and before the penis becomes flaccid. Care needs to be taken during withdrawal that the condom does not come off and that semen does not spill out in the vagina.

Foil wrapped

Partially unrolled

Nipple type

Cap type

Figure 10–2. CONDOMS.

Some of the advantages of the condom are that it is 95 percent effective, the cost is relatively low, no physician's service or prescriptions are necessary, and there are no medical side effects. Another advantage of the condom, which may be less relevant to many Christians, is that it prevents the spread of many venereal diseases.

The condom also has a few disadvantages. One of these is that the male often experiences less sensation. This disadvantage may work as an advantage for some males experiencing premature ejaculation. Another disadvantage is that it requires discipline and "breaks the mood." That is, just when foreplay is producing arousal, the couple must stop for the man to apply the condom. Some couples have the wife apply the condom to her husband's penis as part of foreplay. The fact that the penis must be removed following ejaculation is also seen as a disadvantage by some couples. Partners often enjoy lying together coupled following intercourse.

Diaphragm

The diaphragm is a flexible ring covered with a rubber dome. It is place in the vagina so that it completely encircles the cervix, thus preventing sperm from entering the uterus (see figure 10–3). The diaphragm is generally used in conjunction with a spermicide, a sperm-killing cream or jelly, which is applied to the inside of the dome and the ring.

Diaphragms come in different sizes, from 50 to 105 millimeters. A woman must see a physician who will examine and fit her with the proper size. The physician may supply the diaphragm or give her a prescription to purchase one at a pharmacy. A woman should be refitted every couple of years, following the birth of a child, or after significant weight loss or gain. The physician will usually instruct the woman in how to insert and remove the diaphragm and how to care for it.

The diaphragm may be inserted up to four hours before intercourse and must be left in at least six hours following intercourse. Insertion of the diaphragm is not painful and once in place is usually not felt. It does not interfere with either the male's or female's enjoyment of sex. The diaphragm is the most widely used contraceptive among college-educated women.

The advantages of the diaphragm include its high level of effectiveness, over 98 percent; the fact that it can be inserted well before intercourse and need not interfere with foreplay; there are no medical side effects; and it is a relatively low-cost method. There are also some disadvantages. Two of them are that the services of a physician are needed and a prescription is necessary. Another is that the diaphragm must be cleaned and cared for, since it

Applying spermicidal cream or jelly

Folding for insertion

Inserting diaphragm

Checking diaphragm

Figure 10–3. THE DIAPHRAGM AND ITS APPLICATION.

is reusable—unlike the condom, which is discarded after use. An additional disadvantage is that it interrupts spontaneous sex. If a couple is planning to be intimate the diaphragm may be inserted beforehand, but, if intimacy results spontaneously, foreplay must stop while the woman inserts the diaphragm.

Intrauterine Device

Made of plastic, copper, or stainless steel, an intrauterine device (IUD) is basically an object placed in the uterus by a physician or other health professional (see figure 10–4). Most IUDs have short nylon threads attached to them that hang down into the vagina. The purpose of the threads is for the woman to perform self-examinations to insure the device is in place. The threads do not interfere with intercourse and are not felt by the penis. If the woman desires to have children, a physician can easily remove the IUD.

The IUD is not a *contraceptive* since it does not prevent conception. It is a *contraimplantation* device because it prevents the implantation of the fertilized ovum (zygote) in the uterine wall. It is not known, for sure, how the IUD works, but a widely accepted theory is that it irritates the uterine wall so that the fertilized ovum is rejected. The IUD causes fertilized eggs to be discharged, in fact, causing abortions. For this reason many Christians are opposed to the use of IUDs. We will discuss the issue of abortion later in this chapter.

Lippes Loop   Safe-T-Coil

Copper-T   Copper-7

Figure 10–4. INTRAUTERINE DEVICES (IUD).

The advantages of the IUD include its high level of effectiveness (about 95 percent); the fact that there is nothing to put on, insert, or care for; and its relatively low cost. There are several disadvantages to the use of IUDs. One is the need to see a physician. Another, more serious disadvantage, is the medical side effects. These include increased menstrual flow (24.3 percent of users), irregular flows (26.1 percent of users), abdominal cramping (12.6 percent of users), and involuntary expulsion of the IUD (12.6 percent of users) (Orthner 1981:316). The IUD can also perforate the uterus. In addition, the incidence of pelvic inflammatory disease is up to four times greater for women who use an IUD (*Minneapolis Star and Tribune,* July 9, 1982: 1c). Perhaps the greatest disadvantage of the IUD, at least for Christians and others with a pro-life viewpoint, is that it causes abortions.

Chemical Methods

These methods involve the use of chemical reactions to prevent conception. We will consider two basic methods under this category, the birth-control pills and the spermicides.

Birth-control Pills

The most common form of contraception in the United States is the birth-control pill. Approximately ten million women use birth-control pills, accounting for nearly one out of four users of contraceptives (Golanty and Harris 1982:313). The most commonly used birth-control pills are known as combination pills because they contain estrogen and progesterone. These synthesized hormones inhibit ovulation and thus prevent pregnancy.

In 1973, a second type of birth-control pill was introduced, called the "minipill." This pill contains only progesterone. Because it does not contain estrogen, many of the side effects of the combination pill are eliminated or reduced (see table 10–4) for side effects of estrogen). The minipill, unlike the combination pill, does not suppress ovulation, but affects the lining of the uterus so that a fertilized egg will not be implanted. Because the minipill results in fertilized eggs being aborted, its usage is problematic for many Christians.

A third type of birth-control pill, the postcoital or "morning-after" pill, contains a large dosage of estrogen. This pill also results in the aborting of the fertilized egg. Because of the side effects of this pill, it is not routinely

TABLE 10–4

POSSIBLE ESTROGEN SIDE EFFECTS FROM BIRTH-CONTROL PILLS

1. Nausea, bloating, vomiting
2. Fluid retention
3. Breast tenderness
4. Increased skin pigmentation (cloasma), or "mask of pregnancy," on face
5. Increased mucous discharge from glands of cervix, cervical eversion
6. Headaches during days both on and off the pill
7. Worsening of migraine headaches
8. Increase in blood pressure
9. Change in sugar tolerance and insulin requirements in both diabetics and nondiabetics.
10. Abnormalities in blood clotting tests.
11. Thrombophlebitis (presence of inflamed blood clot in a vein)
12. Pulmonary embolism (passage of blood clot to lung)
13. Cerebral thrombosis (presence of clot in blood vessel in the brain)
14. Myocardial infarction (heart attack due to blood clot in artery of heart)
15. Visual changes, altered contour of the eye and cornea, with contact lens discomfort
16. Changes in certain metabolism tests: thyroid, liver, and fat metabolism
17. Increased growth of benign (noncancerous) fibroid tumors of the uterus
18. Increased growth rate of estrogen-dependent cancers of the breast and uterus (however, estrogen doesn't create new ones)
19. Vitamin deficiencies
20. Possible lowering of the convulsive threshold in sensitive epileptics
21. Urinary tract changes and infection
22. Increased incidence of benign liver tumors and gall bladder disease

Adapted from Shapiro 1977:24

given. The U.S. Food and Drug Administration has approved it only for "emergency" situations.

The advantages of the combination pill include its effectiveness, over 95 percent; its low cost; and the fact that it does not interfere with sexual activity. Again, there are also disadvantages. Two disadvantages are that the services of a physician are required and a prescription is needed. Another is the discipline required in remembering to take the pill daily. Perhaps the major disadvantage is the medical side effects (see table 10–4).

Spermicides

Vaginal spermicides are sperm-killing preparations. They are available in the form of jellies, creams, aerosol foams and suppositories (see figure 10–5). All of these preparations include two compounds: an inert base that keeps the spermicidal agent in the vagina by the cervix and a spermicidal agent. The spermicides come with an applicator (see figure 10–5) and must be deposited at the base of the vagina by the cervix to be effective. The spermicide should be inserted just before intercourse for maximum effectiveness.

The advantages of the spermicides include an effective rate of 97 percent (99 percent if used in conjunction with the condom); neither the services of a physician or a prescription is needed; the cost is low, there are no medical side effects, and the spermicide also functions as a lubricant. There are also disadvantages with this method. One is that the spermicide must be inserted just before intercourse. Another is that this method is messier than other methods. Also, some women have an aversion to placing foreign matter in their vagina.

Surgical Methods

Surgical methods of birth control are those that involve surgical procedures by a physician. We will look at two methods under this category, sterilization and abortion.

Sterilization

The most common form of birth control for couples over thirty years of age is sterilization. Almost 40 percent of all couples choose this method within five years after the birth of their last wanted child (Golanty and Harris 1982:319). While sterilization of females is similar to the sterilization of males in many ways, there are also differences, so we will consider them separately.

The most widely used procedure for the sterilization of women is *tubal ligation,* which involves the cutting and tying of the fallopian tubes (see figure 10–6). This, of course, prevents the egg and the sperm from meeting. A *tubal ligation* does not affect a woman's hormone production, menstrual cycle, or sexual desire. A tubal ligation should be considered permanent. Although it is possible to surgically reconnect the fallopian tubes, this does not insure fertility, since scar tissue in the tubes may prevent conception.

The sterilization procedure for a man is called a *vas-*

Figure 10-5. VAGINAL SPERMICIDES AND THEIR APPLICATION.

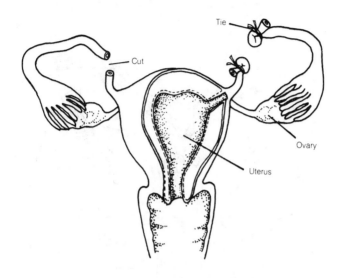

Fallopian tube

Tie

Cut

Ovary

Uterus

Figure 10-6. TUBAL LIGATION.

ectomy. It involves the cutting and tying of the two vas deferens (see figure 10–7). A vasectomy does not affect a man's hormone production, his ability to have an erection, or intercourse. It has no effect on the production of seminal fluid, ejaculation, or orgasm. As with the tubal ligation, a vasectomy is surgically reversible. However, a vasectomy should be considered permanent, since reconnection of the vas deferens does not guarantee the ability to produce children.

The advantages of sterilization are that it is almost 100 percent effective, allows sexual freedom, and it has no medical side effects. There are two major disadvantages. One is that the surgical procedures, though relatively simple, are still costly. Fortunately, many medical insurance carriers will cover the cost because it is much lower than the cost of a pregnancy. The other major disadvantage is that it must be considered irreversible.

Figure 10–7. VASECTOMY.

Abortion

Technically, the term *abortion* refers to the discharge of a zygote, embryo, or fetus. If this occurs naturally, it is referred to as a *spontaneous abortion* or *miscarriage*. If the discharge is produced by artificial means, it is called an *induced abortion*. In our discussion, references to abortion will be to induced abortions.

The three most common methods of induced abortion are the vacuum aspiration, dilation and evacuation, and injection of a saline solution or prostaglandin into the amniotic sac. *Vacuum aspiration* is generally used only during the first trimester of pregnancy. It involves inserting a plastic tube six millimeters in diameter or twelve-millimeter vacurette through the cervix into the uterus. A suction machine is attached to the tube or vacurette and the embryo or fetus is suctioned out. After the twelfth week of pregnancy *dilation and evacuation* may be used. This is a surgical procedure that involves dilating the cervix and mechanically removing the fetus. After the sixteenth week, the most common practice is to remove the amniotic fluid from around the fetus with a syringe and replace it with a *saline solution*. The uterus reacts to the saline solution by contracting and expels the fetus and placenta within a day. An alternative is to inject a hormonal substance called *prostaglandin* into the amniotic sac. This also causes contractions and expulsion.

The medical side effects to abortion involve the possibility of infection and a slightly higher miscarriage rate after two or more abortions. The psychological side effects vary from individual to individual. One study showed that about 21 percent of the women who had an abortion experienced some guilt or other psychological side effects (Shapiro 1977:175).

ABORTION AND THE CHRISTIAN

Abortion presents a theological problem for Christians. As Montgomery (1981:86) indicates, the basic issue centers around the question of when the developing child receives its soul. The two major positions on this question are called *creationism* and *traducianism*. The creationist position

> regards the soul of each human being as immediately created by God and joined to the body either at conception, at birth, or at some time between these two. The advocates of the theory urge in its favor certain texts of Scripture that refer to God as the Creator of the human soul or spirit as well as the fact that there is a masked individuality in the child, which cannot be explained as a mere reproduction of the qualities existing in the parents (Bancroft 1976:189).

The traducianist position

> holds that the human race was immediately created in Adam and, as respects both body and soul, was propa-

gated from him by natural generation. All souls since Adam are only mediately created by God, as the upholder of the laws of propagation which were originally established by Him (Bancroft 1976:190).

We will have to leave the arguments for and against these two positions to the theologians (see, for example, Bancroft 1976:186–91; Berkhof 1949:196–201; Strong 1907:488–97; Thiessen 1951:232–37). However, the implications of these two positions are important for a Christian perspective on abortion. Since those persons holding to traducianism believe the soul is passed on at conception, they generally oppose abortion and see it as the killing of a human soul. On the other hand, those holding to creationism believe God implants the soul some time between conception and birth. Persons holding to creationism and believing the soul is imparted some time after conception generally would have no moral problems with an abortion occurring before the soul is implanted.

While being aware of the arguments in favor of each position and recognizing the problems of each, I am more comfortable with the traducianist position. However, even if one does accept the creationist position, one cannot be certain *when* God imparts the soul. Therefore, to be safe, it seems to me the wisest assumption would be to say that it is at conception (which, in fact, is the view of many who hold the creationist position). If one assumes a later point in prenatal development and if this assumption is wrong, great damage has been done. It is my conviction that Christians ought to be opposed to abortion at any time, from conception onward.

However, Christians need to take responsibility for a prolife position. If we believe that a pregnant teen-ager should bear her child, we need to support her, counsel her, and minister to her, perhaps directing her to a Christian agency that will help her through her time of pregnancy. If we expect the mother who already has five children to bear her sixth, we need to be there with aid to make life worth living. We have no right to be only pro-prenatal life, we must also be pro-postnatal life. We cannot insist that women bear children because of our moral convictions and then walk away. We have to back up our moral convictions with support and action.

ADOPTION

It is estimated that between 10 to 15 percent of married couples cannot conceive because of sterility or low fertility. Many of these couples would like to have children and turn to adoption. Adoptions reached a peak of 175,000 in 1970, but only about 100,000 children were adopted in 1982. There are two primary reasons for the drop in the number of adoptions. First, pregnancies among those single women who would normally give up their children for adoption are down because of birth control and abortions, and records show that 75 percent of legal abortions involve single women. The second reason is that more single women who do bear children are keeping them rather than putting them up for adoption.

Currently, the waiting period for a healthy, white infant is five to ten years, the time varying from one state to another. The waiting time is much shorter, usually only a year or two, for a child over six years of age, a handicapped child, or other hard-to-place child. Many Americans are looking overseas for foreign children because of the lack of American babies available for adoption. However, even this door is closing. The number of foreign children brought into the United States for adoption dropped from almost seven thousand in 1976 to under five thousand in 1979. Many foreign countries are placing severe limits on the number of children adopted by foreigners.

However, for those couples who persevere through the long and tedious adoption process, becoming a parent by adoption brings as much joy as becoming a parent by natural birth. Adopted children function the same as natural-born children. Whether by natural birth or adoption, children are children. The addition of a new child to the family radically changes the relationship. This will be explored in later chapters.

DISCUSSION QUESTIONS

1. Do you believe a Christian couple should choose to remain childless? Give reasons for your answer.
2. What role do you feel social research findings should

play in a couple's decisions concerning timing and number of children? Why?

3. To what extent are humans responsible for the reproductive capacity God has given them?

4. How would you rate, in order of importance, the advantages and disadvantages of the various birth control methods described? Why?

5. Do you think Christians should use sterilization as a birth control method? Why or why not?

6. How do you understand and reconcile God's command to "be fruitful and multiply" with the teaching that people are to subdue nature?

SUGGESTED READING

Linda Ferrill Annis, *The Child Before Birth* (Ithaca, N.Y.: Cornell University Press, 1978). A clear, easy-to-read treatment of prenatal development. The author discusses the effects of nutrition, diseases, and drugs on prenatal development.

Geraldine Flanagan, *The First Nine Months of Life* (New York: Simon and Schuster, 1965). A well-written and readable treatment of prenatal development. It is both sensitive and scientifically accurate.

John Warwick Montgomery, *Slaughter of the Innocents* (Westchester, Ill.: Crossway, 1981). A treatment of abortion from the moral, ethical, theological, legal, and medical perspectives. Montgomery marshalls a number of arguments against legalized abortion.

Francis A. Schaeffer and C. Everett Koop, *Whatever Happened to the Human Race?* (Old Tappan, N.J.: Revell, 1979). A forceful presentation of the dehumanizing aspects of abortion. This book deals with abortion from a biblical perspective.

Howard I. Shapiro, *The Birth Control Book* (New York: St. Martin's, 1977). A readable, basic work on birth control written by a medical doctor. It covers all the major methods.

Walter O. Spitzer and Carlyle L. Saylor (eds.), *Birth Control and the Christian* (Wheaton, Ill.: Tyndale, 1969). A symposium on birth control, with contributions by biblical scholars, theologians, and medical doctors. This is a scholarly work that deals with many critical issues.

11

Child Rearing

*Children, obey your parents in the Lord, for this is
right. "Honor your father and mother"—which is
the first commandment with a promise—"that it
may go well with you and that you may enjoy long
life on the earth." Fathers, do not exasperate your
children; instead, bring them up in the training and
instruction of the Lord.*

EPHESIANS 6:1–4

*You know, before I had children, I used to think
how much fun it would be to have some of my own.
I really enjoyed other people's kids. I didn't realize,
but probably I enjoyed them so much because I was
only around them for short periods of time. I really
love my kids, but sometimes I wish I could get away
from them for just a little while. The responsibility
for raising children is so much greater than I had
ever thought.*

BILL R. WAGONSELLER AND
RICHARD L. MCDOWELL (1979:5)

I CAN IDENTIFY with the second quote above. My wife
and I were married for five years before we had our first
child. During those years we spent a great deal of time
with children. We were houseparents in a children's
home. We ran a day camp. We conducted children's
church. We were sponsors for junior high and senior high
youth groups. Yet, none of those children were our ultimate responsibility. We were more or less free to discontinue our association with them and our care for them at
any time.

Then we became parents, and my lack of preparation
for the role was a real surprise. I had never held a new-

born infant—my motto being "look but don't touch"—
much less changed a diaper before I became a parent. The
first time I changed my newborn son I was literally baptized into the art of diaper changing. My experience
confirmed for me that in the American culture there is
little or no socialization for the role of parent for men and
only haphazard socialization for women as they care for
siblings and babysit.

ROLE OF PARENTHOOD

It is interesting to note than an elementary school
teacher has to have at least a bachelors degree, and in
some states a masters degree, plus be state certified in
order to teach. In most states, day-care facilities and
workers have to be licensed. Child psychologists and
pediatricians must be board certified and state licensed.
In short, most people working with children must be
trained and certified or licensed. However, any couple can
have a child and become parents without regard to
qualifications, training, or fitness. It is incredible how
little socialization and training goes into preparing people
for such a critical role. LeMasters, basing his conclusions
on his research with parents, writes:

> It seemed to us that these couples had received very
> inadequate preparation for the parental role. Most of the
> husbands felt that they had had no preparation whatsoever
> for the father role, and even a majority of the wives felt that
> their preparation for the role of mother had been quite
> inadequate (1970:11).

LeMasters suggests there are three factors missing in
parenthood preparation. The first factor is the lack of formal training for parenthood in secondary schools and
colleges. Generally, courses in this area are either absent
or electives. One college where I teach offers a course
entitled "Parent-Child Relations," but only teacher-
education majors are required to take it. The second factor
is that most Americans grow up in small families with
children closely spaced and, therefore, have little or no
opportunity to care for siblings. The third factor
suggested by LeMasters is what is called the "romantic

complex" about babies and parenthood. Parents, whose children have grown, tend to look back at the infant years and remember only the good times and, therefore, pass on a romanticized view of that stage of life to young couples. The media also encourage this view—examine the advertising for baby products as an example.

Continuing his analysis of parenthood, LeMasters lists thirteen characteristics of this role:

1. The role of parent in modern American is not well defined. It is often ambiguous and hard to pin down.

2. The role is not adequately delimited. Parents are expected to succeed where even the professionals fail.

3. Modern parents are not well prepared for their role as fathers and mothers.

4. There is a romantic complex about parenthood. . . . In some ways the romantic complex surrounding parenthood is even deeper and more unrealistic than that relating to marriage.

5. Modern parents are in the unenviable position of having complete responsibility for their offspring but only partial authority over them. Our thesis on this point is that parental authority has been eroded gradually over the past several decades without an equivalent reduction of parental responsibility.

6. The standards of role performance imposed on modern parents are too high. This arises from the fact that modern fathers and mothers are judged largely by professional practitioners such as psychiatrists and social workers rather than by their peers—other parents who are "amateurs" and not professionals.

7. Parents are the victims of inadequate behavioral science. . . . They have been told repeatedly by psychiatrists, social workers, sociologists, ministers, and others that nothing determines what the child will be like but the influence of the parents . . . this is obviously not true.

8. Parents do not choose their children, unless they are adoptive parents. Thus they have the responsibility for children whether they find them congenial or not. This, of course, is nothing new in parenthood the world over, but the expectations of role performance for modern American parents are such that the nature of the child can impose severe strain.

9. There is no traditional model for modern parents to follow in rearing their children. The old model has been riddled by critical studies, yet a new model that is adequate has not developed. Instead we have had a series of fads and fashions in child rearing based on the research of the moment. . . . This has not been much help to parents who probably need the most help—parents from low income groups.

10. Contrary to what some may think, parenthood as a role does not enjoy the priority one would expect in modern America. The needs of the economic system in particular come first as can be seen in the frequency with which large firms transfer young managers and their families around the country.

11. Other new roles have been assumed by modern parents . . . that are not always completely compatible with the role of parent.

12. The parental role is one of the few important roles in contemporary America that one cannot honorably withdraw from. Most of us can escape from our jobs if they are too frustrating; many of us escape from our parents when we marry; and a considerable number of husbands and wives manage to withdraw with some honor from marriages that they no longer find enchanting. But it is harder to pull out of parenthood, especially for mothers, even when the parent knows he or she is failing.

13. And last but not least, it is not enough for modern parents to produce children in their own image: the children have to be reared to be not only different from their fathers and mothers but also *better* (1970:51–54).

CRISIS OF PARENTHOOD

Several social scientists view the process of becoming a parent as a crisis (e.g., Bigner 1979; Duvall 1977; Eshleman 1981; LeMasters 1970). The addition of a child, a newborn, helpless infant that is in need of constant care, places a strain on a marriage. Two people, who had each other all to themselves now find themselves involved with a third person who demands much of their time and attention. Duvall reports, "Hundreds of couples studied over the years concur that parenthood is a critical experience, and that marital satisfaction drops sharply with the coming of the first baby'' (1977:215). She continues, ''Research finds that having a baby is hard on a marriage in the sense that more sex difficulties arise—problems in which the wife is more concerned and the husband more dissatisfied'' (1977:240). Bigner (1979:105) reports on a large-scale study of married couples that found that marital satisfaction dropped sharply with the birth of the first child and did not return to preparental levels until the last child had left home (see figure 11–1). While the studies cited above show that marital satisfaction falls during the child-rearing years, we should remember that the results are reported in terms of averages. For many couples the child-rearing years are times of joy, and they see these years as some of their happiest. We also need to keep in mind that these are self-reports and individuals' perceptions of their level of marital satisfaction are relative.

The birth of a child brings many disruptions to the marital relationship. The first, at which we have already looked, is the acquisition of a new role, that of parent. Becoming a mother is for a woman usually more of a tran-

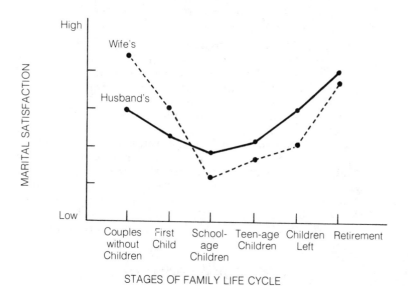

Figure 11–1. LEVEL OF MARITAL SATISFACTION AT VARIOUS STAGES OF THE FAMILY LIFE CYCLE (Adapted from Bigner 1979:106).

sition than becoming a father is for a man. This is because the woman generally ends up with more responsibility for the baby. If both parents have been in the labor force, it is usually the mother who drops out, even if just for a couple of months (maternity leave), to care for the child. The father generally continues his career, with that remaining his primary role while fatherhood becomes a secondary role (Scanzoni and Scanzoni 1981:564–65).

Another area of disruption resulting from the arrival of a new baby is financial. This often is a double blow— the loss of the wife's income and the expenses of a new baby. If the child has been planned for, this disruption is often less severe. However, in the case of an unplanned pregnancy, the financial disruption can be a crisis of major proportions.

Other disruptions involve the interruption of sleep and fatigue, loss of freedom to go places, interference from in-laws, and additional household chores. The new baby also disrupts the relationship between the husband and wife. This is often more problematic for the husband. As Duvall points out, "Few men have been adequately prepared for what to expect when children come" (1977:230). She adds:

> Most difficult of all may be the intimate sharing of his wife with the intrusive little rival that now claims so much of her attention. The husband has had his wife all to himself during their courting and honeymoon days and has learned to take her for granted as his partner and companion during the establishment phase of marriage. He must now see her time, energy, and love directed to the demanding baby in ways that may fill him with intense feelings of being left out and neglected. . . . One of the hazards to be expected . . . is that the mother may devote herself disproportionately to the new baby, and that the young father may retreat emotionally to a doghouse of his own making. Until he can share his wife maturely and participate with her in the experiences of parenthood, he may feel like little more than a fifth wheel around the place (1977:230).

STAGES OF PARENTHOOD

Several schemes for dividing the period of parenthood into various stages have been developed (Duvall

1977; Lamanna and Riedmann 1981; Scanzoni and Scanzoni 1981). Drawing on these schemes, I would like to
suggest five stages of parenthood: (1) New Parent Stage,
(2) Preschool Children Stage, (3) School-age Children
Stage, (4) Teen-age Stage, and (5) Disengagement Stage.

New Parent Stage

This stage, obviously, begins with the birth of the
first child. As we have already seen, this stage is a crisis.
Actually, the birth of the first child, especially if the baby
is healthy, is a moment of elation and rejoicing. The
beaming mother has the assistance of nurses and aids at
the hospital as well as a steady stream of well-wishers.
The proud father is busy calling grandparents, relatives,
and friends. The first few days are quite exciting. It is
when the mother and baby come home from the hospital
that reality sets in. The nursing staff is no longer there to
help with the baby. The full responsibility for around-
the-clock care for the baby falls on the couple.

This stage is a period of adjustment. The couple must
adjust to a third member of the family and to the baby's
schedule. Adjustment to new roles is necessary. The
couple must develop new ways of relating and needs to
work out interpersonal conflicts. Duvall suggests five
major issues a couple needs to work through at this stage:

1. Seeing beyond the drudgeries to the fundamental
   satisfaction of parenthood.
2. Valuing persons above things.
3. Resolving the conflicts inherent in the contradictory
   developmental tasks of parents and young children, and
   of fathers and mothers.
4. Establishing healthy independence as a married couple.
5. Accepting help in a spirit of appreciation and growth
   (1977:245).

Preschool Children Stage

By the time the first child reaches the preschool stage,
about three to five years of age, there may be one or two
younger siblings. The parents have generally adjusted to

their roles as mother and father and are more confident and experienced in dealing with additional children. At this stage the child is able to talk, and patterns of interaction between the child and parents are beginning to develop. Also, by this stage the parents have begun to develop a style of parenting. We will examine various styles of parenting later in this chapter.

The demands and pressures of parenthood at this stage often result in little time for the couple to enjoy each other's company. Research reveals that couples with preschool children have fewer arguments and experience less resentment than earlier in their marriage. On the other hand, they also have less positive support from each other. What has usually happened is that they have settled in a routine of family living that, while producing fewer negative reactions, results in less enjoyment and companionship (Duvall 1977:260–61).

An important task for couples at this stage is to strengthen their relationship. There needs to be creativity and affection in the partnership. Duvall suggests some of the major tasks of this stage include:

1. Supplying adequate space, facilities, and equipment for the expanding family.
2. Meeting predictable and unexpected costs of family life with small children.
3. Assuming more mature roles within the expanding family.
4. Maintaining mutually satisfying intimate communication in the family.
5. Rearing and planning for children.
6. Relating to relatives.
7. Tapping resources outside the family.
8. Motivating family members (1977:261–62).

School-age Children Stage

By this stage most children are fairly self-sufficient. They can dress themselves and care for their basic hygiene. The children need less direct parental care and supervision. In fact, they are gone from the home six to seven hours a day at school. However, the child's life and therefore also the parents' lives become more complex. There are after-school activities—Brownies, Cub Scouts, church activities, and little-league sports. Frequently there are also music lessons, dance classes, or other extracurricular activities.

In fact, Lamanna and Riedmann (1981:409–10) warn that children today face demands from school, church, and recreational organizations that may overextend them. The child is shuffled from one activity to the next. This may produce what they call the "hurried child." They suggest that parents need to take responsibility for seeing that the demands on their children at this stage do not become overwhelming.

This is also a stage when children are starting to make friends outside the home and are becoming more peer conscious. This is another area where parental supervision and guidance are important. Because parents cannot be with their children all the time, it is important for them to help their children find friends who have the same values and standards as they do.

By this stage the parents have been married for at least seven years and have been parents for at least six years. Family routines are probably well established. Duvall sees six major tasks associated with this stage of parenthood:

1. Providing for children's activity and parents' privacy.
2. Keeping financially solvent.
3. Furthering socialization of family members.
4. Upgrading communication in the family.
5. Establishing ties with life outside the family.
6. Developing morally and building family morale (1977:281).

Teen-age Stage

This stage often involves turmoil between parent and child. In fact, both parent and child may be experiencing personal crises at this time. One or both parents may be experiencing the onset of mid-life crises (see chapter 12). The teen-ager is experiencing puberty with its hormonal and physical changes, for the child is beginning the process of becoming an adult. The teen-ager is also beginning the process of cutting the ties with the parents, preparing for the time when he or she will leave home.

Another problem particular to our society is that social change is so rapid that teen-agers today are growing up in a culture that is radically different from that which their parents experienced. I grew up in a world where only the United States had nuclear weapons. My teen-age son is growing up in a world where a dozen nations have the potential to set off a nuclear holocaust. I grew up in a society where drugs were a ghetto problem; my son's middle-class school has a drug program. I grew up in a society that would not let Elvis Presley on television because of the suggestive way he shook his hips, and *Playboy* magazine was sold under the counter. My son lives in a day when R-rated movies are shown on prime-time television, and pornography is displayed in the local corner store. These and many other major differences in the social milieus that parents and teen-agers were raised in adds to the potential for misunderstanding. The widespread drug-usage, permissive sexual attitudes, the epidemic of venereal disease, and the rise of premarital pregnancy make the parenting of teen-agers more difficult than ever.

Some of the tasks parents face at this stage, according to Duvall, include:

1. Providing facilities for widely different needs within the family.
2. Working out ever-changing financial problems.
3. Sharing the responsibilities of family living.
4. Keeping the marriage relationship in focus.
5. Bridging the communication gap between the generations.
6. Maintaining the ethical and moral stance that is meaningful to them (1977:307).

Disengagement Stage

This can often be a difficult stage for parents. They have functioned in the role of father or mother for twenty or more years, in many instances for over half their lives.

When the last child leaves, the role of parent, at least as practiced when the children were at home, abruptly comes to an end. Some of the problems associated with this stage will be discussed in the next chapter.

The tasks facing parents at this stage include:

1. Rearranging physical facilities and resources.
2. Meeting the expenses of a launching-center family.
3. Reallocating responsibilities among grown and growing children.
4. Coming to terms with themselves as husband and wife.
5. Maintaining open systems of communication within the family and between the family and others.
6. Widening the family circle through release of young adult children and recruitment of new members by marriage.
7. Reconciling conflicting loyalties and philosophies of life (Duvall (1977:342).

HUMAN DEVELOPMENT

Before we can go much further in our discussion of parenthood and child rearing, we need to look at human development. An understanding of human development provides a foundation for child rearing. In Luke 2:52 we read, "Jesus grew in wisdom and stature, and in favor with God and men." This verse gives us the four basic aspects of human nature. "Wisdom" refers to the *psychological realm,* "stature" to the *biological,* "in favor with God" to the *spiritual,* and "men" to the *social development.* We need to understand how children develop in each of these areas (see tables 11–1 and 11–2). It is also useful to have an overall model of human development. Perhaps one of the most influential and helpful models is that of Jean Piaget (Pulaski 1980; Singer and Revenson 1978; Wadsworth 1971).

Before we look at Piaget's stages of development, we need to understand some of the presuppositions of his model. One of the foundational premises of Piaget's work is that children are not miniature adults. Their ways of thinking are not merely simplified adult ways. The cognitive processes of children are qualitatively different from

TABLE 11-1
CHILD DEVELOPMENT

Age	Physical	Psychological	Social	Spiritual
0–1 year Infant	Rapid growth — the baby triples its birth weight. Becomes mobile, sits and stands.	Mentally it is a time of discovery. Emotionally the baby is sensitive — capable of anger and joy.	Socially limited. Begins to recognize familiar faces. Coos and babbles at people.	Spiritually dependent on parents.
2–3 years Toddler	Able to walk, beginning to run. Very active. By 2 years, half of adult height is attained.	Mentally — language acquisition, use of symbols. Limited cognitive ability. Emotionally fearful, separation anxiety.	Socially egocentric. Tends to engage in parallel play rather than with peers; i.e., by them rather than *with* them.	Imitates — folds hands, prays, can enjoy Sunday school.
3–5 years Preschool Kindergarten	Growth rate slowing. Large-muscle coordination. Active — playing.	Mentally — explorer and curious. Able to memorize brief items. Emotionally responds to others, still fearful.	Conforming, still egocentric but able to play simple games. Follows older siblings.	Willing to accept whatever taught. Can sing and participate in Sunday school.
6–8 years Primary Grades 1–3	Slow but steady growth. Adult teeth. Small-muscle coordination.	Mentally entering concrete operations stage. Able to manipulate symbols. Learning to read and do math. Emotionally insecure, needs love and security.	Friendly, able to make friends and play organized games. Beginning to see others' point of view.	Able to respond to the gospel. Open to accepting Christ. Eager to please.
9–11 years Junior Grades 4–6	Plateau in growth. Energetic. Able to engage in complex physical activities.	Mentally approaching adult intelligence. Observant and investigative. Emotionally expressive. Able to give and receive affection.	Strong identification with own sex. Socially active, involved in organized sports, clubs, church activities, scouting, etc.	Concerned with relating truth to life. Grasping implications of biblical teachings.

TABLE 11-2
ADOLESCENT DEVELOPMENT

AGE	PHYSICAL	PSYCHOLOGICAL	SOCIAL	SPIRITUAL
12–14 years Early Adolescence Junior High	Puberty, major hormonal and physical changes. Growth spurt. Sexual development.	Mentally critical and testing. Trying out new mental capabilities. Emotionally a period of fluctuations, many ups and downs.	Peer oriented. Need for companionship. Beginning to bceak from parents.	Open to spiritual challenge. Idealistic. Looking for purpose.
15–17 years Middle Adolescence Senior High	Strengthening. Girls reach full adult height and build. Boys grow slowly, and coordination catches up.	Mentally alert. Able to engage in inductive and deductive reasoning. Emotionally experiencing new feelings — love, rejection, loyalty, etc.	Dating — period when boys and girls are interested in each other. Organized sports and clubs.	Looking for reality. Critical period — not interested in pat answers. Time for lifetime commitments.
18–22 years Late Adolescence College and Career	Boys reach full adult height and build. Both sexes at the peak of physical ability.	Mentally involved in synthesizing learned data. Preparation for life career. Emotionally stabilizing. Maturity.	Mate selection. Dating becomes more serious and moves into courtship.	Spiritual growth and commitment. Looking to put faith in action.

that of adults. Much of Piaget's research has centered on the cognitive development of children; that is, how they grow from a child's cognitive processes to adult cognitive processes. Piaget also argues that this development is systematic. Piaget has divided this systematic development into a series of periods. He says that the periods are *sequential* and *necessary*. By sequential he means that they must follow in order; a later period cannot precede an earlier period. By necessary he means that a child cannot skip a period; each period must precede the next. The ages attached to the periods are statistical averages; some children will enter a period earlier, and some later. Each child proceeds at his or her own pace. This leads to another point: Piaget postulates that humans have a *readiness factor;* that is, there are critical periods of development. By readiness factor is meant that at a certain point in his or her development a child is ready to master a specific task. Attempts to teach that behavior to the child before he or she is ready will result in frustration. However, when the critical period of development is reached, the child can readily master the task.

Piaget's Periods of Development

Piaget's model divides the process of cognitive development into four periods: (1) sensorimotor, (2) preoperational, (3) concrete operations, and (4) formal operations. We will look at each of these periods and discuss some of their basic characteristics.

Sensorimotor Period

This period covers the first two years of life. Piaget (1952) has divided this period into six stages. *Stage one,* birth to one month, is characterized by innate reflexes, such as sucking and grasping. Some of these reflexes combine to form primitive schemes, such as the sucking and swallowing reflexes to allow nursing. The infant is totally egocentric and is unable to distinguish between self and the environment. *Stage two,* one to four months, is characterized by the infant's ability to distinguish the limits of his or her own body and engages in repetitious movements. *Stage three,* four to eight months, is characterized by the baby's ability to adopt familiar and simple learned behaviors to new situations. The baby's interest begins to shift from his or her own body to the environment. The baby will grasp for objects within sight, but if the object is put out of sight, under a blanket for example, the baby will act as if it does not exist. *Stage four*, eight to twelve months, is characterized by intentional behavior. At this stage the baby will reach under the blanket for the object. The baby is quite mobile and engages in a great deal of imitative behavior and enjoys imitating sounds. *Stage five*, twelve to eighteen months, finds the child walking, responding to simple verbal directions, and recognizing familiar persons and objects. *Stage six*, eighteen to twenty-four months, is marked by the beginning of the acquisition of language. It is a transition to the next period.

Preoperational Period

This period covers from two years to seven years of age. Piaget has divided this period into *two stages*. The *first stage* is the *preconceptual stage*, two to four years. The main characteristics of this stage are language acquisition and the use of symbols. The child begins the process of conceptualization, such as associating height and age or adding *ed* to verbs for past tense, but tends to overgeneralize. The child is egocentric and assumes that everyone sees the world as he or she does.[1] The child cannot mentally understand another person's point of view. For example, a child at this stage can be taught the behavior of sharing but cannot comprehend the concept of sharing. The child must be taught to share in each specific situation.

The *second stage* of this period is the *prelogical or intuitive stage*, from four to seven years. One of the major characteristics of this stage is that the child cannot master the principle of conversation. This means that he or she

---

[1]There is a difference between being egocentric and selfish. The egocentric person cannot understand another's point of view and so naturally does what he or she wants. The selfish person can understand another's point of view, but disregards it and selfishly does what he or she wants. The egocentric person has no idea the other will be upset. The selfish person does understand but still acts.

cannot conceive of a thing being the same in different states. When my son was about four years old, he saw me put water in an ice-cube tray and put it in the freezer. Later he saw me take out ice cubes. Then he asked me, "Who took the water away and put the ice cubes in the tray?" Piaget uses a classic experiment to demonstrate this point. He takes a tall, thin drinking glass and a short, fat drinking glass, each of which holds the same amount of fluid, and, in front of the child pours water from one to the other. To an adult this would be a clear demonstration that they hold the same amount of fluid. When both glasses are then filled, and a child in this stage is asked which glass has the most water in it, the child invariably replies that the tall glass has the most water.

Another characteristic of this stage is that the child judges naughtiness in terms of damage rather than intention. When a child in this stage is told a story about a boy who breaks a dozen cups accidentally and a boy who breaks one cup intentionally, and then is asked which boy deserves the greater punishment, the child usually replies that the boy who broke twelve cups deserves the greater punishment. When the child is asked why, the response is that he broke more cups.

The child continues to be egocentric at this stage. If you observe parents or other adults dealing with young children, you will frequently hear them ask the child, "How do you think that made Bobby feel?" or some other question that asks the child to see the situation from another person's point of view. They might as well have asked the child to solve an algebraic equation. The child is incapable of seeing another's point of view.

Concrete Operations Period

This period runs from the seventh to the twelfth year. This stage is a giant step toward adult thinking. At this point the child is able to master the principle of conversation, is able to judge naughtiness in terms of intention, and can master what Piaget calls *reversibility*. Reversibility is what makes possible deductions such as "If one plus one equals two, then two minus one must equal one."

From a Christian perspective, one of the interesting characteristics of this stage is that the child becomes less egocentric and is able to see things from another's point of view. This makes it possible for a child to comprehend the message of the gospel. Howard Newsom writes,

> Children in concrete operations are fully capable of understanding their need for a personal Savior. Most children will gladly respond to an invitation to commitment. Studies indicate that a larger percentage of people become Christians during this age span than at any other period of life (1978:40).

Formal Operations Period

Extending from twelve years of age to adulthood, this period involves the ability to reason logically and think abstractly. The youngster is capable of inductive and deductive reasoning. In other words, in this stage there is full adult cognitive ability. While Piaget does not have stages within this period, he points out that not all adults reach the full development of this stage.

STYLES OF PARENTING

As we saw earlier in this chapter, there is not a basic model for parenting in our society. In fact, many different styles of parenting are practiced. LeMasters (1970) has classified styles of parenting into five basic models. While any classification scheme has its limitations and tends to oversimplify, LeMasters' approach is a useful means of organizing a discussion of parenting. His five models are the martyr, the buddy or pal, the policeman or drill sergeant, the teacher-counselor, and the athletic coach.

The Martyr Model

In this model parents have the attitude that nothing is too good for their children, and they claim they would do anything or make any sacrifice for their children. According to LeMasters, there are several characteristics found with this model. One is parental guilt. The parent generally feels he or she is never doing a good enough job.

Another characteristic is overprotection. The overprotection may result from guilt. The parent is afraid that something may hurt the child and attempts to create a super-safe environment for the child. These parents spoil their children, fail to set realistic goals for them, and seldom hold them accountable.

LeMasters found that this model often was used by divorced parents, parents with poor marriages, and parents with handicapped children. The response of the child to this type of parenting is generally either open revolt or meek submission. Whichever outward behavior is exhibited, the child feels hostility and resentment toward the parent. The parent, as a martyr, continues to do "what is best" for the child in the face of this resentment and hostility.

The Buddy or Pal Model

A number of parents in American society have adopted this model. LeMasters suggests that parents who adopt this model are following the expression, "If you can't beat them, join them." The parents are trying to influence and direct their children as a peer. Another reason for the popularity of this model, suggested by LeMasters, is the emphasis on youth in the American culture. Parents may be attempting to recapture some of their own youth.

LeMasters says one of the major problems with the buddy or pal model of parenting is that it is very difficult for the parent to retain authority. If the parent attempts to exercise authority, the child feels betrayed and resentful. LeMasters says it is easier for the traditional authoritarian parent to slacken the rules occasionally than for the buddy or pal parent to pull in the reins when necessary.

The Policeman or Drill Sergeant Model

This model of parenting involves setting strict rules and limits and punishing any and all infractions. The parent is the final authority and expects compliance with his or her rules. LeMasters feels that this model generally will not work in American society for two reasons. First, the culture is antiauthoritarian. As he puts it, Americans are "allergic" to authority (1970:217). Second, adolescent peer influence is too powerful.

According to LeMasters, the only situation in which the policeman or drill sergeant model will work is one with abundant love. "Strict or even harsh discipline will be tolerated by many children," he says, "but warmth and love have to be so obvious and plentiful that the child can never doubt that the parent has the child's best interests at heart" (1970:217). LeMasters's conclusion about strictness and love is supported by more recent research (McClelland et. al. 1978:42–53, 114). From this study the researchers concluded that strictness in parenting inhibited the level of maturity children would attain unless there was love in the home. They write, "Further analysis showed that the impact of strictness depended very much on whether there was love in the home. If the mother really loved the child, how strict the parents were didn't seem to make much difference later on" (McClelland et. al. 1978:46). They add, "Father's affection for the child is also important for thinking maturity . . . it is important to realize that children of affectionate fathers . . . are, in fact, more apt to think and reason in ways that show tolerance and understanding" (McClelland et al. 1978:49).

The Teacher-Counselor Model

LeMasters calls this the developmental model. He says the child is seen as a moldable organism with its potential limited only by its opportunities. While parents practicing this model may be firm in their discipline, they are never harsh. These parents tend to use psychological punishment rather than physical punishment. The parent is viewed as having the right answers and guides the child. A good teacher-counselor puts the needs of the child first.

This model reflects the philosophy of John Dewey. LeMasters says this model has been the dominant one of many middle-class parents, and he believes that this model tends to be too permissive. Also, since the parent is expected to be the expert, it tends to produce anxiety and guilt. LeMasters also feels this model caters too much to the needs of the child, and this is unhealthy because in society there must be a balance between the needs of the individual and the good of society.

The Athletic Coach Model

In this model, the parent functions much as an athletic coach. As a coach prepares his or her players for the game, so a parent prepares his or her child for the game of life. The coach cannot play the game for the players, but only prepares and trains the players for the game. The coach uses discipline, support, training, and example to prepare the players. Again, LeMasters feels that love is an important ingredient for this model.

CHILD ABUSE

Whichever model of parenting they use, parents are supposed to care for and protect their children. While most parents do take care of their children in a reasonable manner, a growing number of parents engage in behavior that is harmful to their child's physical and/or emotional health and welfare. Over two hundred thousand cases of physical abuse and almost one hundred thousand cases of sexual abuse of children are reported each year (Golanty and Harris 1982:257). Another one hundred thousand are neglected each year (Lamanna and Riedmann 1981:417). Approximately six thousand deaths are attributed to child abuse each year. Many experts in this field believe that the reported cases are only the tip of the iceberg. These authorities estimate that the true number of cases of child abuse is closer to two million incidents a year. One researcher believes that the actual number of deaths from child abuse may be as high as fifty thousand a year. He says that many of these deaths are reported as "accidents" (Lamanna and Riedmann 1981:418). Whatever the true figures may be, this is a serious problem of significant magnitude.

Types of Child Abuse

Although there is not an agreed-upon definition or categories of child abuse, one commonly used typology looks at four areas of child abuse: (1) physical abuse, (2) sexual abuse, (3) psychological abuse, and (4) neglect (Dworetzky 1981:401).

Physical Abuse

One study found that 3.5 percent of the parents surveyed admitted they had reacted with physical violence sufficient to cause injury toward at least one of their children in the past year (Dworetzky 1981:401). Of those cases of child abuse reported by physicians, approximately 67 percent had bruises and/or welts; 32 percent had abrasions, contusions, or lacerations; 10 percent had been burned or scalded; 8 percent had wounds or punctures; and 5 percent had skull fractures (Dworetzky 1981:401).

Sexual Abuse

In the early 1980s in Minnesota, in a well-publicized case involving several sensational trials, two brothers, their wives, and the brothers' parents were all sentenced to jail for having sexual relations with their children and grandchildren. It was alleged that the children were forced to engage in sexual acts with their parents, aunts and uncles, and grandparents in a group setting. I know a therapist who counseled with a young father who had been the victim of sexual abuse by his father and had just discovered his father was abusing his son. He also counseled with two girls who had been sexually abused by their fathers. In one case the girl was a pastor's daughter who feared her father was now abusing her younger sister. Are these isolated instances? Unfortunately they are not. One authority has concluded that at least one out of every hundred women in the United States has been sexually abused by her father (Press, Morris, and Sandza 1981:30). Other researchers say it is one woman in seventy-five (Herman and Hirschman 1980: 266). These researchers report on a study of court cases involving incest that found 90 percent of the cases involved fathers or stepfathers and daughters. Homosexual abuse of sons by fathers accounted for 5 percent of the cases. The remainder involved mothers and sons. They also cite another study that found that 92 percent of the victims of sexual abuse were girls; however, 97 percent of the offenders were men (Herman and Hirschman 1980:266).

In researching the case histories of sexual abuse, which usually involves fathers or stepfathers and daughters, researchers have found a familiar pattern. The victims are generally the eldest or only daughters. They were first approached sexually between the ages of six and nine. Sexual contact was usually continuous, lasting an average of three years. Psychological rather than physical force was generally used, and the relationship was kept secret. In more than half the cases the mothers were incapacitated by illness or mental problems or absent from the home due to work. The daughters had taken over many of the mothers' household tasks. The relationship between the mothers and daughters frequently was strained.

Sexual abuse is often difficult to uncover for two reasons. First, the victim must describe to strangers intimate and embarrassing incidents. Second, the victim must betray his or her parent and risk destroying the family. With this problem being brought out into the open and the victims being able to realize they are not the only ones in this type of situation, it is hoped that victims may be more willing to confide in others who can help them.

Psychological Abuse

Parents who would never think of physically harming their children may engage in behavior that results in emotional damage. Dr. Shirley O'Brien, a human development specialist, writes:

> Emotional abuse comes in many forms and disguises, such as the following: teasing, yelling, desertion, disinterest, name calling, downgrading, continual criticism, scary threats, and any other behavior that destroys or damages a child's self-esteem or self-image.
>
> The type of emotional abuse that is especially detrimental is verbal abuse that bombards the child until he not only has lost his self-esteem but develops a negative self-image because of constant negative reinforcement (1980:20).

In psychological abuse the distinction between normal and abnormal behavior is often difficult to define. Most parents tease, yell at their children, are disinterested, criticize, and use threats from time to time. If this type of behavior is continual and not offset by positive behaviors and results in psychological harm to the child, it may be diagnosed as psychological abuse.

Neglect

Some authorities treat neglect as a separate topic; others include it under child abuse. Wherever it is considered, the effect is the same on its victims. O'Brien defines neglect as "withholding necessary food, clothing, shelter, and education opportunities, or other forms of inadequate care and supervision that might lead to endangering the child's well being" (1980:9). She adds, "Neglect also means withholding love, socialization, and proper stimulation" (1980:9). It is estimated that as many as one third of abused children also suffer from some form of neglect (Justice and Justice 1976:19). For example, in the United States, it is estimated that 40 percent of all children have not been properly immunized against disease (Dworetzky 1981:401). Due to neglect many children have never been seen by a dentist, and almost a third of the children in the United States have an iron-deficient diet (Bee 1981:125).

Abusive Parents

What type of person would abuse his or her own child? Child abusers come from all social classes, races, ages, and both sexes. There is no typical child abuser. However, there are some social factors that are associated with child abuse. Abuse is highest among young parents, the unemployed, those in lower socioeconomic levels, and those who were abused themselves as children (Scanzoni and Scanzoni 1981:586–87).

Abused Children

Again, children of all races, ages, and social classes are the victims of abuse. However, there are certain social factors that are often associated with child abuse. Young children between the ages of three months to three years are the most susceptible to physical abuse (Scanzoni and Scanzoni 1981:587). Children in large families (four or more siblings) are more frequently subject to abuse. The children of unwed mothers and those resulting from an unwanted pregnancy have a greater chance of being victims of abuse (Scanzoni and Scanzoni 1981:587).

According to one researcher, there are three reasons why young children under four years of age are more frequently the victims of physical abuse. First, a small child is more susceptible to injury from physical punishment because of its frailty. Infants are particularly prone to head injuries. Second, parents easily become frustrated with very young children because they cannot reason or communicate with them. Third, the young child, by its very presence, may be creating economic hardship, disrupting the marital relationship, or in other ways creating stress for the parents (Scanzoni and Scanzoni 1981: 581–88).

CHRISTIAN CHILD REARING

We have looked at the role of parenthood, various models of parenting, and some malfunctions of parenting. Parenting is a topic that the Bible also addresses. Parents are instructed to teach their children the Word of God (Deut. 6:6–9; 11:18–21; Prov. 22:6; Eph. 6:4). Parents are also told to discipline their children (Prov. 13:24; 23:13–14; 29:15, 17). In addition, parents are commanded to instruct and discipline their children in a way that does not provoke them (Eph. 6:4; Col. 3:21).

Several Christian authors have written on the application of these principles. Paul Meier (1977) a psychiatrist, drawing on his psychiatric training and his study of the Word of God, has come up with five principles for Christian child rearing: (1) love, (2) discipline, (3) consistency, (4) example, and (5) the father.

Love

Meier says that two types of love are necessary for effective parenting. First, the mother and father must love each other, and second, the parents must love the child. He argues that love is the basis of Christianity. God demonstrated His love by sending His Son to die for our sins (John 3:16). As God loves His children, so parents should love their children. The essence of love is found in 1 Corinthians 13:4–7. We saw earlier that social research on parenting recognizes the importance of love in child rearing.

Love also helps a child develop a good self-image and self-confidence. We love what we value. As parents show their children that they love them, they are showing them that they value them. As parents value their children, the children will come to value themselves. When we love someone, we want to do what is best for that person. One of the best ways to build self-worth and self-confidence in a youngster is by the use of sincere praise. Flattery will backfire but sincere praise will build up the child. Every child has characteristics and behaviors that are praise-worthy. If parents would be just half as quick with praise as they are with criticism, they would see tremendous changes. Actually, a good rule might be to use twice as much praise as criticism. Where flattery builds false pride, praise will build a positive self-image.

Discipline

Meier agrees with Dobson (1970) that a quick spanking is an effective means of disciplining young children. Dobson expands on this. He feels that spankings should be restricted to incidents of rebellion. However, Dobson believes that parents should use positive reinforcement where possible. That is, parents should reinforce desired behaviors.

Discipline involves teaching correct behavior as much as it involves correcting wrong behavior. Many times it is more profitable to concentrate on the correct behavior rather than on the wrong behavior. By way of example, a parent asks a child to straighten up her bedroom. The parent comes to check on the bedroom and finds the job well done—except for some items left on the dresser. What is the parent most likely to say to the child? You are right. The parent will probably comment on the dresser, pointing out what was not done. What would be more effective in this case would be to praise the child for the work that was done correctly. That is reinforcing the behavior the parent wants to see continued. Psychological research clearly indicates that in most situations rewards are more effective behavior modifiers than punishment.

Discipline also involves setting guidelines and limitations. Guidelines and limitations not only function to keep the child in line but also to keep problems out. Boundaries provide security and protection. No matter how hard young people fight against the boundaries parents set for them, they need them and want them. It is a paradox, but there can be freedom only within boundaries. Without boundaries you do not have freedom but anarchy. Parents need to provide their children with guidelines and limitations in order for them to develop healthy and happy lives.

Consistency

Parents need to be consistent in their discipline as well as consistent with each other. They should agree on rules and punishment. If one is lenient and the other is strict, the child learns that discipline is arbitrary. If parents have a disagreement about discipline, they should deal with it privately.

Parents also need to be consistent with discipline from situation to situation and time to time. Children are smart. My children will ask my wife for something when she is on the phone or busy with something because they believe she will say yes to get rid of them. It is important for parents to be consistent and fair.

Example

It really does not matter what we *say;* children learn from what we *do.* Most values are caught—not taught. We are all familiar with the expression, "Do as I say, not as I do." Unfortunately, it does not work that way. Modeling is one of the most powerful teaching methods. It can be used for good or harm.

Father

Not only does the Bible put a great deal of emphasis on the father, but social research confirms the importance of the father in child rearing. In our society many fathers have abdicated their responsibilities. They may still be feeding and clothing their children, but they are not involved with child rearing. It is important for the father to be involved in his children's lives. He should be involved in discipline, spiritual development, education, and recreation.

Dan Kiley (1978), a child psychologist, has written a book entitled *Nobody Said It Would Be Easy*. There is a lot of truth in that title. Parenting is hard work and requires responsibility and dedication. It is also a rewarding experience.

DISCUSSION QUESTIONS

1. Why do you think American society provides so little preparation for the role of parenthood?
2. What, in your opinion, is the reason that the role of parent is not well defined in the North American culture?
3. Do you believe that fathers should be entitled to maternity leaves from work, the same as mothers, to help care for the new baby? Why?
4. Which of LeMasters's five models of parenting do you believe would be most effective? Why?
5. In your opinion why is there so much child abuse in the American society and what can be done about it?
6. What principles for parenting do you find in Deuteronomy 6:6–9; Proverbs 2:1; 3:1; 13:24; 22:6; and Ephesians 6:4?

SUGGESTED READING

Jerry J. Bigner, *Parent-Child Relations: An Introduction to Parenting* (New York: Macmillan, 1979). A good basic introduction to parenting; the book deals with the role of parenthood. It also deals with child development and the role and responsibilities of the parent at each stage.

James Dobson, *Dare to Discipline* (Wheaton, Ill.: Tyndale, 1970). A popular work on child rearing in general and discipline in particular. Written from a Christian viewpoint, it draws heavily on a behaviorist perspective.

_____. *Hide or Seek* (Old Tappan, N.J.: Revell, 1974). This book deals with building self-esteem in children—an important topic, particularly for the Christian community.

John P. Dworetzky, *Introduction to Child Development* (St. Paul:

West, 1981). A good basic introduction to child development, it deals with the various stages of development, with good coverage of Piaget's theory of cognitive development.

Paul D. Meier, *Christian Child-Rearing and Personality Development* (Grand Rapids: Baker, 1977). Written by a Christian psychiatrist, this book covers self-concept, human development, spiritual development, and parenting. Useful and informative, but weak on biblical application.

Shirley O'Brien, *Child Abuse* (Provo, Utah: Brigham Young University Press, 1980). A good introduction to child abuse, this book deals with the history and definition of child abuse and offers some good suggestions for dealing with it. The work discusses the abuser as well as the abused.

12

The Middle Years

The middle of the thirties is literally the mid point of life. The halfway mark. No gongs ring, of course. But twinges begin. Deep down a change begins to register in those gut-level perceptions of safety and danger, time and no time, aliveness and stagnation, self and others.

GAIL SHEEHY (1976:242)

MIDDLE AGE, WHAT is it? Some people speak of mid-life, middlescence, and middle age as interchangeable concepts; others see them as being distinct. We will treat them as synonymous concepts. But to what do they refer? One writer sees this period as beginning when we have completed our preparation for life and ending at retirement (Howe 1959). Other writers see this period covering the years from thirty to seventy (Maas and Kuypers 1974; Hulme 1962). Still others see it as the forties (Fried 1967; Peterson 1967; Goolrick 1975), while yet another writer puts it as forty to sixty-five (Clinebell 1977). A friend of mine suggests that people should multiply their age by two at every birthday, and when the result is more years than they expect to live, they have arrived at middle age. A survey of the literature indicates that there is no general agreement on the beginning or ending of middle age. For our purposes, we will consider middle age as the years from thirty-five to fifty-five.[1]

---

[1]It should be noted that the U.S. Census Bureau uses forty-five to sixty-four as middle age, and many sociologists follow this because that is the way data is collected by the Census Bureau. However, these ages do not cover the years when many crises occur—the late thirties and early forties. Psychologists generally prefer to use thirty-five to fifty-five or other years in this range.

Who are the people that make up this age group? According to 1980 census figures, about 52 percent are women and 48 percent are men. They are generally economically well-off and have the lowest unemployment rate of all age groups. Their income is at or near their lifetime peak. Chief executives and members of corporate boards have generally reached those positions by age fifty-five; their average annual compensation is about three hundred thousand dollars a year. While that kind of income is not typical of most middle-aged people, the average income of middle-aged people is well above the national average. People between forty-five to fifty-four years of age head about 15 percent of all households, but account for almost 21 percent of all household income. Middle-aged couples are more likely to own their own home. More than three out of four families headed by a person age fifty-five live in their own home. Middle-aged persons are less likely to be victims of crime than the general population. They also have a higher voter turnout rate—almost 70 percent compared to a national average of under 55 percent.

More than eight out of ten persons in their middle years live in a family. The divorce rate for this age group is well below the national average, but it has doubled since 1950. Almost two out of three couples have no children under eighteen years of age living at home by the time the couple reaches age fifty-five. It is during this period of life that many individuals face a series of crises. In this chapter we will examine some of these crises and see how they affect marriage and the family.

Before we look at these crises, it should be pointed out that we will be dealing with generalizations, statistical norms, averages, and case studies. The reader should be careful not to stereotype persons in this age range or assume that everyone will go through each of these crises with equal intensity. For some persons middle age is a smooth transition with few problems. However, for many others it is a turbulent time with significant crises and problems. Because many readers of this book are college students whose parents are in this age bracket and because individuals and couples in this age range make up a significant part of most of our churches and hold many of the offices and positions of responsibility, it is important for us to understand this age group. We will explore some of the unique crises of this stage of life and offer some suggestions for dealing with them.

PHYSICAL-PSYCHOLOGICAL DIMENSION

As one considers the human life cycle, there are two periods or stages that involve major physiological changes with accompanying emotional crises. The first of these periods is puberty. During this stage the physical changes are rapid and obvious. Both males and females develop pubic hair. Females develop breasts, experience the onset of menses, and in general begin the process of becoming women. Males develop facial hair; experience growth of the larynx, which leads to a change of voice; experience the enlargement of their genitals as well as the ability to ejaculate; and in general begin the process of becoming men.

While the physiological changes that take place during puberty are fairly rapid and obvious, the changes that take place during the second stage that involves major physiological changes—middle age—are more gradual and not always obvious. The years between these two stages are active years. The person is preparing for his/her life work, entering the courtship process, marrying, having and raising children, as well as making a drive for occupational success.

The emotional dimension is closely tied to the physical dimension of change. It is impossible to separate the emotional and physical dynamics in middle life. Edmund Bergler thinks that this stage of life has two desperations. "One is acute tiredness. The other is the need to affirm masculinity (or femininity) and self-worth" (Bergler 1958:2).

Some physiological changes that take place during this stage are common to both men and women, and some are unique to each sex. First we will look at those changes that are common to both sexes. For most persons the peak of physical strength and stamina comes in the late twenties and early thirties. By age thirty-five most adults begin to notice a slight decline in both strength and stamina. For example, very few professional athletes are still competing after age thirty-five, and those few who do continue to play usually play "skill" positions where their experience can make up for loss of speed and strength. Fran Tarkenton, a quarterback for the Minnesota Vikings played injury-free football until his mid-thirties but was injured his last two seasons, was unable to throw long passes, and finally retired at the old age of thirty-nine.

Discussing Tarkenton's injuries raises another characteristic of middle age; people become more prone to major illness. As Rouch points out:

> Our first major illness is likely to occur in middlescence. Whether it does or not, we will be confronted with the deaths of relatives or close friends. Death thus becomes more immediate than before . . . combined with our natural bodily changes, (it) is a powerful force pulling us toward inwardness (1974:122).

Sheehy sees facing one's death as the major issue or crisis of middle age. She says:

> Each of us stumbles upon the major issue of midlife somewhere in the decade between 35 and 45. Though this can also be an ordinary passage with no outer event to mark it, eventually we all confront the reality of our own death. And somehow we must learn to live with it. The first time that message comes through is probably the worst (1976:8).

Not only do individuals face declining physical strength and well-being in themselves, but, for the married, also in their partner. In addition, married people are confronted not only with their own death but also with the death or loss of their partner.

Other physical changes that are common to both men and women are changes in appearance. The body metabolism in both sexes changes during this period, and there is a tendency to put on weight. This tendency is so common it has come to be called "middle-aged spread." Women's breasts and buttocks, which were firm and well shaped, begin to sag. Women experience menopause during this period, and this can result in both physical and emotional changes. Both men and women begin to get double and triple chins, wrinkles, facial sags, and graying hair. Many men will begin to bald during this period. These physical changes are related to those aspects of an appearance that are associated with "sex appeal," or attractiveness to the opposite sex. Frequently, during this stage both men and women feel that they are losing their attractiveness to the opposite sex, and there is a tendency to want to "prove they still have it." While it is more common for a man to have an affair during this stage, women are also prone to extramarital affairs.

On the other hand, the failing attractiveness of a marriage partner along with declining physical stamina can often cause the sexual dimension to become a growing problem for the married couple. With the lessening of sexual drive comes an added need for closeness, stability, acceptance, and companionship. All of these changes subtly put additional burden on a marriage and the relationship between marriage partners.

As Belkin and Goodman point out, middle age is a period of adjustments. They believe that middle-aged couples are often caught between two conflicting expectations. They write:

> For many years the sexual expectations of married couples in middlescence were consistent with the myth of less sexual activity. Therefore, they were not at least superficially, troubled by the decline in their marital sex life. But things have changed, middle-aged couples now have greater sexual expectations, but they may find themselves confused about their new roles and the "new norms" of middle-age sexuality . . . to some extent these new norms may be just as unrealistic as the old ones, and they may place just as many social pressures upon couples to conform to values they do not feel comfortable with (1980:357).

It is a myth that couples become asexual in their middle years. Clinebell reports on a study that found that couples between forty-five and fifty-four had a median frequency of sexual intercourse of once a week (1977:50). Clinebell argues that sex in middle age can be rich and rewarding. He suggests eight guidelines for sexual enrichment in the middle years:

1. Liberate your attitudes about sex.
2. Keep your total relationship growing, and sex will tend to improve.

3. Discover and enjoy the special romance and new meanings that are possible in mid-years sex.

4. Create new ways to let your inner "child" sides play.

5. Discover what you enjoy most and coach each other on how to give maximum mutual enjoyment.

6. Enjoy leisurely nondemanding pleasuring.

7. Avoid the triple traps of hurry, fatigue, and too much alcohol.

8. If do-it-yourself methods such as those described above do not enhance your sex life sufficiently, get the help of a trained sex therapist who is also trained in marriage counseling (1977:51–58).

CAREER DIMENSION

Some time between the ages of thirty-five and fifty-five both men and women will face a crisis period in their careers. Thirty or thirty-five is usually felt to be a turning-point age when a person is no longer "young" or "just starting out" or "preparing for a career" but has reached a climactic point of readjustment. The woman, if married, may feel a little desperate about soon becoming too old to return to her career. The working wife realizes that if she doesn't quit work and have a family soon, it will be too late. The single woman in her early thirties can no longer "mark time" waiting for the "right man" to come along. She suddenly realizes that she may never be married, and she must make a life for herself alone.

The married man in his early thirties now tries to refine and narrow his goals. He feels the pressure to put everything into his goal of reaching the top. The early thirties are usually not as great a crisis time for a man as they are for a woman. He will hit the mid-life career crisis in his early forties. He suddenly realizes that he may never reach the top, or that the goal he set has been reached (or is within reach), and it brings no satisfaction, or he feels bored and in a dead-end, locked-in position. He knows that the early goals and values have to be adjusted.

Age becomes the enemy for both men and women as they realize half of their lives are over, and there is a desperate "now or never" feeling about life. The family budget is under heavy strain as the children go to college. The "nest is empty," or almost, and the woman's all-consuming mothering roles come to an end. Now is the switch time, a time of readjustment for the couple and their family. The woman, after years of nurturing, now starts to build her self-identity. The man after years of building his self-identity now reexamines his values and often seeks deeper meaning in life through relationships and causes.

During middlescence the person has usually finished raising his or her children and probably has reached a plateau in occupation. At this point in life most people have a good picture of what they can accomplish occupationally. This insight, along with the empty-nest syndrome with all the role reversals that go with it, is very traumatic. The family has to be reorganized, and new roles and expectations must be accepted.

"It is not through more caregiving that a woman looks for a replenishment of purpose in the second half of her life," says Gail Sheehy. "It is through cultivating talents left half-finished, permitting ambition once piggybacked, becoming aggressive in the service of her own convictions rather than a passive-aggressive party to someone else's" (1976:294). When the period of procreation ends for the woman, her creative energies can be poured into new pursuits. Sheehy states, "If the struggle for men in mid-life comes down to having to defeat stagnation through generativity, I submit that the comparable task for women is to transcend dependency through self-declaration" (1976:294).

Marriages can be shaken by the mid-life crisis. The husband can become envious of the time his wife now spends on herself and her new career. He is used to being the center of her life and can't help thinking rather selfishly, "She should be here when I need her." The wife in her anxiety as she goes "back to work" becomes self-absorbed and a little frantic as she tries to fit into the academic or working world. The husband, instead of being supportive as she was when he was starting out, often sees her excitement and self-awareness as a threat. After the crisis period and adjustments are made, the husband and grown children experience pride in the wife and mother's accomplishments. They are pleased that she is not dependent on them for her identity and happiness and that she is becoming an ever more interesting person.

Emotional stability during this period is threatened. Life often centers around the children of the home; so when they go out on their own, it brings on a need for reordering expectations and roles. Many people have so much emotional involvement invested in their children that letting loose of their hold on them and a reordering of expectations and roles is difficult. This situation threatens the very personhood of many parents. These problems of emotional instability can creep into a marriage relationship and have the potential to be devastating. At the time children leave home it is usually when occupational concerns and business are at a peak. This concern occupies the attention of one or both spouses while at the same time as marriage partners they are in deep need for renewed companionship. This need for companionship is multiplied by the fact that the children have left the home.

The man in his mid-life crisis often cries out from boredom and frustration, "I need a change!" This is the same cry of the woman who has spent her married life in one occupation—that of homemaker. Each needs to see his or her work as having purpose. Attitudes have a great deal to do with dissatisfaction and boredom. Reuel Howe in *The Creative Years* describes some ways that attitudes must change:

1. Our attitude toward ourselves as persons in a world of things. Rather than resent this person-thing dilemma, we should expect it. Much of our time is devoted to the business of living in which our relation to one another is relatively impersonal and functional.

2. We need to change our attitude toward work to one of acceptance because it is socially necessary and meets some aspect of human need.

3. We need to see our work as a part of God's work. A job, any job that serves a constructive purpose, even a menial job, has the meaning of a ministry; and by our faithfulness to it, we serve both God and man (1959:176–80).

Understanding is necessary on the part of husband and wife as each goes through the mid-life crisis.

> The intensity of the middle-age crisis depends on the need-satisfyingness of the relationship and particularly on the success achieved in the previous stages of intimacy. If the basic art of loving mutually was learned during the young adult years, most couples take the middle-years crisis in stride. They reexamine their relationship and shift some patterns, but they know how to relate and how to go about changing and deepening their marriage to meet the needs of the second half of life. . . .
>
> The middle years can be highly productive and creative in which each partner finds new stimulation in developing interests and activities. Some of the energy that was formerly invested in the children is available for reinvestment in a second career for the wife, new hobbies for the husband, and joint projects in which the couple finds new meanings by giving themselves to meet some need in society (Clinebell and Clinebell 1970:127–30).

FAMILY DIMENSION

Married couples do not live in isolation. Each partner is a member of two families: the family of orientation, the one they are born into; and the family of procreation, the one they form by marriage. Changes take place in both of these families during the middle years.

As we have previously pointed out, during the parents' middle years children have usually grown and are in the process of leaving home. Ideally, parents are to give their children room to become autonomous throughout their childhood development. This is not an easy task because our nature is to cling to those we love rather than giving them opportunity to become independent. But no matter how good of a job the parents have done at making this transition more bearable, it still hurts. As James Peterson has so vividly expressed it, "Often both parents wander about the home and look at mementos from an exhilarating past—and try to remember how these rooms, now so still, used to echo with rock and roll, loud laughter, or singing" (1968:42).

This transition is much more difficult when the husband and wife have for the past eighteen or twenty years made their relationship revolve around the children instead of the enhancement of their own lives together. We often see that divorce occurs during this time of life because when the children leave, the parents are often left facing each other, asking the question, "Who are you?" It is most important that the husband and wife regularly evaluate their relationship with one another. They need to keep the lines of communication open so they can grow together, rather than apart.

This crisis we have been discussing is commonly referred to as the "empty-nest syndrome." It is a phenomenon of the last half of the twentieth century. In previous generations women continued to bear children throughout their fertile years, often having their last child in their late thirties or early forties. By the time the last child left home, the couple were at or near the end of their life. However, today most couples have had their last child before they are thirty and have life expectancies in the mid seventies. That means the last child will leave home before they are fifty, leaving them with twenty to thirty years of life remaining.

If the couple have built their lives around their children, there may be little left to their relationship. In fact, couples who have stayed together "for the sake of the children" may have little or no incentive to maintain the relationship after the nest is empty. At this time a couple can easily lose touch with each other. They may either divorce or live together as roommates, but not as husband and wife.

On the other hand, research indicates that marital satisfaction often increases during this period (Green 1978:326). The couple is usually reasonably well off financially, still in relatively good health, and with productive years left. These years can be a time of growth for them both as individuals and as a couple. They can be a period when the couple can spent time and resources on themselves that had been spent previously on the children. This can be an exciting time for couples that are committed to each other and their relationship.

While children are leaving home, changes are also taking place in their families of orientation. About the time a couple become free from the responsibilities of child rearing, they may find that they have to pick up responsibilities related to aging parents. Again, this is an area where recent changes in life expectancy and family size will have profound implications. In 1900, only about 42 percent of the population lived to be sixty-five, and life expectancy was forty-seven years. By 1973, over 70 percent of the population lived to be sixty-five. In 1973 that meant that out of four parents, a couple could expect three or four of their parents to live to age sixty-five. That means a couple may end up with double the number of aged parents to care for. Also, family size has been reduced since 1900. This means that there are fewer brothers and sisters to share the responsibility for aged parents. Couples are frequently faced with the agonizing decision of placing aged parents in a nursing home or bringing them into their home. Middle-aged couples also face the deaths of their parents.

HUSBAND AND WIFE RELATIONSHIP

We have examined some of the crises and problems faced by couples during their middle years. We have discussed some ways these changes may impact the husband-wife relationship. The various crises of middle age may act as a wedge to drive a couple apart, or as an opportunity to pull them together. Actually, a couple will most likely respond to the crisis of mid-life in the same ways they have learned to respond to crises earlier in their relationship. However, couples can develop strategies for dealing with the crises of middle age. Nelson Foote, a sociologist who has pioneered the developmental approach to the study of marriage and the family, says:

> To expect a marriage to last indefinitely under modern conditions is to expect a lot. Certainly marriage counselors report many cases of mates who disclose no specific cause of dissatisfaction, yet complain that they have lost interest in their marriage. Successful marriage may thus come to be defined, both by married people and students of marriage, in terms of its potential for continued development, rather than in terms of momentary assessments of adjustment (Quoted in Kephart 1981:377).

Reuel Howe, in his book *The Creative Years* (1959: 119–25), suggests five strategies for developing a creative marriage in the middle years. These strategies consist of five affirmations. We will discuss each of them and see how they apply.

1. *Since we are made in the image of God, there is more to each of us than the other sees.* After having lived with another person for twenty or more years, it is easy to believe we know all about our spouse and to take him or her for granted, forgetting that he or she was created in God's image. Even as we can never fully understand or know God so we can never fully understand or know another person. However, in the marriage relationship that understanding and knowledge should be growing. The more we seek to know and understand our partner, the deeper the relationship will grow.

This is expecially true because people are always changing. My wife and I have been married for eighteen years. I am not the same person I was eighteen years ago. There have been many changes in my personality. The same is true for my wife. In essence, we have to keep rediscovering each other. We are both growing people and need to keep up with each other's growth.

2. *You will find life by giving yourself and cherishing the other person.* As we saw in chapter 3 on dating (pp. 55–76), authentic love is not primarily an emotion but an act of the will. Love is behavior, thoughts, and actions. Emotions are the by-products of thoughts and actions. Authentic love is a commitment that carries married partners through crises so that they come out closer for the experience.

As we saw above, people are constantly changing, growing, and developing. The girl I "fell in love" with and married is now a mature woman and mother. She is not the same person that I first met. It is my opinion that, in a good marriage, a couple continually "refall in love." The commitment made at marriage needs to be constantly reconfirmed.

3. *The differences between man and woman can be good.* While I believe men and women are equal, I also recognize differences. The mistake of radical feminism has been to see *equal* and *same* as equivalent. Things and people can be different and of equal value and worth.

Without getting into the debate concerning whether the differences are genetic or cultural, there are differences between men and women. These differences can bring added dimensions to a relationship. The husband has the additional benefit of a female perspective on issues, and the wife has the benefit of a male perspective. I have four eyes to see the world with, my own and my wife's. She sees things I do not see and that is my gain. For a creative marriage, each partner needs to accept his or her own uniqueness and the uniqueness of the partner.

4. *Compatibility is the achievement of marriage, not a condition necessary to its beginning.* In many states incompatibility is grounds for divorce. Incompatibility, rather than being the basis for the destruction of a marriage, should become the dynamic for the growth of a marriage. Two normal, healthy human beings are not going to be able to live together in the intimacy of marriage and not have differences. These differences should not become obstacles that divide, but building blocks for growth.

5. *It takes time to be married.* We have an expression in the American culture that says, "Time is money." If that is so, then marriage requires a large investment. It may be said that one will get out of marriage what one puts into it. Some will argue that it is the quality of the time and not the amount of time that counts. They are half correct. The quality of the time is what counts, but it is not possible to have quality without sufficient quantity.

I once heard a chapel speaker say that he was glad to be married and past the dating stage of his life. I am married but have not passed the dating stage—and hope I never do. My wife and I go out on a date at least once a week. We make time for each other. Time is necessary for a good relationship.

Harold Myra, publisher of *Christianity Today* and a middle-aged married man, has written a poem, "An Ode to Marriage," about marriage in the middle years. This poem catches the problems and potentials of mid-life marriage and reflects Howe's five affirmations:

"You know, it could happen to us,"
  you said to me,
    sitting in your favorite chair as we sipped coffee,
    digesting the news of the latest couples splitting up.

"No matter how great we think we have it,
 if all *those* people can break up
 it could happen to us.
We're humans like them.
It is possible."

I didn't answer for awhile.
We were both incredulous at the news.
Men and women of maturity
 decades-long marriages
 so many have exploded, one after another.
Almost every week, another set of names.
Not him! Not her!
They're too sensible, too solid.

"You're right," I finally admit.
We've never joked about divorce,
 never brought it up as an option.
We declared total commitment to each other
 and must reaffirm that always.
But maybe realizing it could happen to us
 helps us make sure it won't.

How terrible to think of an argument
 someday when one of us feels
 the need for the ultimate weapon,
"Well, obviously there's no sense staying
together. We're just hurting each other,
 just keeping each other trapped."
Those are words mouthed in kitchens
 and bedrooms of "mature" Christian homes.

Remember how our love began?
Years ago, I offered you my arm
 that September night we first went out.
You reached for it
 as we leaped a puddle together.
Then you walked just close enough
 to show you liked it.
I glimpsed your face under the streetlight,
 excitement splashing gently on it. . . .
No commitment—just beginnings.

My arm pulled you that January eve
 tight beside me in that car.
Midnight. Time to leave.
"Good night" wasn't quite enough,
 and our lips touched gently
 in a kiss as light as angel cake.

"I like you," it said,
  but nothing more.

November air had rough-scrubbed our faces.
As we wrestled playfully
  in your parent's farmhouse.
That moment I knew
  and breathed into your hair,
"I LOVE YOU."
The words exploded around us.
They meant far more than "you're nice."
They meant commitment.
Your words came back to me
  in firm, sure sounds:
"I love you too."
And our kiss of celebration
  was the beginning of a new creation.

Yes, I chose you.
Out of all the lovely girls I knew.
I chose you.
How marvelous are the women of planet Earth,
  hair flaring in the wind
  rich browns and golds
  a thousand delicious shapes
  girls who laugh saucily
  girls who read Browning
  girls who play sitars
  girls who fix carburetors.
Of all those fascinating possibilities,
I chose you.
Decisively. Permanently.
Is that self-entrapment?
Was a commitment made in youth
  to bind me a lifetime?
Ah, but it was as strong as birth,
  a fresh creation,
  soon to be a new flesh,
  you and I as one.

We chose each other.
We created something new under the sun.
You to shape me
  and I you,
  like a Luther Burbank original.
We, our own new creation,
  to produce fruit wholly unique,
UNIQUE IN THE UNIVERSE!

Then the wedding
    flying rice and honeymoon
    days and nights together.
Two persons
    as unalike as birch and cypress
    had chosen each other.
The heavens laughed
    and the sands of earth
    lay ready for the tender feet
    of our newborn self.
Does time change all that?
Were we naive? Now, after we have
    loved, argued, laughed, given birth,
what does it mean
    when I hold you and say,
    "I love you"?
Without the young-love ecstasy,
    is it required rote
    or reaffirmation of our new creation?

"I love you."
My temples don't pulse as I say it.
My body does not ache for coupling,
    not as it did.
Yet the words carry more fact
    than ever they did in courtship.
They embrace a million moments shared. . . .

Standing together
    atop Cadillac Mountain
    and aching to absorb the blue-white-green beauty. . . .
Or angrily expounding to each other in the kitchen
    about our particular stupidities,
    then sharing a kiss ten hours later. . . .
Bonding moments, holding us together.
How easily those bonds could be tyrannical.
"You always forget. . . ." "You never think. . . ."
And bitter moments bite into their flesh
    with binding ropes that tie them to the
    time and place instead of to each other.
Yet bonds can be a
    thousand multicolored strands
    of sorrow, joy, embarrassment,
    of anger, laughter shared
    as we watch God maturing us,

as we gently tell each other
of our joys, our fears,
even of our fantasies.
Rope is rope.
Experiences are much the same:
   crabby days
   laughing days,
   boring days.
We'll go through them "in love,"
   by commitment to each other,
   sharing, forgiving,
   not blaming, not hurting.
Yet when we do hurt,
   we ask forgiveness,
   so the ropes will bind us together.

For if they don't
   they'll wrap around our throats,
   so that each struggle will tighten the noose,
   and we'll have to reach for the knife to cut the bonds.
"I love you."
It sounds trite—
   but not if it's remembering
   the thousands of strands
   of loving each other when we don't feel lovely,
   of holding each other,
   of winking across a room,
   of eating peanut butter sandwiches besides the surf.
   and of getting up in the morning
   thousands of times, together,
   and remembering what we created
   the day we first said "I love you,"
Something permanent
   and growing
   and alive (1979:60–62).

DISCUSSION QUESTIONS

1. What do you think of when you think of a middle-aged person? Are your thoughts positive or negative? Why?

2. Male movie stars often retain their appeal to females into their fifties and sixties while female stars rarely retain their appeal past their forties. Why do you think this happens?

3. A recent study found that a sample of college students considered their parents sexually inactive. When the

parents of these students were surveyed, they were found to be, for the most part, sexually active. Why, do you think the college students thought their parents were sexually inactive?

4. Do you believe the empty-nest syndrome affects men or women more? Career women or homemakers? Why?

5. What do you see as the implications of longer life expectancies coupled with women having fewer children and completing their families before age thirty?

6. What do you see as the biblical response to the aging process? How should Christians react to middle age?

SUGGESTED READING

Reuel L. Howe, *The Creative Years* (Greenwich, Conn.: Seabury, 1959). A well-written captivating treatment of middle age. Writing from a Christian perspective, Howe deals with the crises of mid-life marriage and offers biblical, practical counsel for dealing with them.

Daniel J. Levinson et al. *The Seasons of a Man's Life* (New York: Knopf, 1978). A classic work dealing with middle age. It contains interesting case studies illustrating the phases of aging.

Henry S. Maas and Joseph A. Kuypers, *From Thirty to Seventy* (San Francisco: Jossey-Bass, 1974). A forty-year longitudinal study of adult lifestyles and personality. It deals with major issues related to both men and women.

Gail Sheehy, *Passages* (New York: Dutton, 1976). A well-written and popular book that is fast becoming a classic. This work contains a number of case studies and deals with the major crises of mid-life.

13

Aging and Death

Is not wisdom found among the aged?
Does not long life bring understanding?

JOB 12:12

Rise in the presence of the aged,
show respect for the elderly.

LEVITICUS 19:32

WHAT IS OLD AGE? When I was a teen-ager, I thought thirty was old. Now that I am forty, I think fifty is still young. Obviously, old age is relative. However, we have to make an arbitrary determination in order to be able to discuss this stage of life. If we call the years from thirty-five to fifty-five the middle years, then we might view the years from fifty-six to sixty-five as the *mature years*, and after age sixty-five, the *senior years*.

In one sense, we might say that people begin aging as soon as they are born. However, when we use the term *aging*, we are generally referring to a process of deterioration and movement toward death rather than just getting older. The first half of life is usually marked by growth and increasing strength, whereas the second half of life is marked by decline and increasing weakness. During the middle years this decline is generally gradual and often made up for by experience and knowledge. But as the person moves into the mature years, and especially the senior years, the rate of decline increases. Even experience and knowledge cannot always make up for diminished capacities.

As we discuss the characteristics of people in the mature and senior years, we need to be reminded again that we will be looking at generalizations, statistical averages, and norms. We need to be careful not to stereotype older persons. While one seventy-year-old during the 1980s was infirm, senile, and in a nursing home, another seventy-year-old served as president of the United States.

The senior years, or old age, begin at sixty-five. Who are the people of this age group? They make up 11 percent of the population of the United States, some twenty-five million strong. In 1900, only four out of ten people reached age sixty-five. By 1980, eight out of ten persons live to be sixty-five. It is estimated that by the year 2000, the over-sixty-five population in the United States will reach thirty million and by the year 2030, it will reach forty-three million (Golanty and Harris 1982:420).

While almost three-fourths of the men over sixty-five are living with their spouses, only a little more than a third of the women in this age bracket are living with a spouse. The reasons for the disparity in these figures is that men make up just over 40 percent of this age group and women almost 60 percent. In 1977, at age sixty-five, the life expectancy for white males was 13.9 more years, for white females, it was 18.4 more years (Eshleman 1981:515). Almost 40 percent of the women live alone as compared to only 16 percent of the men.

Only about 6 percent of the population over sixty-five live in nursing homes, or about 1.5 million persons in 1980. Because of their longer life expectancy, there are more than two women for every man in nursing homes. Over 40 percent of nursing home residents are over eighty years of age. On the other hand, more than 11 percent of persons over sixty-five are active in the labor force— almost three million persons. However, roughly the same number of persons over sixty-five are living below the poverty level.

Perhaps the greatest effect on aging and population trends has been the dramatic increase in life expectancy (see figure 13–1). As this segment of the population increases, there will be major changes in America's culture and lifestyles. We are already seeing senior citizens becoming a powerful political force. Social Security was a major campaign issue in the 1982 national elections in the United States. Those industries that serve the needs of the aging will be growth industries, and the job market for those serving the elderly will be expanding. The fields of *gerontology*, the study of aging and the problems of the aged, as well as *geriatrics*, the treatment of the aging, are rapidly expanding.

Figure 13-1. GROWTH IN THE UNITED STATES OF THE POPULATION 65 YEARS AND OVER, 1900–2030 (Adapted from Eshleman 1981:514; Golanty and Harris 1982:420).

While in many cultures the aged are looked up to, honored, and revered, the American culture tends to disparage the old. It has generally been a youth-oriented culture, and aging is seen as a negative process. All one has to do is look at the commercials for hair dyes, wrinkle removers, and other products designed to remove the signs of aging to realize that aging is undesirable. These negative attitudes toward aging and the aged may be summed up in the term *agism*. Agism is the stereotyping of and discrimination against persons because they are old. As Orthner points out:

Stereotypes of the elderly abound. Once people reach their sixties, they are supposed to graciously give up their jobs, their sex life, their sporty cars, their in-style clothing, and their time in favor of sitting, watching television and rocking on their porch eagerly waiting for someone to visit them. The popular image of the elderly in the media, including children's books and programs, portrays them as being sickly, passive, incompetent, and less self-reliant than other adults (1981:427).

In spite of recent federal legislation forbidding age discrimination in hiring and allowing persons to work past age sixty-five, age discrimination is a continuing problem for the elderly. However, today more and more older people are advocating their rights and demanding the same respect and opportunities as other people. Examples of this movement are organizations such as the Gray Panthers, the National Council of Senior Citizens, and the American Association of Retired Persons—all formed to fight for the rights of the elderly. The Bible clearly teaches we are to respect, honor, and care for the elderly (i.e., Lev. 19:32; 1 Tim. 5:1–3; James 1:27).

THEORIES OF AGING

A number of theories have been developed in an attempt to study and better understand aging. Two of the more accepted theories, *activity theory* and *disengagement theory*, take contrasting views of aging. There seems to be some evidence to support each theory; however, neither theory seems to fully explain the aging process. We will briefly examine each of these perspectives.

Activity Theory

Activity theory is based on the premise that satisfaction is related to a high level of social activity. Those who hold to this theory argue that, except for physical changes, the elderly are not significantly different from middle-aged adults. They believe that social and psychological needs remain the same. Therefore, the need for social activity is still necessary. The elderly should continue an active lifestyle and maintain social contacts. The aging should participate in the labor force as long as possible and substitute activities should replace work when retirement is necessary. The secret to successful aging according to this theory is to remain active (Green 1978:332).

Disengagement Theory

The disengagement theory views successful aging in terms of gradual disengagement from society. Those who hold to this theory believe that a process of gradual disengagement is healthy for both the individual and society. The person begins to have a natural preoccupation with self while decreasing emotional involvement with others (Green 1978:333). This theory postulates a double withdrawal—the society from individual as well as individual from society. Those who hold to this theory believe that people will experience peace and contentment with age (Kephart 1981:387).

Whichever theory of aging one accepts, there are many factors that characterize the mature and senior years. We will look at some of the major ones: grandparenthood, retirement, death, widowhood, and remarriage.

GRANDPARENTHOOD

Whereas grandparenthood was once reserved for the senior years, it has now moved into the mature years and even the middle years. We have seen that in 1960 the median age at first marriage for men was approximately twenty-three and for women approximately twenty (table 6–1, p. 128). If the first child was a daughter and was born two years after the marriage, she would be twenty-two in 1984. If the daughter married at that time (twenty-two is the current median age at first marriage for women) and had her first child two years later, her father would become a grandfather at age forty-seven and her mother would become a grandmother at age forty-four. In fact, many Americans will become grandparents in their forties (Eshleman 1981:510).

With people becoming grandparents earlier and with increased life expectancies, more and more youngsters will have all or most of their grandparents alive while they are growing up. Ironically, while children have more grandparents living than previous generations did, they are having less contact with their grandparents (Green 1978:326). In our highly mobile society children frequently live hundreds or thousands of miles from their grandparents and see them only occasionally. Both of my grandmothers were frequently long-term residents in our home when I was growing up. My wife's grandparents lived across the street when she was growing up. Now my mother and my wife's parents live on the East Coast and we live in the Midwest; our children see their grandparents only once a year for a week when we go east on vacation.

Grandparenthood as a Status

While grandparenthood is a status with its associated role behavior, surprisingly little sociological research has been conducted on grandparenthood. One of the few studies to examine the role of grandparenthood was carried out by Bernice Neugarten and Karol Weinstein (1964). They discovered that approximately a third (36 percent of the grandmothers and 29 percent of the grandfathers) experienced some role strain or role conflict. Some of the grandparents found the role of grandparenthood alien to their self-image. Others were not sure of how involved they should be in the rearing of grandchildren. And some felt imposed upon with care-taking or responsibility for grandchildren.

In their research, Neugarten and Weinstein found that grandparents played one of five major roles. The first is the *Formal* role. Grandparents in this role carefully distinguish between parenting and grandparenting. They will provide special treats and indulge their grandchildren and provide babysitting. However, they are careful to leave parenting strictly to the parents. While they show an interest in their grandchildren, they avoid becoming involved in child rearing directly or by giving advice.

The second grandparent role is the *Fun Seeker*. This role is characterized by an informal and playful relationship with the grandchildren. The grandparent joins in the child's activities as a playmate. These grandparents tend to view their grandchildren as a source of leisure activity. The relationship is based on mutuality rather than authority. The goal of the relationship is for both parties to derive fun from it.

The *Surrogate Parent* is the third role grandparents may take. If this role is played, it is done so primarily by grandmothers. The grandmother assumes the actual child rearing responsibilities for the grandchild. This role often develops when the mother works outside the home and the grandmother provides child care. This role is also common when the mother is unwed. Green reports that one out of eight grandmothers have unwed daughters. He also writes that 52 percent of single teen-age mothers receive help from their own mothers (1978:326).

The fourth role is the *Reservoir of Family Wisdom*. This tends to be an authoritarian matriarchal or patriarchal role. Grandparents who play this role are involved in the child rearing of their grandchildren. When the parents do not want interference in child rearing, this role can result in resentment and conflict.

The last grandparent role suggested by Neugarten and Weinstein is the *Distant Figure*. In this role, the grandparent has only limited and brief contact with the grandchildren. The grandparent may see the grandchild only at Christmas or on his or her birthday. The grandparent is generally benevolent, but distant and remote. The grandparent is not part of the grandchild's everyday life.

One of the interesting findings in Neugarten and Weinstein's study is the relation between the age of the grandparents and the roles they played. They found that the majority of the Fun Seeking and Distant Figure grandparents were under sixty-five years of age, whereas the majority of the Formal grandparents were over sixty-five. Apparently age did not affect the other two roles.

Another of the few sociological studies of grandparenthood deals specifically with grandmotherhood (Robertson 1977). This study concludes that the role of grandmother can be understood in terms of two dimensions, personal and social. The social dimension results from social and normative forces—society's expectations. The personal dimension stems from personal forces and needs. The study involved administering a scale to a sample of grandmothers. The answers to the items on the scale permitted the assigning of respondents to a high or low rating on each dimension. Combining the two dimensions resulted in four categories or grandmother roles (see figure 13–2).

PERSONAL DIMENSION

		High	Low
SOCIAL DIMENSION	High	Apportioned (29%)	Symbolic (26%)
	Low	Individualized (17%)	Remote (28%)

Figure 13–2. ROBERTSON'S FOUR GRANDMOTHER ROLES
(Adapted from Robertson 1977).

The first role category is the *Apportioned* grandmother. These women scored high on both the social and personal dimensions and were equally concerned with doing what was morally right for their grandchildren and indulging them. Grandmothers in this category are the most involved with their grandchildren. They also tend to be widowed and not participating in the labor force. This apparently leaves them more time to be involved with their grandchildren.

The second type of grandmother role is the *Symbolic* type. These women scored high on the social dimension and low on the personal dimension. Grandmothers in this category were more concerned with what was morally good for their grandchildren. They wanted their grandchildren to have a good education, to develop good manners, to be polite, to have moral values and a good reputation. The grandmothers in this group were the youngest, and the majority were married and in the labor force.

The third role is the *Individualized* grandmother. These women scored low on the social dimension and high on the personal dimension. These grandmothers were not as concerned with norms but were more concerned with companionship. The grandmothers in this group were the oldest, with an average age of almost seventy. There seems to be an indication that as grandparents become older their roles change.

The fourth role group is the *Remote* grandmother. These women scored low on both the social and the personal dimensions. These grandmothers were the least involved with their grandchildren. They carried out their grandmother role in a distant, impersonal, and ritualistic manner. This group obviously found little meaning or satisfaction in their grandmother role.

From both studies we have looked at (Neugarten and Weinstein 1964; Robertson 1977), it is clear that most grandparents are involved with their grandchildren and most enjoy their roles. Lasswell and Lasswell conclude that "most middle-aged parents enjoy becoming grandparents even though they may not always like to think of themselves as old enough for this to happen" (1982:457). Commenting on these studies, Orthner writes, "The majority of grandparents . . . expressed only comfort, satisfaction, and pleasure with their grandparent role" (1981:420).

RETIREMENT

Retirement as an extended stage of life is a recent occurrence. In 1900, the average man lived only 2.8 years after retirement. Today, by age sixty-five, 80 percent of all men and 90 percent of all women are retired and have fifteen or more years of life ahead of them (Orthner 1981:431). While some people want to keep working after age sixty-five, the majority of workers want to retire before then. On the one hand, recent federal legislation has made it possible for most workers to keep their jobs until at least age seventy. On the other hand, some unions have negotiated a "thirty and out" pension program in their contracts that allows workers to retire even as soon as their early fifties. Many union contracts permit early retirement, and Social Security retirement benefits can be collected at age sixty-two.

While both men and women are in the work force and both retire, retirement affects a man more because his self-image is closely related to his occupation. Men have been socialized to see their identity in their career and judge their value in terms of their work (Green 1978:327).

Crises of Retirement

Reporting on studies related to retirement, Lasswell and Lasswell (1982:459–60) present the following five major crises faced in retirement.

Loss of Finances

As many as 80 percent of retired persons have Social Security as their only source of income. Most private and corporate pension programs were not started until after World War II, so most workers eligible for these programs have not reached retirement age yet. For many workers retirement means a loss of income and a lowered standard of living. The vast majority of nursing home residents receive public assistance, and many of the elderly are on welfare.

For those who have adequate income, retirement is often welcomed. It is an opportunity to travel, pursue hobbies, or engage in other activities that had to be put off during the working years. The greater the resources older people have, the more likely they are to view retirement as a pleasant experience.

Loss of Self-esteem

We have already seen that workers have their identity in their occupation. When people retire, to the extent their identity was related to the job, there is a loss of identity. Green (1978:328) points out that frequently blue-collar workers have a more difficult time than white-collar workers making the adjustment from worker to retiree.

Loss of Work-oriented Social Contacts

For many workers, both male and female, most of their social relationships have centered around their work. They may have been part of a company or union bowling league or played golf with business associates. While both men and women develop social relationships through their work, research indicates that women who retire from the work force have a harder time than men adjusting to the loss of social contacts (Lasswell and Lasswell 1982:460). This may be due to the nature of these relationships. In the American culture relationships among men tend to be more instrumental; however, among women they tend to be more emotional.

Loss of Meaningful Tasks

A person who has gone to work for forty or more years suddenly discovers that the meaning of life was related to a career. Even stable marriages may be shaken by the retirement of the husband. When a man retires, it changes not only his lifestyle but that of his wife also. If she has been a homemaker, her daily routine has more than likely centered around the husband's work schedule. If they are both in the work force, they have most likely developed a division of labor in the home. Generally, the man is older than his wife and retires first. Tensions may result as the wife looks for a shift in the division of labor. A major task of retirement is to discover rewarding and meaningful interests to replace work. This may involve such activities as hobbies, volunteer work, or even starting a new career.

Loss of Reference Group

Many workers, particularly those in professions, have identified with their peers. They have thought of themselves as doctors, lawyers, professors, bankers, or stockbrokers; now they are retired persons. Retired persons need to develop new reference groups. While they were in the work force, their reference groups were occupational, but now new reference groups need to be formed. These may center around hobbies or other interests.

Types of Retired Families

Retired families may be studied in terms of the resources they have for their retirement years. One study

(Streib 1971) classified older families in terms of four categories of resources: (1) physical health, (2) emotional well-being, (3) economic resources, and (4) social resources. On the basis of these four categories of resources, Lasswell and Lasswell discuss five types of retirement families. These types may be summarized as follows:

> Type I: "The golden sunset family" has all four necessary resources: good physical health, good emotional health, adequate economic resources, and good social resources.
>
> Type II: Those who are physically incapacitated but who are emotionally stable, have financial security, and who have family and friends for support.
>
> Type III: These are older persons who are both physically and emotionally unhealthy, but who have enough money and family resources to take care of themselves.
>
> Type IV: This type includes those who have only family to care for them. They are in poor physical and emotional health and have no money.
>
> Type V: This type is "the totally deprived family," who end their years in misery. These are the families that present the most serious problems in old age because many of them lack any of the four important resources (1982:461–62).

DEATH

In the Bible we read, "The days of our years are threescore years and ten; and if by reason of strength they be fourscore years" (Ps. 90:10 KJV). The Bible also says, "It is appointed unto men once to die" (Heb. 9:27 KJV). If it has not happened before old age, death certainly follows old age. While death can occur suddenly, for many it is an extended process. One researcher who has extensively studied the process of death and dying is Elisabeth Kubler-Ross (1969, 1974, 1975). She has discovered that the process of dying generally involves five stages: (1) denial and isolation, (2) anger, (3) bargaining, (4) depression, and (5) acceptance (1969). She points out that not all dying persons go through all five stages and not all go through them in the order given. However, enough people do go through all five stages in the order given to make her stages a valid generalization. We will examine each of the stages.

Stages of Dying
Denial and Isolation

Frequently a person's first reaction to a diagnosis of a terminal disease or medical problem is one of denial. The individual may respond with comments such as "The lab people made a mistake," or "The technician must have gotten my x-ray confused with someone else's," or "The doctor is overreacting." Some people will go from one physician to another seeking a different diagnosis. A more subtle type of denial involves carrying on business as usual while ignoring the diagnosis and its implications.

It is usually a shock to a person to learn of his or her impending death, even if it has been suspected. Denial is a psychological defense mechanism for handling shock. One therapist calls denial the shock absorber for human tragedy (Wright 1977b:134). Denial allows people to adjust gradually to the situation as they are able to cope. Joyce Landorf watched her mother pass through the five stages of dying. In her book *Mourning Song,* she shares with us valuable lessons about denial:

> I know that denial is needed in our emotions to act as a buffer or safety zone after we see the reality of someone else's (or our own) death. It gives a temporary measure of healing. It can be used in our lives as a God-given diversion.
>
> Somewhere along the line we as Christians have been given the general feeling that if you are a Christian denial is not a problem, or in some cases, shouldn't even exist. What happens when a Christian does experience denial? And what if, in his denial, his actions do not appear to be too Christian?
>
> We need denial to help us through the most shocking moments of our painful knowledge.
>
> We need denial—but we must not linger in it. We must recognize it as one of God's unique tools and use it. . . . We do not need to feel guilty or judge our level of Christianity. . . . However, after . . . the initial danger has passed, we need not be dependent on it (1974:47–53).

As Kubler-Ross points out, it is not only the dying persons who pass through these stages but also close family and friends. One form denial can take with the close family and friends is isolation from the dying person. The more these people can avoid or isolate the dying person, the less they have to face the reality of their loved one's impending death. Writing about isolation, Wright indicates:

> One of the problems that can occur is the Abandonment Syndrome. Dying people express the fear that their condition will make them so unacceptable to others around them that they will be abandoned, and in many cases studies have confirmed their fears.
>
> Sometimes . . . terminally ill patients are actually abandoned. . . . Often this is a reaction to the fears the person has of one's own death. Because of the implications of the loved one's death, we have to try to separate ourselves from him in some way (1977b:136).

Norman Cousins, who was faced with a terminal diagnosis, has written:

> Death is not the ultimate tragedy of life. The ultimate tragedy is depersonalization—dying in an alien and sterile area, separated from the spiritual nourishment that comes from being able to reach out to a loving hand, separated from a desire to experience the things that make life worth living, separated from hope (1979:133).

Anger

When the reality of one's death breaks through the defense of denial, often the next reaction is anger. Anger is the usual response to frustration, and death may be the ultimate frustration. There may be many targets for the person's anger. The dying person may become angry with himself or herself, with loved ones, with physicians and nurses, or even with God Himself. This anger may boil under the surface or it may explode in words and actions.

Bargaining

This stage generally follows the anger stage. The dying person begins to realize that anger, especially if it is directed at God, is not going to help him. Then he decides to attempt to bargain with God: "If you will let me live God, I'll do such and such for you."

We find a classic case of bargaining in the Old Testament:

In those days Hezekiah became ill and was at the point of death. The prophet Isaiah . . . went to him and said, "This is what the Lord says: Put your house in order, because you will die; you will not recover." Hezekiah turned his face to the wall and prayed to the Lord, "Remember, O Lord, how I have walked before you faithfully and with wholehearted devotion and have done what is good in your eyes." And Hezekiah wept bitterly (2 Kings 20:1–3).

We also find examples of bargaining in the New Testament where close family and friends came to Jesus on behalf of dead or dying persons (e.g., the centurion, Matt. 8:8–13; Peter's mother-in-law, Matt. 8:14–15; Jairus's daughter, Mark 5:21–43; Lazarus, John 11:1–14). As with the case of Hezekiah, each was allowed to live longer.

As Christians, what should our response be to bargaining with God for our lives or the lives of our loved ones? The Bible teaches that God answers prayer and that He does heal. We also must realize that everyone eventually will die. As one pastor phrased it:

God heals you of every sickness but your last. For the Bible says, "It is appointed unto man to die." In other words, should Jesus Christ tarry, every one of us here tonight at some time is going to die. Some bodily organ will cease functioning—it will break down and we will die. Think of the healing results during the ministry of Jesus. There were lepers cleansed of their diseases, but they are not living today. Something else happened to them and they died. The woman with the issue of blood was healed of her disease but something else happened to her and eventually she died. They are not around today. God heals us of every disease, but "it is appointed unto man once to die" (Lyons 1973).

Depression

People generally reach this stage when they have exhausted their energy and resources on anger and bargaining. Kubler-Ross (1969:86) distinguishes between two types of depression. The first she calls *reactive depression*. This type results from the losses the person is experiencing in the process of dying. These losses include such things as self-esteem, self-reliance, job, physical strength, and physical appearance. The second type she labels *pre-

paratory depression. This results from anticipated losses and separation from all that is cherished.

Acceptance

This is the final stage. This stage is reached when the person accepts his or her death. Joyce Landorf writes of her mother's acceptance of death:

> During the last week of my mother's life, we could distinctly feel her God-given confidence in dying. Even though she did not always understand the ways and workings of God, she spent the last week alive and in great beauty. The dignity of her inner confidence was apparent to all who saw her (1974:113).

Christians are able to accept death because of their new life in Christ and their hope of resurrection. As the apostle Paul writes:

> I declare to you, brothers, that flesh and blood cannot inherit the kingdom of God, nor does the perishable inherit the imperishable. . . . For the perishable must clothe itself with the imperishable, and the mortal with immortality. When the perishable has been clothed with the imperishable, and the mortal with immortality, then the saying that is written will come true: "Death has been swallowed up in victory." "Where, O death, is your victory? Where, O death, is your sting?" The sting of death is sin, and the power of sin is the law. But thanks be to God! He gives us the victory through our Lord Jesus Christ (1 Cor. 15:50, 53–57).

Death, Dying, and the Family

We have already seen that close family and friends, as well as the dying person, usually experience the stages of dying. However, the dying person and the family members may not all go through the stages at the same rate. Joyce Landorf recounts that when her mother was in the depression stage, she herself was already at the acceptance stage. However, her father was still back at the denial stage, and her sister was at the bargaining stage. Joyce Landorf shares some of the tensions and conflicts that arose because different family members were at different stages.

It is probably easier for most people to accept their parents' death than to accept a spouse's death. We all recognize that if life follows its normal course we will bury our parents. We are prepared and socialized to experience the death of parents. But most people are not prepared to experience the death of a spouse. We are not socialized to bury our mates.

When a parent dies in old age, the child is usually married and has a family of his or her own. The demands and responsibilities of that family, as well as the support and nurture of that family, usually limit grief and hasten acceptance. However, when a mate dies, there is a major void for the surviving spouse. Widowhood is a major crisis and a stage of adjustment for most people.

WIDOWHOOD

In the United States there are some ten million widows and two million widowers (see table 13–1). While persons can become widowed in young adulthood and middle age, 69 percent of the widowed are over sixty-five. Among women sixty-five and older, a third are widows (Eshleman 1981:530). Becoming a widow or widower in the American culture can be difficult transition because families rarely discuss or prepare for the death of any of their members unless there is a terminal illness. Usually there is not preparation for death. As Eshleman writes:

TABLE 13–1
NUMBER OF WIDOWERS AND WIDOWS IN THE UNITED STATES
FROM 1900 TO 1978

Year	Widowers	Widows
1900	1,178,000	2,155,000
1910	1,471,000	2,718,000
1920	1,758,000	3,176,000
1930	2,025,000	3,918,000
1940	2,144,000	4,734,000
1950	2,296,000	5,700,000
1960	2,112,000	6,967,000
1970	2,103,000	8,064,000
1978	1,800,000	10,100,000

Source: Adapted from Nye and Berardo 1973:601; Eshleman 1981:530.

Society compounds the difficulty of adjusting to the widowed status by placing an unstated taboo on the discussion of death between husband and wife or parents and children while they are alive. As a result, the widow or widower is often unprepared for the decisions that need to be made. Even if discussion preceded the death, the likelihood is great that loneliness, social isolation, and a need for major readjustments in living patterns will result. There is probably no other period in one's life where there is a greater effort at self-awareness. Feelings of inadequacy and guilt, which lead to depression, are frequent occurrences after the death of a spouse (1981:530).

Widowers

Because women generally marry men who are older than they are and because women have a longer life expectancy than men do, the probability of a woman's becoming a widow is five times as great as that of a man's becoming a widower. While many more women than men lose their spouses, research indicates that men have a more difficult time adjusting to their mate's loss than women do (Nye and Berardo 1973:602; Kephart 1981:392). One of the reasons is that in many ways the role of a wife does not change in widowhood. A woman continues to cook, keep the house, and perform other household tasks, much as she did before her husband's death. In fact, the maintenance of routine can be a source of security and comfort in dealing with grief. On the other hand, a widower has lost his cook and housekeeper as well as his partner. It is generally easier for a widow than a widower to maintain separate living quarters. Also, married children are generally more open to having a widow than a widower come to live with them. In addition, widowers are more likely to be socially isolated. They are less likely to be living with children, to maintain relationships with the extended family, to have friends in the community, to attend church, or belong to formal organizations or groups (Nye and Berardo 1973:605). One of the consequences of this isolation is that widowers have high suicide rates.

Widows

To say that widowers have a more difficult time than widows in adjusting to losing a mate is not to suggest that widows have an easy time. They also experience their particular problems. Traditionally, in North American society, women have placed greater value in their role as a wife than men have in their role as a husband. While women have often been identified as the wife of such and such a man, men have generally been identified by their profession or occupation. When a woman becomes a widow, she may, therefore, suffer more of a loss of status than a man who becomes a widower.

Another problem that widows have is the responsibility for the business and financial affairs of the family. While women are moving into the labor force in greater numbers and are learning to handle business and financial affairs, in many homes these matters are still cared for by the husband, with the wife having little or no knowledge in these areas. This is particularly true for couples who were married in the forties and fifties and have more traditional marriages. It is these couples who now make up the segment of our population entering the retirement years. Most retired people today grew up in traditional homes where the husband handled business and financial matters.

Because of the imbalance in the sex ratio (about seventy men for every one hundred women), widows over age sixty-five have much less opportunity for remarriage than widowers. Also, as we have already seen, over 70 percent of the men over sixty-five are married. It is also interesting to note that the children and friends of a widow do not give her as much encouragement to remarry as they do a widower (Nye and Berardo 1973:605).

REMARRIAGE OF THE WIDOWED

Over thirty-five thousand marriages a year involve at least one partner over the age of sixty-five (Kephart 1981:393). However, the percentage of men remarrying is much greater than the percentage of women. Almost 50 percent of all widowed men under age seventy remarry

(Golanty and Harris 1982:438), whereas only about 5 percent of the widowed women over fifty-five will remarry (Lamanna and Riedmann 1981:528). Golanty and Harris (1981:438–39 suggest that there are at least three factors that account for this imbalance in remarriage rates between widowers and widows. First, as we have already seen, widows greatly outnumber widowers, and this means that there are fewer potential mates for widows than widowers. Second, it is more socially acceptable for older men to marry younger women than for older women to marry younger men. This provides widowers with a larger pool of potential mates than widows have. Third, widowed men may be more motivated than widowed women to remarry. Because the older men generally have a weaker social network than women, they may have greater desire for the companionship of marriage. Also, the men have a greater need for cooking and housekeeping help than women do. Another reason may be that widows, recognizing the odds against remarriage, adjust better to widowhood and are not as interested in remarriage.

One study of remarriages in the senior years found five factors that were related to marital success:

1. The bride and groom had known each other for a long time.
2. The marriage was approved by their children and friends.
3. Both partners had adjusted well to other facets of retirement and aging.
4. The couple disposed of previously owned property and bought or rented a home for themselves.
5. There was sufficient income to live without economic hardship (McKain 1969 in Lasswell and Lasswell 1982:471).

This study rated 74 percent of these remarriages successful on this five-factor scale: (1) showing respect and affection for each other, (2) enjoying each other's company, (3) having no serious complaints about each other (4) being proud of each other, and (5) being considerate of each other (Lasswell and Lasswell 1982:471). It appears that the widowed may find remarriage is a viable option for them and that they can find happiness the second time around.

DISCUSSION QUESTIONS

1. Why do you think the aged tend to be disparaged in the American culture, whereas other cultures honor them?

2. Which theory of aging—activity or disengagement —do you think would best lead to successful adjustment to aging? Why?

3. In your opinion why is there so little social research conducted on grandparenthood?

4. Why do you believe the children of the widowed are less likely to take in a widower? Why are they more likely to encourage a widower than a widow to remarry?

5. Why do you think some family members may work through the stages of dying sooner than others when a loved one is terminally ill?

6. What do Psalm 23 and 1 Corinthians 15 have to say about the process of death and dying?

SUGGESTED READING

Jean Beaven Abernethy, *Old Is Not a Four Letter Word* (Nashville, Abingdon, 1975). A positive view of aging. The author refutes many of the stereotypes about the process and attempts to develop a meaningful view of aging.

Zena Smith Blau, *Old Age in a Changing Society* (New York: New Viewpoints, 1973). While the research in this book is a decade old, much of it is still relevant. This work is a classic sociological study that is widely cited in current literature.

Douglas C. Kimmel, *Adulthood and Aging* (New York: John Wiley, 1974). A social psychological view of aging. This work deals with Erikson's adult stages, retirement, the aging process, death, and bereavement.

Elisabeth Kubler-Ross, *On Death and Dying* (New York: Macmillan, 1969). A classic treatment of death and dying. The author deals with the five stages of dying, fear of death, the dying person's family, and therapy for the dying. This book is basic to an understanding of this topic.

Joyce Landorf, *Mourning Song* (Old Tappan, N.J.: Revell 1974). A well-written and sensitive account of the death of the author's mother. This is an excellent illustration of Kubler-Ross's five stages. Landorf traces her mother's and the rest of the family's working through the stages.

14

Divorce and Remarriage

> When Jesus had finished saying these things. . . . Some Pharisees . . . asked, "Is it lawful for a man to divorce his wife for any and every reason?"
>
> "Haven't you read," he replied, "that at the beginning the Creator 'made them male and female,' and said, 'For this reason a man will leave his father and mother and be united to his wife, and the two will become one flesh'? So they are no longer two, but one. Therefore what God has joined together, let man not separate."
>
> "Why then," they asked, "did Moses command that a man give his wife a certificate of divorce and send her away?"
>
> Jesus replied, "Moses permitted you to divorce your wives because your hearts were hard. But it was not this way from the beginning. I tell you that anyone who divorces his wife, except for marital unfaithfulness, and marries another woman commits adultery."
>
> MATTHEW 19:1–9

WHAT GOD HAS joined together, let man not separate." Unfortunately we are seeing more and more marriages break up. There are a number of types of marital dissolution. In *annulment* a marriage is ruled invalid and for legal purposes never took place. Some of the grounds for annulment include bigamy, one of the parties being still legally married to someone else; incompetency on the part of one or both parties; deception; coercion; or one or both parties being minors. *Desertion* is a separation that is not legally sanctioned and is against the will of one spouse. Since desertion is not a legal process, there are no statistics on the extent of this type of separation. It is thought to be quite widespread, especially among the lower classes. In fact, it is often referred to as the "poor man's divorce" (Orthner 1981:373). On the other hand, a *legal separation* involves the agreement of both parties, a separation agreement spelling out the conditions of the separation. A legal separation is a dissolution of the marital relationship, either temporarily or permanently, but not the dissolution of the legal marriage. *Divorce* is the legal termination of a marriage.

DIVORCE RATES

What is the extent of divorce in the United States? What percentage of marriages end in divorce? That depends on which statistics one uses. There are at least four types of divorce statistics. The first is the *number of divorces per year* (see table 14–1). This figure does not really tell us much because it does not take into account increases or decreases in either the general population or married population. The second is the *ratio of marriages to divorces per year* (see table 14–1). This statistic is also unreliable because it compares marriages taking place in one year with divorces from marriages that took place over many years. If the number of marriages in a given

TABLE 14–1
MARRIAGES, DIVORCES, AND THE RATIO BETWEEN THEM
IN THE UNITED STATES

Year	Number of Marriages	Number of Divorces	Marriage/Divorce Ratio
1900	709,000	55,751	12.7/1
1910	948,166	83,045	11.4/1
1920	1,274,476	170,505	7.5/1
1930	1,126,856	195,961	5.8/1
1940	1,595,879	264,000	6.0/1
1950	1,667,231	385,144	4.3/1
1960	1,153,000	393,000	3.9/1
1970	2,158,802	708,000	3.0/1
1980	2,413,000	1,182,000	2.0/1

Source: National Center for Health Statistics, U.S. Department of Health and Human Services.

year decreases, the divorce rate will appear to rise, even if the number of divorces decreases at a slower rate or remains stable.

A more accurate measure is the *crude divorce rate* (see table 14–2). This is the number of divorces per one thousand persons in the population that year. While this rate does take into account increases and decreases in the general population, it does not take into account age changes in a population. For example, an aging population, such as in America, will have a greater percentage of its population married each year. Therefore, even if the percentage of marriages ending in divorce remained constant, the crude divorce would rise.

TABLE 14–2
CRUDE AND REFINED DIVORCE RATES IN THE UNITED STATES

Year	Crude Divorce Rate	Refined Divorce Rate
1920	1.6	7.0
1930	1.6	7.5
1940	2.0	8.5
1950	2.6	9.8
1960	2.2	9.2
1970	3.5	15.0
1980	5.3	23.5

Sources: (Crude Rates) National Center for Health Statistics, U.S Department of Health and Human Services.

(Refined Rates) Lamanna and Riedman (1981:460) 1980 rates are projected from 1977 rates.

The most accurate and useful measure of divorce is the *refined divorce rate* (see table 14–2). This is the number of divorces a year per one thousand married women over age fifteen. This is the most valid statistic on divorce because it measures divorces by the number of women eligible for divorce. This measure allows an accurate comparison of divorce rates from one year to another without having to be concerned about age, size of population, or marital changes in the population.

One problem with all of these divorce rates is that they do not distinguish between first, second, and more divorces. That is, a few people having several divorces would produce the same rates as many people having one divorce. For example, of every one hundred women who marry for the first time, thirty-eight will have their marriages end in divorce. Of these thirty-eight women, twenty-nine will remarry. Of those twenty-nine remarriages, thirteen will end in divorce. Therefore, out of one hundred women who marry, sixty-two will never experience a divorce, and yet those one hundred women between them will account for fifty-one divorces (thirty-eight plus thirteen). Actually, sixty-two married women had no divorces, while thirty-eight married women had fifty-one divorces (Belkin and Goodman 1980:427).

People who divorce give various reasons for their divorces. Some of the more common ones are listed in table 14–3. However, not all of these reasons are legitimate grounds for divorce in every state. As with marriage laws, each state enacts its own divorce laws. A summary of the divorce laws in each state is presented in table 14–4.

TABLE 14–3
REASONS GIVEN FOR FAILURE OF FIRST MARRIAGES

REASON	PERCENTAGE OF TIMES LISTED FIRST	PERCENTAGE OF TIMES LISTED[1]
Infidelity	34%	52%
No longer in love	21%	38%
Emotional problems	11%	38%
Financial problems	6%	28%
Physical abuse	6%	15%
Alcohol	5%	10%
Sexual problems	4%	23%
Problems with in-laws	3%	17%
Other	10%	30%

[1]This column adds up to more than 100% since some people listed more than one reason.

Source: Lamanna and Rietmann (1981:468).

THE DIVORCE EXPERIENCE

Paul Bohannan, a social scientist who has conducted a good deal of research on marriage and the family, has argued that divorce is a process. He also says, "Divorce is

TABLE 14-4
GROUNDS FOR DIVORCE AND RESIDENCE REQUIREMENT BY STATES[1]

State	Adultery	Breakdown of Marriage/ Incompatibility	Cruelty	Desertion	Non-Support	Alcohol &/or Drug Addiction	Felony	Impotency	Insanity	Other Grounds	Living Separate and Apart	Residence Time
Alabama	X	X	X	X	X	X	X	X	X	X		1 Year
Alaska	X	X	X	X		X	X	X	X	X		1 Year
Arizona	X	X										90 Days
Arkansas	X		X	X	X	X	X	X	X	X	3 Years	3 Mos.
California	X	X							X			6 Mos.
Colorado	X	X										90 Days
Connecticut	X	X	X	X	X	X	X		X	X	18 Mos.	1 Year
Delaware	X	X									18 Mos.	3 Mos.
Dist. of Columbia	X			X			X	X		X	6 Mos.-1 Yr.	6 Mos.
Florida	X	X							X			6 Mos
Georgia	X	X	X	X		X	X	X	X	X		6 Mos.
Hawaii	X	X								X	2 Years	6 Mos.
Idaho	X	X	X	X	X	X	X		X	X	5 years	6 Wks.
Illinois	X		X	X		X	X	X				3 Mos.
Indiana	X	X					X	X	X			6 Mos.
Iowa	X	X										1 Year
Kansas	X	X	X	X		X	X	X	X	X		60 Days
Kentucky	X	X										180 Days
Louisiana	X						X			X	2 Years	1 Year
Maine	X	X	X	X	X	X		X			3 Years	6 Mos.
Maryland	X			X			X	X	X	X	1-3 Yrs.	1 Year
Massachusetts	X	X	X	X	X	X	X	X			6 Mos.-1 Yr.	2 Years
Michigan	X	X										6 Mos.
Minnesota	X	X								X	6 Mos.	6 Mos.
Mississippi	X	X	X	X		X	X	X	X	X		6 Mos.
Missouri	X	X									1-2 Yrs.	3 Mos.
Montana	X	X										3 Mos.
Nebraska	X	X										1 Year
Nevada	X	X							X		1 Year	6 Wks.
New Hampshire	X	X	X	X	X	X	X	X		X		1 Year
New Jersey	X		X	X		X	X		X	X	6 Mos.	1 Year
New Mexico	X	X	X	X								6 Mos.
New York	X		X	X			X			X	1 Year	1 Year
North Carolina	X							X	X	X	1 Year	6 Mos.
North Dakota	X	X	X	X	X	X	X	X	X	X		1 Year
Ohio	X	X	X	X		X	X	X	X	X	2 Years	6 Mos.
Oklahoma	X	X	X	X	X	X	X	X	X	X		6 Mos.
Oregon	X	X										6 Mos.
Pennsylvania	X		X	X			X	X	X	X	3 Years	1 Year
Rhode Island	X	X	X	X	X	X	X	X			3 Years	1 Year
South Carolina	X		X	X		X					3 Years	1 Year
South Dakota	X		X	X	X	X	X					Actual
Tennessee	X	X	X	X	X	X	X	X		X		6 Mos.
Texas	X	X	X	X			X		X		3 Years	1 Year
Utah	X		X	X	X	X	X	X	X	X		Actual
Vermont	X		X	X	X		X			X	6 Mos.	6 Mos.
Virginia	X		X	X							1 Year	6 Mos.
Washington	X	X									2 Years	Actual
West Virginia	X		X	X		X	X		X		2 Years	2 Yrs.-S
Wisconsin	X	X								X	1 Year	6 Mos.
Wyoming	X	X							X		2 Years	60 Days

[1]As of 1978.

a complex social phenomenon as well as a complex personal experience" (1970:30). He sees the complexity of divorce arising from the number of things happening at once. To better understand divorce, Bohannan has the process divided into six overlapping experiences: (1) the emotional divorce, (2) the legal divorce, (3) the economic divorce, (4) the coparental divorce, (5) the community divorce, and (6) the psychic divorce. This approach to understanding divorce has proven useful and is widely accepted (Cox 1981; Golanty and Harris 1982; Lamanna and Riedmann 1981; Orthner 1981; Scanzoni and Scanzoni 1981). We will look at each of these experiences individually, but in doing so, we must remember that they are overlapping experiences often occurring simultaneously.

The Emotional Divorce

When someone is courting, becomes engaged, and is married, it is an exciting time. The other person is treating him or her as someone special. The person realizes that someone has chosen and wants to make a commitment to him or her. When someone is going through a divorce, they are being rejected and treated as a problem. It is easy to see why divorce is an emotional experience.

The emotional divorce generally is the initial experience in the divorce process. It consists of a chain of events that lead up to divorce in the same way that a chain of events led to marriage. Even as neither party realized on the first date that their relationship would lead to marriage, so neither party may realize a given event in their marriage is the first link in a chain leading to divorce.

Almost every married person, even after only a few months of marriage, knows what to say or do to hurt his or her partner. Each knows where to hit the other to "draw blood." As a couple learns each other's weaknesses and sensitivities, each gains in the ability to hurt the other.

Disagreements and fights occur in every marriage. Even healthy marriages have their times of conflict. However, in a healthy marriage the conflict tends to clarify issues, increase understanding, and lead to a developing relationship. But if the conflict results in hurting the other and undermining the relationship, then the process of emotional divorce has begun. Often when this happens, the couple fights over issues that are cover-ups for the real problem, which may be power, self-esteem, status, or some other such issue. Two issues over which couples frequently fight, that often are cover-ups for deeper concerns are finances and sex.

As we saw in chapter 8, money represents a number of things including power, love, and status. Because money represents more than dollars and cents, it can easily become a cover-up for other issues. In one study reported by Belkin and Goodman, of couples seeking divorce, over a third claimed that finances were the source of their conflict (1980:433). While money management and budgeting are the source of endless discussion in most homes, it is when this area is used as a means for one party to attack the other that problems begin.

Sex is often used as a weapon in a conflict between a couple. Frequently sexual symptoms are the first indication to a couple that there is a problem. On the other hand, there are some couples for whom their sexual relationship is the only part of their marriage that seems to work. However, those types of relationships are the exception. Generally, when a couple's communication becomes strained, their sexual relationship is the first to suffer. Because sexual intercourse is one of the most intimate social relationships, emotional problems and misgivings generally show up here.

Sexual problems may take many forms. A sexual problem may manifest itself as general sexual dysfunction in women and impotence in men. On the other hand, it may result in adultery, which may be an attempt to hurt or humiliate the other. Adultery, as we have seen in table 14–4 is grounds for divorce in all fifty states.

The emotional divorce usually involves the couple's growing apart. One or both partners feel a lessening of commitment. Partners may feel cramped by the marriage or cheated by the other. Eventually one or both parties feel the need to dissolve the relationship. Sometimes a couple may experience an emotional divorce, yet never get a legal divorce. They live under the same roof and remain husband and wife in name, but emotionally they are divorced.

Another aspect of emotional divorce is loss and grief. Emotional divorce results in the loss of a loved one that is just as real as a loss by death. In some ways the loss from divorce may be worse, since in death the person is gone. Also, while friends, family, and church provide support for dealing with the bereavement of death, a person usually receives little or no support during the bereavement of divorce. In fact, the person going through the bereavement of divorce may in addition be the object of condemnation from family, friends, and the church.

The Legal Divorce

Judicial divorce is the legal dissolution of a relationship that often has already experienced its emotional dissolution. There are two types of legal divorces: *fault* and *no-fault*. In fault divorces one party sues the other party for divorce on legal grounds (see table 14–4). Fault divorce may be *contested* or *uncontested*. While most divorces are uncontested, in some instances a spouse may not agree to the divorce and contest or challenge the grounds.

There are several reasons why a divorce may not be granted in a contested fault suit. One is *recrimination,* meaning the partner being sued for divorce countercharges an accusation in return. For example, a wife may sue her husband for divorce on the grounds of adultery. He may be guilty of adultery and admit it, but countercharge that his wife withheld affection from him. If he can prove his countercharge, the court may deny his wife a divorce.

A second reason for not granting a divorce in a fault proceeding is *collusion*. This means that the spouses cooperated in getting the divorce. Fault divorce is an adversarial procedure, and the two parties are not permitted to cooperate with each other. If the court discovers that collusion has taken place, a divorce may be denied. There are three types of collusion. In one type of collusion the couple submits false evidence. For example, they may submit evidence that the husband committed adultery though the act never took place. In the second type of collusion one party engages in an act solely for the purpose of providing grounds for divorce. For instance, a husband and wife want a divorce in a state where the only grounds for divorce is adultery, so the husband has an affair strictly for the purpose of having grounds for a divorce. In the third type of collusion the accused party does not offer an adequate defense. In states that do not have no-fault divorce, many fault cases involve collusion, but these practices seldom are brought to light or used to deny a divorce.

Connivance is a third reason for not granting a divorce in a fault suit. Connivance is similar to collusion. It involves one partner's encouragement of the other partner's act of marital offense in order to obtain a divorce. For example, a husband might arrange for another man to seduce his wife so he could catch her in adultery.

Another reason for not granting a fault divorce is *condonation*. In some states the court will grant the innocent partner a divorce only if the innocent partner has not forgiven the offending partner. Because it is difficult to define forgiveness, condonation is generally assumed if the couple have continued to live together or had sexual relations since the commitment of the offending act.

Today most states have some form of no-fault divorce (see table 14–4, Breakdown of Marriage Incompatibility). In a no-fault case the adversarial nature of divorce is absent, and there is no concern with "guilty" or "innocent" parties. Rather, a couple is allowed to dissolve a marriage without concern for fault finding if it has irretrievably broken down. In no-fault cases both parties agree to the divorce. Advocates of no-fault divorce argue that it has made divorce simpler, cheaper, and less traumatic; has eliminated accusations and recriminations; and has done away with the duplicity of collusion (Golanty and Harris 1982:372). However, other authorities warn of some of the problems associated with no-fault divorce. These include rising divorce rates, inequitable property settlements, and less consideration of the consequences of divorce (Cox 1981:460–61).

The Economic Divorce

Many states have what are called *community property laws*. This means that most items owned by either party are considered community property—that is, the property of the couple. In the case of a divorce, the community property and assets must be divided between the divorcing parties. Besides the division of current assets, most divorce settlements involve future assets. For example, if a wife worked to help her husband through medical school and then he divorces her, is she entitled to only half of their current financial assets or is his education an asset and is she entitled to a portion of his future earnings? There are two basic types of payments that involve future assets.

One of these payments involving future assets is *alimony*. This term is derived from the Latin word meaning sustenance or nourishment. Alimony is based on the idea that a husband, or a wife in some cases, has taken on the obligation of supporting a spouse and that obligation continues even after a divorce. The other type of payment is *child support*. This involves one spouse, generally the husband, paying for the support of the children who are living with the other spouse, usually the wife. Today more and more courts are awarding joint custody, whereby both parties have to share equally the cost of child support.

The Coparental Divorce

Children under eighteen years of age are involved in 60 percent of all divorces (Orthner 1981:393). Bohannan uses the term *coparental divorce* to indicate that while parents divorce each other, they do not divorce their children. Even though a couple is no longer husband and wife after a divorce, they are still father and mother.

Divorce is every bit as much a trauma for the children as it is for the parents. In some cases it is more traumatic since the parents are divorcing by choice, but the children have no say in the matter. The children are often the center of long custody battles, used as pawns to seek revenge on a partner, and subject to dislocation and drastic changes in lifestyle. Some researchers in this area feel that the children of divorce go though a series of phases related to the loss of their family. These phases are similar to Kubler-Ross's five stages of dying, examined in the last chapter.

It is also quite common for children of divorced parents to experience guilt. They may believe that they are in some way responsible for the divorce. This problem is particularly true for younger children who have trouble comprehending what is happening. The children of divorce are also subject to other psychological problems. One is the fear of desertion. "After all, if mom and dad could just leave each other, why couldn't they just leave me?" thinks the child. There is also resentment and a feeling of betrayal when one parent begins dating or remarries. Many children want mom and dad to get together again and they realize that a new suitor interferes with that hope.

Custody

Until recently, mothers were generally given custody of the children in the case of a divorce. This was particularly true of young children under what came to be known as the *tender years doctrine*. Most courts held that children in their "tender years," preteens, were all but automatically placed in their mother's custody. However, today nearly every state has changed its divorce laws to eliminate the biases of the tender years doctrines. These laws now direct the courts to consider "the best interests of the child." That is, the parent best able to care for the child should receive custody (Orthner 1981:394).

The courts are also moving toward more liberal *visitation rights*. Visitation rights are the rights of the parents who do not receive custody of their children to visit their children, to have their children with them for holidays and vacation periods, that is, to spend time with their children.

The courts are also granting *joint custody* in more cases. In this situation, each parent has the children an equal share of the time, and the parents share equal responsibility for the children. Joint custody, when it is granted, is frequently associated with no-fault divorce, since neither party has accused the other with any type of violation.

Consequences for Children

In a major longitudinal study of a group of children of divorce, researchers (Wallerstein and Kelly) found that five years after the divorce, the child could be classified as belonging to one of three groups. About a fourth of the children were adjusting successfully. They appeared to be well adjusted and had fully recovered from the divorce experience. About half were coping with the after-effects of the divorce. They were not fully recovered from the experience and were dealing with lingering problems. The other fourth had not recovered from the divorce. They were not well adjusted and were not coping well with the after-effects of the divorce.

The research found three basic factors associated with good adjustment to the divorce by the children. The first was psychologically healthy parents. The second factor was a lack of rancor and revenge between the divorced parents and regular and dependable visitation by the parent who had not been given custody. The third was that the children had an emotionally nurturant relationship with the father. According to the researchers, this was critical for good adjustment for both sexes (Wallerstein and Kelly 1980:71).

The Community Divorce

Becoming divorced not only changes one's relationship to one's spouse, it also changes one's status from married person to single person. In most of their social circles, the couple had related to others as couples. When a person is divorced, those relations are not the same. In fact, divorced persons, particularly women are often suspect. Divorced persons move from the world of married back to the world of singles. However, if they have children, they do not really fit in with the premarried singles.

Today many organizations have been formed to provide support and social outlets for single parents. Perhaps the best known of these is Parents Without Partners. These organizations provide information, discuss common problems, engage in civic projects, and sponsor social activities for their members. Whether they have children or not, the newly divorced face many adjustments in relating to the community.

The Psychic Divorce

Bohannan suggests that this may be the most difficult of the six aspects of divorce and continues after the legal divorce is final. The psychic divorce involves emotionally and psychologically separating oneself from the other person. If two people have shared life as intimately as a married couple does for an extended period of time, it is often difficult for the one person to get the other "out of his or her system." In marriage, people have become one, and in divorce, they must become autonomous again. Divorced persons must get over the positive feelings they have for each other; however, attachment often continues for some time following a divorce. One study found that 86 percent of divorcing people still had some attachment for their spouse (Kitson 1982:379). But perhaps more importantly, divorced persons need to get over any negative feelings resulting from the divorce. Those negative feelings are much more harmful and create more problems than any lingering feelings of affection can ever overcome.

REMARRIAGE

Divorce apparently does not sour most people on marriage. The vast majority of divorced people remarry. In fact, 83 percent of all divorced men and 75 percent of all divorced women remarry. Not only do most divorced people remarry, they do so quite soon after their divorces. About 25 percent are remarried less than six months after their divorce. Another 25 percent are remarried within a year, and 25 percent more are re-married within three years after their divorce. Remarriages are so popular they constitute 30 percent of all marriages performed annually. Divorced persons are also more likely to have a civil ceremony than first marrieds (Kephart 1981:485–86).

How do remarriages compare with first marriages on happiness and stability? When it comes to happiness, remarried couples report similar levels of happiness with their marriages as first married couples report with theirs (Lamanna and Riedmann 1981:491). However, it is difficult to compare these results because remarried persons are more likely to enter their second marriage with different expectations than people entering a first marriage. When we look at stability, we are looking at hard statistics rather than self-reports; so we can be on more certain ground. Divorce statistics indicate that while 38 percent of first marriages end in divorce, 44 percent of second marriages end in divorce (Lamanna and Riedmann 1981:493). It appears that remarriages are not generally as stable as first marriages.

RECONSTITUTED OR BLENDED FAMILIES

When Ralph and Sonja were divorced, Ralph received custody of their three-year-old daughter, Judy, because of Sonja's emotional instability. A few years later Ralph met Sue, who was also divorced and had custody of her two-year-old son, Jason. A year later Ralph and Sue were married, and Sue became Judy's "mother," and Ralph became Jason's "father." Together they form what is called a *reconstituted* or *blended family*. Some thirty million adults and one out of every five children in America live in reconstituted families (Einstein 1983:67).

Reconstituted families face some unique problems. One is that children end up with two "fathers" or two "mothers," their biological parent and their stepparent of the same sex. Children generally end up being members of two households with two distinct sets of rules. The role of a stepparent is poorly defined, and the stepparent has little or no authority. Children in reconstituted families also end up with extra grandparents. Some of the major problems parents encounter in reconstituted families are presented in table 14–5.

DIVORCE, REMARRIAGE, AND THE BIBLE

While there is sincere disagreement among Christians on the issues of divorce and remarriage, most agree that God's ideal plan is for a couple united in marriage to remain so for life (Gen. 2:24; Matt. 19:5–6; Rom. 7:2; 1 Cor. 7:39). Most also agree that divorce is a consequence or a result of sin (Deut. 24:1; Matt. 19:8). Also, most agree that divorce is displeasing to God (Mal. 2:16).

TABLE 14-5
MAJOR PROBLEMS ENCOUNTERED BY PARENTS
IN RECONSTITUTED FAMILIES

Problem	Husbands	Wives
Child rearing	35%	35%
Financial	20%	16%
Sexual	11%	6%
Religion	10%	6%
Political	9%	11%
Outsiders	9%	14%
Recreation	6%	11%

Source: Adapted from Lamanna and Riedmann 1981:497.

However, after these points of agreement comes much controversy. There are two basic issues involved. The first relates to whether divorce is always a sin or is wrong only under certain circumstances. The second relates to whether remarriage is ever permitted, and if so, under what circumstances. For both the Old Testament and New Testament Hebrews, these two questions would generally run together, since divorce presupposed remarriage and was customary (Ellison 1977:63; Martin 1974: 18–19).

Jesus dealt with the issue of divorce and remarriage (Matt. 5:31–32; 19:3–9; Mark 10:2–11; Luke 16:18). The accounts in all three synoptic Gospels are similar. Jesus deals with both divorce and remarriage and presumes divorce will result in remarriage. He argues that remarriage results in adultery because divorce does not break the marriage bond. In the Matthew account He includes an exception, and that is the case of fornication.

To understand Jesus' teaching we need a little background information. In the Matthew 19 and Mark 10 passages He is responding to a question from the Pharisees. Deuteronomy 24:1 reads, "If a man marries a woman who becomes displeasing to him because he finds something indecent about her, and he writes her a certificate of divorce, gives it to her and sends her from his house. . . ." A major debate existed in Jesus' day as to what was meant by "something indecent." The conservative rabbinical school of Shammai argued it referred to sexual immorality, whereas the liberal rabbinical school of Hillel argued it meant anything that displeased the husband, even burning the supper. Many scholars believe that this debate was the basis and context for the Pharisees' question to Jesus (Bustanoby 1978; Duty 1967; Ellisen 1977; Martin 1974; Woodson 1979).

It is interesting to note that Jesus, in His response to the Pharisees' question concerning the correct interpretation of the law of Moses, did not appeal to Moses, but to the creation account. In essence, Jesus said, "Let's see what God's original intention was." Moses' teaching on divorce, according to Jesus, was an accommodation to human sinfulness, not part of God's original plan. As in so many other areas where the Pharisees questioned and challenged Jesus, He responded by referring to God's purposes and plans rather than to the law. Jesus appeared to be more concerned with the spirit of the law as a reflection of God's purposes than with the letter of the law.

Those who believe that divorce and remarriage are always wrong and that only death can break the marriage bond have to deal with the exception clauses in Matthew 5 and 19. This is generally done in one of two ways. The first is to claim that since the clauses are not recorded in Mark or Luke, they were probably never uttered by Jesus. They were either an explanatory note added by Matthew that eventually became part of the text or they were added by the early church to soften Jesus' teaching on divorce and remarriage. The fact is that there is not a shred of evidence that the exception was added later. The exception clauses have been accepted as genuine by the translation committees for the King James Version, the American Standard Version, the New American Standard Bible, and the New International Version. They have been accepted as genuine by the Roman Catholic church (see Duty 1967:73–76 for a more detailed discussion). Some may ask why the exception clause was recorded by Matthew but not by Mark and Luke. The basic explanation was that each of the gospel accounts was written with a different primary audience in mind. Matthew wrote for Jewish believers, Mark for Roman believers, and Luke for Greek believers. Each writer included or omitted material as it was relevant to the message he was attempting to communicate. The Gospels are not basically biographies but theologies. The Greeks and Romans, with no awareness of the rabbinical debate that was the context for Jesus' response, did not require those comments. The Jewish readers, who were aware of the debate, needed those comments (see Duty 1967:77–83 for a further discussion of this issue).

The other major New Testament passage dealing with divorce and remarriage is 1 Corinthians 7:12–16, verses 12 and 15 in particular: "If any brother has a wife who is not a believer and she is willing to live with him, he must not divorce her. . . . But if the unbeliever leaves, let him do so. A believing man or woman is not bound in such circumstances." While everyone agrees a believer cannot prevent a nonbelieving mate from leaving, the issue is whether or not the remaining believing mate is free to remarry. Again, scholars are divided on this question. The majority of the works I consulted felt the believer was free to remarry.

Divorce and remarriage is a difficult and controversial issue in many of our churches. There is no question that divorce is a major issue and a destructive force in our society. There is no question that Christians must be pro-family and do everything possible to prepare young people for marriage and help couples maintain their marriages. Yet, when divorce does occur, what should our response be? It is not my purpose to develop or defend a position on this question. That has been done quite thoroughly by others (see Suggested Reading at the end of the chapter). However, I would challenge each reader to study the Word of God, read the scholars, and come to his or her own convictions.

MARRIAGE AND THE FAMILY: A FINAL THOUGHT

In this book we have looked at many facts and figures, theories and models, as well as problems and opportunities related to marriage. However, behind the statistics and theories are real men and women, real boys and girls. There are joys and tears, hopes and fears, love and hate, happiness and misery. While God does not promise us a problem-free life, it is my conviction that if we will faithfully and diligently apply God's Word in our personal lives and family lives, we can have marriages and homes that will be places of opportunity and challenge, love and wholeness. It is my prayer that all readers will make the Lord Jesus Christ a part of their life and family.

DISCUSSION QUESTIONS

1. Do you believe that no-fault divorce is helpful or harmful? Why?
2. Should parents who want a divorce but have young children stay together for the sake of the children? Why?
3. Should divorced couples with children be automatically given joint custody unless there is a compelling reason for one spouse or the other to have custody?
4. Why do you think so many divorced people remarry soon after their divorce?
5. Do you believe it is ever permissible for a believer to divorce his or her spouse? Is it ever permissible for a divorced Christian to remarry? On what do you base your views?
6. What, if any, do you see as biblical grounds for remarriage following divorce?

SUGGESTED READING

André Bustanoby, *But I Didn't Want a Divorce* (Grand Rapids: Zondervan, 1978). Written by a Christian marriage counselor, this book deals with the aftermath problems of divorce. It covers biblical teaching on divorce, single parenthood, loneliness, and remarriage.

Andrew J. Cherlin, *Marriage, Divorce, Remarriage* (Cambridge, Mass.: Harvard 1981). A sociological analysis of marriage, divorce, and remarriage. The major emphasis of this work is on the consequences of divorce and remarriage.

Lucile Duberman, *The Reconstituted Family* (Chicago: Nelson-Hall, 1975). A sociological study of reconstituted families. The book deals with special problems faced by reconstituted families; demographic factors; husband-wife relationships; and stepparent-stepchild, as well as step-sibling, relationships.

Guy Duty, *Divorce and Remarriage* (Minneapolis: Bethany, 1967). A classic work on the topic. This is a well-documented and thorough biblical study of the issue.

Stanley A. Ellisen, *Divorce and Remarriage in the Church* (Grand Rapids: Zondervan, 1977). A biblical study of the issue that also looks at the role of divorced and remarried people in the church.

Larry Richards, *Remarriage: A Healing Gift From God* (Waco: Word, 1981). From the pen of a well-known Bible student, theologian, and educator comes a work typical of a number of current writers on this subject. The basic thesis is that God's grace is sufficient to cover any sin, and God gives us the opportunity to start over again.

Appendix:
Venereal Disease

I. GONORRHEA

Gonorrhea is the disease that is largely responsible for the VD epidemic. Although it is curable by penicillin (and other drugs for those who must not use penicillin), recently strains of gonorrhea that are resistant to treatment have evolved. Persons who treat themselves with nonprescribed penicillin may use the wrong type of drug, or may stop taking the drug before all the organisms that cause the disease have been killed. The surviving organisms are the strongest of those that caused the infection. The disease progresses in infected individuals, who pass the hardy strain of gonorrhea on to others through sexual contact.

A. Transmission of Gonorrhea

The organism that causes gonorrhea can be transmitted only through sexual intercourse, including vaginal, anal, or oral-genital intercourse. Outside of the body, it dies almost immediately. A man has a 20 to 50 percent chance of contracting gonorrhea from one act of intercourse with an infected partner; a woman has a more than 50 percent chance after one act of vaginal intercourse with an infected man.

B. Symptoms of Gonorrhea

Although many men first notice symptoms of gonorrhea within three to five days after exposure to it, asymptomatic (lacking symptoms) gonorrhea is becoming more common among men. Symptoms may appear as soon as one day or as late as two weeks before exposure. When symptoms appear in the male, he first has a thin, clear discharge seeping from the opening of his penis. After a day or two the discharge becomes heavy and creamy. It is usually white but may be yellow or yellow-green. The tip of the penis becomes swollen, with the lips of the urethral opening standing out from the glans. Urination is painful or causes a burning sensation and may become difficult.

If treatment is delayed for more than a few days, the infection spreads up the urethra, and may eventually invade the prostate gland and the epididymis, or symptoms of gonorrhea may seem to go away. If untreated, however, the man can still spread the disease to his sexual partners. The untreated man may also become sterile.

Most women who contract gonorrhea experience no symptoms at all for the first weeks or months of their disease. Before the disease is discovered, permanent damage may be done to the Fallopian tubes, causing sterility. Some women, however, do notice a change in the vaginal secretions from the normal clear or white to a yellow-green or greenish color. The gonorrheal discharge is rarely noticeable unless another infection is present at the same time.

C. COMPLICATIONS OF GONORRHEA

If left untreated, gonorrhea can cause severe pain and infection in both men and women. Damage to the reproductive system is not reversible, and sterility results. In women who have had such damage, the likeliness of an ectopic pregnancy (pregnancy that occurs outside of the uterus, in the Fallopian tube or abdominal cavity) is greatly increased. Fertilization occurs in the Fallopian tubes. If the tubes are partially blocked by scar tissue from the gonorrheal infection, the fertilized egg cannot pass to the uterus and develops elsewhere instead. Eventually, the area hemorrhages and the woman experiences severe pain and internal bleeding. If she does not receive immediate medical attention, she may die.

D. TREATMENT OF GONORRHEA

The best treatment for gonorrhea is penicillin, given in injections in the buttocks. The *VD Handbook* discusses which types of penicillin are most effective in the treatment of gonorrhea. Tetracycline is the best for persons who are allergic to penicillin.

E. PREVENTION OF GONORRHEA

The condom is the best means of preventing transmission of the disease, but it is not 100 percent effective. Many birth control clinics include a test for gonorrhea as a part of a routine checkup. VD clinics test for gonorrhea and other venereal diseases, often without charge. Routine checks for gonorrhea and syphilis are important for sexually active persons, especially women. However, it should be emphasized that increasing numbers of men are contracting gonorrhea without the warning symptoms.

II. SYPHILIS

Although syphilis is not as widespread a disease as gonorrhea, it is more serious because of the excessive damage that it can do when untreated. It may affect any of the body's organs when in the late stage. The diagnosis of syphilis is difficult because symptoms at various stages resemble the symptoms of other diseases.

A. Transmission of Syphilis

Syphilis is highly contagious for about the first year of the disease, if untreated. It is most commonly passed from one person to another through vaginal, anal, or oral-genital intercourse. It can travel from one partner to the other through the intact skin of the sexual organs. A man wearing a condom can contact syphilis from his partner, "since the organism can enter at the junction of the penis and rest of the body." The syphilitic rash is also highly contagious. Within a few hours after the organisms enter the body, they are carried by the bloodstream to all parts of the body.

B. Stages and Symptoms of Syphilis

1. *Primary Syphilis.* Around three or four weeks after exposure to syphilis (or as early as ten days or late as three months), a chancre or sore appears on the body at the point of entry of the organism. On a man it is usually on the glans of the penis, but it may be elsewhere. A woman who has had vaginal intercourse usually does not notice the chancre, since it usually develops on her cervix or vaginal walls. Many women, therefore, are not aware when they have primary syphilis unless informed by their sexual partners.

When the chancre first appears, it is a dull red bump about as large as a pea. The bump's surface becomes eroded, and the chancre becomes a dull red, open sore that may be covered by a scab. The chancre does not hurt, and does not bleed easily. It may have a rubbery pink border. If left untreated, the chancre heals by itself within one to five weeks after its appearance.

2. *Secondary Syphilis.* The infected person continues to infect his or her sexual partners, even when symptoms do not exist. The disease usually progresses to its second stage about six months after exposure, when a skin rash develops. The rash is extremely contagious to other people. It may not be obvious or may not appear at all. Nevertheless the syphilitic person is still able to infect others.

3. *Latent Syphilis.* If secondary syphilis is not treated, it may become dormant or hidden for many years. About a year after the initial infection, the individual is no longer infectious to others, with one exception. A pregnant woman passes the disease to her fetus.

4. *Late Syphilis.* A number of years after exposure, the untreated individual may develop a number of complications, including heart disease, blindness, paralysis, insanity, and other serious complications.

C. Treatment of Syphilis

A complete physical examination should be given to persons who believe that they may have syphilis. If sores or rash exist, fluid taken from them is examined under a microscope.

For years, blood tests have been given routinely to persons applying for marriage licenses in most states. Such a test is required in all but two states.

As with gonorrhea, the first choice in antibiotics to treat syphilis is penicillin (though a different type than the type used to treat gonorrhea), and the second choice is tetracycline.

III. VENEREAL HERPES*

Venereal or genital herpes is caused by a virus, herpes simplex type II. It is closely related to herpes simplex type I, a virus that causes fever blisters. According to the Center for Disease Control in Atlanta, 20 million Americans had genital herpes in 1982 and a half million additional cases are expected each year. According to *Newsweek* (April 12, 1982:75–76), some experts are estimating that almost a third of all adult Americans have some form of herpes infection.

A. TRANSMISSION OF VENEREAL HERPES

Venereal herpes is transmitted through sexual contact—oral, anal, or vaginal. It can also be transmitted to the genitals by hand if one has ordinary cold sores. About one-third of the women under twenty-four with venereal herpes suffer from herpes simplex Type I (*Time*, August 2, 1982:62). The virus attacks the skin and particularly mucous membranes.

B. SYMPTOMS OF HERPES

The early symptoms consist of a tingling or itching sensation. Two to fifteen days later, fluid-filled blisters appear on the genitals or buttocks, sometimes accompanied by feverishness and headaches. The first outbreak generally lasts about three weeks, then the lesions harden, scab over, and heal. Unfortunately the infection has not been cleared up. Rather, the virus travels from the genitals along nerve pathways to the base of the spinal cord. It lies dormant there until it is ready to break out again on the genitals. Researchers are not sure what triggers the recurrence of break-outs.

C. COMPLICATIONS OF VENEREAL HERPES

In addition to the physical pain and discomfort of venereal herpes, there are more serious consequences. Women with venereal herpes have a cervical cancer rate four times greater than that of noninfected women. Also a pregnant woman with an active case of venereal herpes may pass the virus to her baby during delivery. The virus can cause a severe and potentially fatal form of encephalitis. It can also cause brain damage and/or blindness.

---

*Research on venereal herpes has progressed significantly in the past eight years. Therefore this section has been rewritten by Dr. Grunlan.

D. Treatment of Venereal Herpes

As of the writing of this material there is no known cure for herpes. As someone has said, "Herpes is forever." There are some medications that relieve the symptoms in some cases, but a permanent cure has yet to be discovered.

E. Prevention of Venereal Herpes

The best way to prevent venereal herpes is to avoid sexual intimacy with an infected partner. Work is under way on a vaccine to prevent the spread of herpes. At this time it has not been tested on humans. Abstinence is still the best prevention.

IV. OTHER VENEREAL DISEASES

Both men and women may develop irritating genital diseases that may be spread through sexual contact or other means (such as a washcloth) as well. These diseases may be confused with gonorrhea and often develop in conjunction with it. In the male, the disease is know as *urethritis* (inflammation of the urethra), and in the female, *vaginitis* (inflammation of the vagina). The affected area burns or itches, and there may be an abnormal discharge from the male's urethra or female's vagina. Females may have itching or burning sores on the clitoris, inner lips, vestibule, cervix, or vagina. Urethritis and vaginitis are caused by a numer of different organisms, and treatment for the different organisms varies. Therefore, medical examination and diagonsis are essential.

V. CONCLUSIONS

Venereal diseases are usually spread by sexual contact, and vary in severity from being merely annoying to causing severe injury or death. Ignorance is the biggest factor in the spread of venereal disease, which is reaching epidemic proportions. The person who believes that he or she is infected with any kind of venereal disease should seek immediate medical attention and should inform his or her sexual partners when a disease is confirmed. Sexual contact should be avoided until the disease is cured.

By law, all information regarding the patient's condition is kept confidential. In all states but Wisconsin, it is unlawful for authorities to inform parents that their children, minor or otherwise, have a venereal disease. Most states have free VD clinics. To find out the laws and availability of clinics in a particular state, the reader should contact the state health service.

Bibliography

Abernethy, Jean Beaven
  1975   Old Is Not a Four-Letter Word. Nashville: Abingdon.

Annis, Linda Ferrill
  1978   The Child Before Birth. Ithaca, N.Y.: Cornell University.

Bach, George R., and Peter Wyden
  1968   The Intimate Enemy: How to Fight Fair in Love and Marriage. New York: Avon.

Bancroft, Emery H.
  1976   Christian Theology: Systematic and Biblical (2nd rev. ed.). Grand Rapids: Zondervan.

Basso, Ellen B.
  1973   The Kalapalo Indians of Central Brazil. New York: Holt, Rinehart and Winston.

Bee, Helen
  1981   The Developing Child (3rd ed). New York: Harper & Row.

Begley, Sharon, and John Carey
  1982   "How life begins." Newsweek (January 11):38–43.

Belgum, David
  1972   Why Marry? Minneapolis: Augsburg.

Belkin, Gary S. and Norman Goodman
  1980   Marriage, Family, and Intimate Relationships. Chicago: Rand McNally.

Bem, Sandra Lipsitz
  1977   "Beyond androgyny: Some presumptuous prescriptions for a liberated sexual identity." Pages 204–21 in Arlene Skolnick and Jerome Skolnick (eds.), Family in Transition (2nd ed.). Boston: Little, Brown.

Berelson, B., and G. A. Steiner
  1964   Human Behavior. New York: Harcourt.

Bergler, Edmund
  1958   The Revolt of the Middle-aged Man. New York: Hill and Wang.

Berkhof, L.
  1949   Systematic Theology. Grand Rapids: Eerdmans.

Berscheid, Ellen, and Elaine Walster
    1969   Interpersonal Attraction. Reading, Mass.: Addison-
               Wesley.

Bigner, Jerry J.
    1979   Parent-Child Relations: An Introduction to Parenting. New
               York: Macmillan.

Black, Eric
    1982   Marriage counselors hear an earful about failure to com-
               municate. Minneapolis Star and Tribune (June 3) 1B–5B.

Blau, Zena Smith
    1973   Old Age in a Changing Society. New York: New View-
               points.

Bohannan, Paul
    1970   "The six stations of divorce." Paul Bohannan (ed.), Divorce
               and After. Garden City, N.Y.: Doubleday.

Brandt, Henry and Phil Landrum
    1976   I Want My Marriage to Be Better. Grand Rapids: Zonder-
               van.

Brim, Orville G.
    1966   "Socialization through the life cycle." Pages 3–49 in O. G.
               Brim and S. Wheeler (eds.), Socialization After Childhood.
               New York: Wiley.

Broom, L., P. Selznick, and D. Darroch
    1981   Sociology (7th ed.). New York: Harper & Row.

Broom, Leonard, and Philip Selznick
    1979   Essentials of Sociology. (2nd ed.) New York: Harper &
               Row.

Brunner, Emil
    1952   The Christian Doctrine of Creation and Redemption.
               Dogmatics: Volume 2. Philadelphia: Westminster.

Bustanoby, André
    1978   But I Didn't Want a Divorce. Grand Rapids: Zondervan.

Cherlin, Andrew J.
    1981   Marriage, Divorce, Remarriage. Cambridge, Mass.: Har-
               vard.

Christenson, Larry
    1970   The Christian Family. Minneapolis: Bethany.

Clayton, Richard R.
    1979   The Family, Marriage, and Social Change. Lexington,
               Mass.: Heath.

Clinebell, Howard J.
    1977   Growth Counseling for Mid-life Couples. Philadelphia:
               Fortress.

Clinebell, Howard J., and Charlotte H. Clinebell
1970   The Intimate Marriage. New York: Harper & Row.

Collins, Gary R.
1972   Effective Counseling. Carol Stream, Ill.: Creation House.

Conger, John J.
1977   Adolescence and Youth. New York: Harper & Row.

Coombs, Robert
1966   "Value consensus and partner satisfaction among dating couples." Journal of Marriage and the Family 28:166–73.

Cosgrove, Mark P.
1977   The Essence of Human Nature. Grand Rapids: Zondervan.

Cousins, Norman
1979   Anatomy of an Illness. New York: Norton.

Cox, Frank D.
1981   Human Intimacy: Marriage, the Family, and Its Meaning. St Paul: West.

Dale, Robert D., and Carrie K. Dale
1978   Making Good Marriages Better. Nashville: Broadman.

Dayton, Howard L.
1979   Your Money: Frustration or Freedom. Wheaton, Ill.: Tyndale.

DeJong, Peter, and Donald R. Wilson
1979   Husband and Wife: The Sexes in Scripture and Society. Grand Rapids: Zondervan.

Dobson, James
1970   Dare to Discipline. Wheaton, Ill.: Tyndale.
1974   Hide or Seek. Old Tappan, N.J.: Revell.
1978   Preparing for Adolescence. Santa Ana, Calif.: Vision House.

Downs, James F.
1977   "The Navajo." G. Spindler and L. Spindler (eds.), Cultures Around the World. New York: Holt, Rinehart and Winston.

Driscoll, R., K. E. Davis, and M. E. Lipetz
1972   "Parental interference and romantic love: The Romeo and Juliet effect." Journal of Personality and Social Psychology 24:1–10.

Duberman, Lucile
1975   The Reconstituted Family. Chicago: Nelson-Hall.

Duty, Guy
1967   Divorce and Remarriage. Minneapolis: Bethany.

Duvall, Evelyn Millis
1977   Marriage and Family Development (5th ed.). Philadelphia: Lippincott.

Dworetzky, John P.
  1981   Introduction to Child Development. St. Paul: West.

Edwards, John N.
  1969   "Familial behavior as social exchange." Journal of Marriage and the Family 31:518–26.

Einstein, Elizabeth
  1983   Stepfamilies—dealing with anger and disappointment. U.S. News and World Report (January 17):67–68.

Elder, Carl A.
  1976   Values and Moral Development in Children. Nashville: Broadman.

Ellisen, Stanley A.
  1977   Divorce and Remarriage in the Church. Grand Rapids: Zondervan.

Eshleman, J. Ross
  1981   The Family: An Introduction. Boston: Allyn and Bacon.

Feldman, Francis
  1976   The Family in Today's Money World. New York: Family Service Association.

Flanagan, Geraldine
  1965   The First Nine Months of Life. New York: Simon and Schuster.

Florio, Anthony
  1978   Two to Get Ready. Wheaton, Ill.: Victor.

Fooshee, George
  1976   You Can Be Financially Free. Old Tappan, N.J.: Revell.

Fried, Barbara
  1967   The Middle-Age Crisis. New York: Harper & Row.

Gangel, Kenneth
  1972   The Family First. Minneapolis: HIS International.

Garrett, William R.
  1982   Seasons of Marriage and Family Life. New York: Holt, Rinehart and Winston.

Getz, Gene
  1972   The Christian Home in a Changing World. Chicago: Moody.

Golanty, Eric, and Barbara B. Harris
  1982   Marriage and Family Life. Boston: Houghton Mifflin.

Goolrick, William K. (ed.)
  1975   The Adult Years. New York: Time-Life.

Gordon, Michael
  1978   The American Family: Past, Present, and Future. New York: Random House.

Gough, E. Kathleen
    1959   "The Nayars and the definition of marriage." Journal of
                Royal Anthropological Institute 89:23–34.

Graburn, Nelson (ed.)
    1971   Readings in Kinship and Social Structure. New York:
                Harper & Row.

Green, Ernest J.
    1978   Personal Relationships: An Approach to Marriage and
                Family. New York: McGraw-Hill.

Grunlan, Stephen A.
    1972   "Terms of address among American college students."
                Unpublished paper.
    1982   "Sociology and the Christian." Pages 401–14 in S. Grunlan
                and M. Reimer (eds.), Christian Perspectives on Sociology.
                Grand Rapids: Zondervan.

Grunlan, Stephen A., and Daniel H. Lambrides
    1983   Effective Lay Counseling. Harrisburg, Pa.: Christian Pub-
                lications.

Grunlan, Stephen A., and Marvin K. Mayers
    1979   Cultural Anthropology: A Christian Perspective. Grand
                Rapids: Zondervan.

Grunlan, Stephen A., and Milton K. Reimer (eds.)
    1982   Christian Perspectives on Sociology. Grand Rapids: Zon-
                dervan.

Gundry, Patricia
    1977   Woman, Be Free! Grand Rapids: Zondervan.
    1980   Heirs Together. Grand Rapids: Zondervan.

Hendricks, Howard G.
    1973   Heaven Help the Home. Wheaton, Ill.: Victor

Herman, Judith, and Lisa Hirschman
    1980   "Incest between fathers and daughters." P. H. Mussen,
                J. J. Conger, and J. Kagan (eds.), Readings in Child and
                Adolescent Psychology. New York: Harper & Row.

Hess, Beth B., E. W. Markson, and P. J. Stein
    1982   Sociology. New York: Macmillan.

Hite, Shere
    1976   The Hite Report. New York: Macmillan.

Hoebel, E. A.
    1972   The Study of Man. New York: McGraw-Hill.

Horton, Paul B., and Chester L. Hunt
    1980   Sociology (5th ed.). New York: McGraw-Hill.

Howe, Reuel L.
    1959   The Creative Years. Greenwich, Conn.: Seabury.

Howell, John C.
    1979   Equality and Submission in Marriage. Nashville: Broad-
                man.

Hughes, Philip Edgcumbe
1969   "Theological principles in the control of human life." Pages
        93–149 in Walter O. Spitzer and Carlyle L. Saylor (eds.),
        Birth Control and the Christian. Wheaton, Ill.: Tyndale.

Hulme, William E.
1962   The Pastoral Care of Families. Nashville: Abingdon.

Jeeves, Malcom
1976   Psychology and Christianity: The View Both Ways. Down-
        ers Grove, Ill.: InterVarsity.

Johnson, Winston A.
1982   "Groups." Pages 150–66 in S. Grunlan and M. Reimer
        (eds.), Christian Perspectives on Sociology. Grand Rapids:
        Zondervan.

Jones, W. H., R. O. Hansson, and A. L. Phillips
1978   Physical attractiveness and judgments of psychopathology.
        Journal of Social Psychology 105:79–85.

Justice, Blair, and Rita Justice
1976   The Abusing Family. New York: Human Sciences.

Kaplan, Helen Singer
1974   The New Sex Therapy. New York: Brunner/Mazel.

Koteskey, Ronald L.
1980   Psychology From a Christian Perspective. Nashville:
        Abingdon.
1981   "Growing up too late, too soon." Christianity Today
        (March 13).

Kelley, Robert K.
1969   Courtship, Marriage and the Family. New York: Harcourt,
        Brace and World.

Kephart, William M.
1972   The Family, Society, and the Individual (3rd ed.). Boston:
        Houghton Mifflin.
1981   The Family, Society, and the Individual (5th ed.). Boston:
        Houghton Mifflin.

Kiley, Dan
1978   Nobody Said It Would Be Easy. New York: Harper & Row.

Kimmel, Douglas C.
1974   Adulthood and Aging. New York: Wiley.

King, K., J. O. Balswick, and I. E. Robinson
1977   "The continuing premarital sexual revolution among col-
        lege females." Journal of Marriage and the Family
        39:455–59.

Kinsey, A. C., W. B. Pomeroy, C. E. Martin, and P. H. Gebhard
1953   Sexual Behavior in the Human Female. Philadelphia:
        Saunders.

Kitson, Gay C.
   1982   "Attachment to the spouse in divorce." Journal of Marriage
            and the Family 44 (2):379–93.

Kubler-Ross, Elisabeth
   1969   On Death and Dying. New York: Macmillan.
   1974   Questions on Death and Dying. New York: Macmillan
   1975   Death: The Final Stage of Growth. Englewood Cliffs, N.J.:
            Prentice-Hall.

LaHaye, Tim, and Beverly LaHaye
   1976   The Act of Marriage. Grand Rapids: Zondervan.

Lamanna, Mary Ann, and Agnes Riedmann
   1981   Marriages and Families. Belmont, Calif.: Wadsworth.

Lambrides, Daniel
   1982   Lecture given at St. Paul Bible College.

Landorf, Joyce
   1974   Mourning Song. Old Tappan, N.J.: Revell.

Lasswell, Marcia
   1974   "Is there a best time to marry?" The Family Coordinator, 23
            (3):237–42.

Lasswell, Marcia, and Thomas E. Lasswell
   1982   Marriage and the Family. Lexington, Mass.: Heath.

Lee, Mark W.
   1976   "Reasons marriages fail—communication." Cary Collins
            (ed.), Make More of Your Marriage. Waco: Word.

LeMasters, E. E.
   1970   Parents in Modern America: A Sociological Analysis.
            Homewood, Ill.: Dorsey.

Levinson, Daniel J. et al.
   1978   The Seasons of a Man's Life. New York: Knopf.

Levy, M. J.
   1949   Family Revolution in Modern China. Cambridge, Mass.:
            Harvard.
   1955   "Some questions about Parsons' treatment of the incest
            problem." British Journal of Sociology 6:277–85.

Linton, Ralph
   1936   The Study of Man. New York: Appleton.

Lyons, Christopher A.
   1973   "The Healing Ministry of the Holy Spirit." Sermon deliv-
            ered at the Wheaton Bible Church, Wheaton, Ill., Sep-
            tember 23.

Mass, Henry S., and Joseph A. Kuypers.
   1974   From Thirty to Seventy. San Francisco: Jossey-Bass.

MacGregor, Malcolm and Stanley G. Baldwin
   1977   Your Money Matters. Minneapolis: Bethany.

MacKay, Donald M.
    1979   Human Science and Human Dignity. Downers Grove, Ill.:
                InterVarsity.

McClelland, David et al.
    1978   Making it to maturity. Psychology Today (June): 42–53,
                114.

McKain, W.
    1969   Retirement Marriages. Storrs, Calif.: Storrs Agricultural
                Experiment Station, Monograph 3.

Martin, John R.
    1974   Divorce and Remarriage. Scottdale, Pa.: Herald.

Masters, William H., and Virginia E. Johnson
    1966   Human Sexual Response. Boston: Little, Brown and Com-
                pany.

May, Rollo
    1969   Love and Will. New York: Norton.

Mayers, Marvin K.
    1976   Christianity Confronts Culture. Grand Rapids: Zondervan.

Meier, Paul D.
    1977   Christian Child-Rearing and Personality Development.
                Grand Rapids: Baker.

Menchar, J. P.
    1965   "The Nayars of South Malakar." M. F. Nimkoff (ed.),
                Comparative Family Systems. Boston: Houghton Mifflin.

Merriam-Webster Dictionary
    1974   New York: Pocket Books.

Miles, Herbert J.
    1971   Sexual Understanding Before Marriage. Grand Rapids:
                Zondervan.

Miles, Herbert J., and Fern H. Miles
    1978   Husband-Wife Equality. Old Tappan, N.J.: Revell.

Minirth, Frank B. and Paul D. Meier
    1978   Happiness Is a Choice. Grand Rapids: Baker.

Minneapolis Star and Tribune
    1982   "Use of diaphragm cuts women's risk of pelvic disease,
                new study says." (July 7): 1C.

Mischel, Walter
    1981   Introduction to Personality. New York: Holt, Rinehart and
                Winston.

Montgomery, John Warwick
    1981   Slaughter of the Innocents. Westchester, Ill.: Crossway.

Morgan, Marabel
    1973   The Total Woman. Old Tappan, N.J.: Revell.

Murdock, George Peter
    1949   Social Structure. New York: Macmillan.

Murstein, Bernard
   1976   Who Will Marry Whom? New York: Springer.

Myra, Harold
   1979   Love Notes to Jeanette. Wheaton, Ill.: Victor.
   1979   "An ode to marriage." Moody Monthly (May): 60–62.

Neugarten, Bernice L., and Karol K. Weinstein
   1964   "The changing American grandparent." Journal of Mar-
             riage and the Family 26:199–204.

Newsom, Howard
   1978   "How little Christians grow." Eternity (September): 39–
             40, 45.

Nye, F. Ivan, and Felix M. Berardo
   1973   The Family: Its Structure and Interaction. New York: Mac-
             millan.

O'Brien, Shirley
   1980   Child Abuse. Provo, Utah: Brigham Young University
             Press.

Orthner, Dennis K.
   1981   "Intimate Relationships: An Introduction to Marriage and
             the Family." Reading, Mass.: Addison-Wesley.

Otterbein, Keith F.
   1977   Comparative Cultural Analysis. New York: Holt, Rinehart
             and Winston.

Parsons, Talcott, and Robert F. Bales
   1955   Family, Socialization and Interaction Process. Glencoe, Ill.:
             Free Press.

Penner, Clifford, and Joyce Penner
   1981   The Gift of Sex. Waco: Word.

Peterson, James
   1968   Married Love in the Middle Years. New York: Association.

Peterson, Robert
   1967   Life Begins at Forty. New York: Trident.

Pfouts, Jane H.
   1980   "Birth order, age-spacing, IQ differences, and family rela-
             tions." Journal of Marriage and the Family 42:517–31.

Piaget, Jean
   1952   The Origins of Intelligence in Children. New York: Norton.

Piehl, J.
   1977   "Integration of information in the courts: Influence of
             physical attractiveness on amount of punishment for traffic
             offenders." Psychological Reports 41:551–56.

Plog, Fred, and Daniel G. Bates
   1976   Cultural Anthropology. New York: Knopf.

Press, Aric, Holly Morris, and Richard Sandza
   1981   "An epidemic of incest." Newsweek (November 30): 68.

Pulaski, Mary Ann
    1980   Understanding Piaget. New York: Harper & Row.

Queen, S. A., and R. W. Haberstein
    1971   The Family in Various Cultures. (4th ed.) Philadelphia: Lippincott.

Reimer, Milton K.
    1982   "The study of sociology: An introduction." Pages 11–27 in S. Grunlan and M. Reimer (eds.), Christian Perspectives on Sociology. Grand Rapids: Zondervan.

Reiss, Ira L.
    1980   Family System in America (3rd ed.). New York: Holt, Rinehart and Winston.

Richards, Larry
    1981   Remarriage: A Healing Gift From God. Waco: Word.

Robertson, Joan F.
    1977   "Grandmotherhood: A study of role conceptions." Journal of Marriage and the Family 39:165–74.

Robinson, Ira E., and Davor Jedlicka
    1982   "Change in sexual attitudes and behavior of college students from 1965 to 1980: A research note." Journal of Marriage and the Family 44 (1): 237–40.

Rouch, Mark
    1974   Competent Ministry. Nashville: Abingdon.

Rubenstein, Carin
    1981   "Practice marriages don't make perfect." Psychology Today (July): 19.

Sanford, John A.
    1982   Between People. Ramsey, N.J.: Paulist.

Saxton, Lloyd
    1972   The Individual, Marriage, and the Family (2nd ed.). Belmont, Calif.: Wadsworth.
    1980   The Individual, Marriage, and the Family (4th ed.). Belmont, Calif.: Wadsworth.

Scanzoni, John
    1979   Love and Negotiate: Creative Conflict in Marriage. Waco: Word.

Scanzoni, Letha D., and John Scanzoni
    1981   Men, Women, and Change (2nd ed.). New York: McGraw-Hill.

Scanzoni, Letha, and Nancy Hardesty
    1975   All We're Meant to Be. Waco: Word.

Schaeffer, Francis A., and C. Everett Koop
    1979   Whatever Happened to the Human Race? Old Tappan, N.J.: Revell.

Schoen, Robert
   1975   "California divorce rates by age at first marriage and dura-
             tion of first marriage." Journal of Marriage and the Family
             37:548–55.

Schultz, Duane
   1981   Theories of Personality. Monterey, Calif.: Brooks Cole.

Schusky, Ernest L.
   1965   Manual for Kinship Analysis. New York: Holt, Rinehart
             and Winston.

Seamands, David A.
   1977   "Is masturbation sinful?" J. Allan Petersen (ed.), For
             Families Only. Wheaton, Ill.: Tyndale.

Shapiro, Howard I.
   1977   The Birth Control Book. New York: St. Martins.

Shedd, Charlie W.
   1965   Letters to Karen. Nashville: Abingdon.
   1968   Letters to Philip. New York: Doubleday.
   1976   The Stork Is Dead. Waco: Word.

Sheehy, Gail
   1976   Passages. New York: Dutton.

Shepard, Jon M.
   1981   Sociology. St. Paul: West.

Singer, Dorothy G., and Tracey A. Revenson
   1978   A Piaget Primer: How a Child Thinks. New York: Interna-
             tional Universities Press.

Sperry, Len
   1978   The Together Experience. San Diego: Beta.

Spiro, Melford
   1968   "Is the family universal?—the Israeli case." N. W. Bell and
             E. F. Vogel (eds)., A Modern Introduction to the Family
             (rev. ed.). New York: Free Press.

Steelman, L. C. and J. A. Mercy
   1980   "Unconfounding the confluence model: A test of sibship
             size and birth order effects on intelligence." American
             Sociological Review 45:571–82.

Stephan, C., and J. C. Tully
   1977   "The influence of physical attractiveness of a plantiff on the
             decision of simulated jurors." Journal of Social Research
             101:149–50.

Stephens, William N.
   1963   The Family in Cross-cultural Perspectives. New York: Holt,
             Rinehart and Winston.
   1970   "Predictors of marital adjustment." L. Saxton (ed.), A Mar-
             riage Reader. Belmont, Calif.: Wadsworth.

Stewart, C. W.
   1970   The Minister as Marriage Counselor. Nashville: Abingdon.

Streib, G.
  1972   "Older families and their troubles: familial and social re-
              sponses." Family Coordinator 21:5–19.

Strong, August H.
  1907   Systematic Theology. Valley Forge: Judson.

Strong, Bryan, Sam Wilson, Mina Roberts, and Thomas Johns
  1981   Human Sexuality: Essentials (2nd ed.). St Paul: West.

Taylor, Jack
  1974   One Home Under God. Nashville: Broadman.

Thiessen, Henry C.
  1951   Introductory Lectures in Systematic Theology. Grand
              Rapids: Eerdmans.

Tillich, Paul
  1957   Dynamics of Faith. New York: Harper and Brothers.

Turner, Jonathan H.
  1981   Sociology: Studying the Human System. Santa Monica:
              Goodyear.

U.S. Bureau of the Census
  1977   Current Population Reports, Series P-20, No. 311.
              Washington, D. C.: U.S. Bureau of the Census.

Vander Zanden, James W.
  1979   Sociology (4th ed.). New York: Wiley.

Wadsworth, Barry J.
  1971   Piaget's Theory of Cognitive Development. New York:
              Longman.

Wagonseller, Bill R., and Richard L. McDowell
  1979   You and Your Child. Champaign, Ill.: Research.

Walker, Graham
  1982   The Christian case for military service. Moody Monthly
              (July/August): 6–8.

Waller, Willard
  1937   "The dating and rating complex." American Sociological
              Review 2:727–34.

Wallerstein, Judith S. and Joan B. Kelly
  1980   "California's children of divorce." Psychology Today
              (January): 67–76.

Walster, Elaine, and G. William Walster
  1978   A New Look at Love. Reading, Mass.: Addison-Wesley.

Waltke, Bruce K.
  1969   "Old Testament texts bearing on the problem of the control
              of human reproduction." Pages 7–23 in Walter O. Spitzer
              and Carlyle L. Saylor (eds.), Birth Control and the Chris-
              tian. Wheaton, Ill.: Tyndale.

Wheat, Ed, and Gaye Wheat
  1977   Intended for Pleasure. Old Tappan, N.J.: Revell.

White, John
　1977　　　Eros Defiled. Downers Grove, Ill.: Inter-Varsity.

Winch, Robert F.
　1958　　　Mate Selection. New York: Harper and Brothers.
　1963　　　The Modern Family. New York: Holt, Rinehart and Winston.

Winch, Robert F., Thomas Ktsanses, and Virginia Ktsanses
　1954　　　"The theory of complementary needs in mate selection: An analytic and descriptive study." American Sociological Review 19:242.

Wolf, Harold A.
　1975　　　Personal Finance. Boston: Allyn and Bacon.

Woodson, Les
　1979　　　Divorce and the Gospel of Grace. Waco: Word.

Wright, H. Norman
　1974　　　Communication: Key to Your Marriage. Glendale, Calif.: Regal.
　1977a　　Premarital Counseling. Chicago: Moody.
　1977b　　Training Christians to Counsel. Denver: Christian Marriage Enrichment.

Wright, H. Norman, and Marvin Inmon
　1978　　　Dating, Waiting, and Choosing a Mate. Irvine, Calif.: Harvest House.

Yang, Martin
　1971　　　"The Chinese family pattern." W. Goldschmidt (ed.), Exploring the Ways of Mankind (2nd ed.). New York: Holt, Rinehart and Winston.

Yankelovich, Skelly, and White, Inc.
　1975　　　The General Mills American Family Report, 1974–75. Minneapolis: General Mills.

Zajonc, Robert B.
　1975　　　"Dumber by the dozen." Psychology Today (January).

Zajonc, R. B. and G. B. Markus
　1975　　　"Birth order and intellectual development." Psychological Review 82:74–88.

Zelditch, Morris
　1964　　　"Cross-cultural analyses of family structure." H. T. Christensen (ed.), Handbook of Marriage and the Family. Chicago: Rand McNally.

AUTHOR INDEX

SUBJECT INDEX